l 50
ωιο

SKELETONS IN THE CLOSET, SKELETONS IN THE GROUND

CW01083815

The Cañada Blanch / Sussex Academic Studies on Contemporary Spain

General Editor: Professor Paul Preston, London School of Economics

Richard Barker, *Skeletons in the Closet, Skeletons in the Ground: Repression, Victimization and Humiliation in a Small Andalusian Town – The Human Consequences of the Spanish Civil War.*

Germà Bel, *Infrastructure and the Political Economy of Nation Building in Spain, 1720–2010.*

Gerald Blaney Jr., *"The Three-Cornered Hat and the Tri-Colored Flag": The Civil Guard and the Second Spanish Republic, 1931–1936.*

Michael Eaude, *Triumph at Midnight in the Century: A Critical Biography of Arturo Barea.*

Soledad Fox, *Constancia de la Mora in War and Exile: International Voice for the Spanish Republic.*

Helen Graham, *The War and its Shadow: Spain's Civil War in Europe's Long Twentieth Century.*

Angela Jackson, *'For us it was Heaven': The Passion, Grief and Fortitude of Patience Darton – From the Spanish Civil War to Mao's China.*

Gabriel Jackson, *Juan Negrín: Physiologist, Socialist, and Spanish Republican War Leader.*

Sid Lowe, *Catholicism, War and the Foundation of Francoism: The Juventud de Acción Popular in Spain, 1931–1939.*

Olivia Muñoz-Rojas, *Ashes and Granite: Destruction and Reconstruction in the Spanish Civil War and Its Aftermath.*

Linda Palfreeman, *¡SALUD!: British Volunteers in the Republican Medical Service during the Spanish Civil War, 1936–1939.*

Cristina Palomares, *The Quest for Survival after Franco: Moderate Francoism and the Slow Journey to the Polls, 1964–1977.*

David Wingeate Pike, *France Divided: The French and the Civil War in Spain.*

Isabelle Rohr, *The Spanish Right and the Jews, 1898–1945: Antisemitism and Opportunism.*

Gareth Stockey, *Gibraltar: "A Dagger in the Spine of Spain?"*

Ramon Tremosa-i-Balcells, *Catalonia – An Emerging Economy: The Most Cost-Effective Ports in the Mediterranean Sea.*

Dacia Viejo-Rose, *Reconstructing Spain: Cultural Heritage and Memory after Civil War.*

Richard Wigg, *Churchill and Spain: The Survival of the Franco Regime, 1940–1945.*

Published by the Cañada Blanch Centre for Contemporary Spanish Studies in conjunction with Routledge / Taylor & Francis

1 Francisco J. Romero Salvadó, *Spain 1914–1918: Between War and Revolution.*
2 David Wingeate Pike, *Spaniards in the Holocaust: Mauthausen, the Horror on the Danube.*
3 Herbert Rutledge Southworth, *Conspiracy and the Spanish Civil War: The Brainwashing of Francisco Franco.*
4 Angel Smith (editor), *Red Barcelona: Social Protest and Labour Mobilization in the Twentieth Century.*
5 Angela Jackson, *British Women and the Spanish Civil War.*
6 Kathleen Richmond, *Women and Spanish Fascism: The Women's Section of the Falange, 1934–1959.*
7 Chris Ealham, *Class, Culture and Conflict in Barcelona, 1898–1937.*
8 Julián Casanova, *Anarchism, the Republic and Civil War in Spain 1931–1939.*
9 Montserrat Guibernau, *Catalan Nationalism: Francoism, Transition and Democracy.*
10 Richard Baxell, *British Volunteers in the Spanish Civil War: The British Battalion in the International Brigades, 1936–1939.*
11 Hilari Raguer, *The Catholic Church and the Spanish Civil War.*
12 Richard Wigg, *Churchill and Spain: The Survival of the Franco Regime, 1940–45.*
13 Nicholas Coni, *Medicine and the Spanish Civil War.*
14 Diego Muro, *Ethnicity and Violence: The Case of Radical Basque Nationalism.*
15 Francisco J. Romero Salvadó, *Spain's Revolutionary Crisis, 1917–1923.*
16 Peter Anderson, *The Francoist Military Trials. Terror and Complicity, 1939–1945.*

To
NOELIA RODRÍGUEZ ESCOBAR
granddaughter of Manuel Escobar Moreno, 1906–1936,

SARA REBOLLO TEBAS
granddaughter of Manuel Tebas Escobar, 1898–1936,

*and to all those who, like Noelia and Sara,
seek to rescue their grandparents from oblivion.*

SKELETONS IN THE CLOSET, SKELETONS IN THE GROUND

Repression, Victimization and Humiliation
in a Small Andalusian Town

The Human Consequences of the Spanish Civil War

RICHARD BARKER

sussex
ACADEMIC
PRESS
Brighton • Portland • Toronto

Cañada Blanch Centre
for Contemporary
Spanish Studies

Copyright © Richard Barker, 2012.

The right of Richard Barker to be identified as Author of this work has been asserted in accordance with the Copyright, Designs and Patents Act 1988.

2 4 6 8 10 9 7 5 3 1

First published in 2012 in Great Britain by
SUSSEX ACADEMIC PRESS
PO Box 139
Eastbourne BN24 9BP

and in the United States of America by
SUSSEX ACADEMIC PRESS
920 NE 58th Ave   Suite 300
Portland, Oregon 97213-3786

and in Canada by
SUSSEX ACADEMIC PRESS (CANADA)
8000 Bathurst Street, Unit 1, PO Box 30010, Vaughan, Ontario L4J 0C6

Published in collaboration with the Cañada Blanch
Centre for Contemporary Spanish Studies.

All rights reserved. Except for the quotation of short passages for the purposes of criticism and review, no part of this publication may be reproduced, stored in a retrieval system, or transmitted, in any form or by any means, electronic, mechanical, photocopying, recording or otherwise, without the prior permission of the publisher.

British Library Cataloguing in Publication Data
A CIP catalogue record for this book is available from the British Library.

Library of Congress Cataloging-in-Publication Data
Barker, Richard.
Skeletons in the closet, skeletons in the ground : repression, victimization and humiliation in a small Andalusian town : the human consequences of the Spanish Civil War / Richard Barker.
pages   cm. — (The Canada Blanch/Sussex Academic Studies on Contemporary Spain)
Includes bibliographical references and index.
ISBN 978-1-84519-536-6 (p/b : alk. paper)
  1. Castilleja del Campo (Spain)—History—20th century. 2. Castilleja del Campo (Spain)—Social conditions—20th century. 3. Spain—History—Civil War, 1936–1939—Social aspects. 4. Spain—History—Civil War, 1936–1939—Influence. I. Title.
DP402.C43625B37 2012
946.081′1—dc23

2011051607

MIX
Paper from
responsible sources
FSC
www.fsc.org   FSC® C013056

Typeset & designed by Sussex Academic Press, Brighton & Eastbourne.
Printed by TJ International, Padstow, Cornwall.

Contents

The Cañada Blanch Centre for Contemporary Spanish Studies

In the 1960s, the most important initiative in the cultural and academic relations between Spain and the United Kingdom was launched by a Valencian fruit importer in London. The creation by Vicente Cañada Blanch of the Anglo-Spanish Cultural Foundation has subsequently benefited large numbers of Spanish and British scholars at various levels. Thanks to the generosity of Vicente Cañada Blanch, thousands of Spanish schoolchildren have been educated at the secondary school in West London that bears his name. At the same time, many British and Spanish university students have benefited from the exchange scholarships which fostered cultural and scientific exchanges between the two countries. Some of the most important historical, artistic and literary work on Spanish topics to be produced in Great Britain was initially made possible by Cañada Blanch scholarships.

Vicente Cañada Blanch was, by inclination, a conservative. When his Foundation was created, the Franco regime was still in the plenitude of its power. Nevertheless, the keynote of the Foundation's activities was always a complete open-mindedness on political issues. This was reflected in the diversity of research projects supported by the Foundation, many of which, in Francoist Spain, would have been regarded as subversive. When the Dictator died, Don Vicente was in his seventy-fifth year. In the two decades following the death of the Dictator, although apparently indestructible, Don Vicente was obliged to husband his energies. Increasingly, the work of the Foundation was carried forward by Miguel Dols whose tireless and imaginative work in London was matched in Spain by that of José María Coll Comín. They were united in the Foundation's spirit of open-minded commitment to fostering research of high quality in pursuit of better Anglo-Spanish cultural relations. Throughout the 1990s, thanks to them, the role of the Foundation grew considerably.

In 1994, in collaboration with the London School of Economics, the Foundation established the Príncipe de Asturias Chair of Contemporary Spanish History and the Cañada Blanch Centre for Contemporary Spanish Studies. It is the particular task of the Cañada Blanch Centre for Contemporary Spanish Studies to promote the understanding of twentieth-century Spain through research and teaching of contemporary Spanish history, politics, economy, sociology and culture. The Centre possesses a valuable library and archival centre for specialists in contemporary Spain. This work is carried on through the publications of the doctoral and post-doctoral researchers at the Centre itself and through the many seminars and lectures held at the London School of Economics. While the seminars are the province of the researchers, the lecture cycles have been the forum in which Spanish politicians have been able to address audiences in the United Kingdom.

Since 1998, the Cañada Blanch Centre has published a substantial number of books in collaboration with several different publishers on the subject of contemporary Spanish history and politics. A fruitful partnership with Sussex Academic Press began in 2004 with the publication of Christina Palomares's fascinating work on the origins of the Partido Popular in Spain, *The Quest for Survival after Franco. Moderate Francoism and the Slow Journey to the Polls, 1964–1977*. This was followed in 2007 by Soledad Fox's deeply moving biography of one of the most intriguing women of 1930s Spain, *Constancia de la Mora in War and Exile: International Voice for the Spanish Republic* and Isabel Rohr's path-breaking study of anti-Semitism in Spain, *The Spanish Right and the Jews, 1898–1945: Antisemitism and Opportunism*. 2008 saw the publication of a revised edition of Richard Wigg's penetrating study of Anglo-Spanish relations during the Second World War, *Churchill and Spain: The Survival of the Franco Regime, 1940–1945* together with *Triumph at Midnight of the Century: A Critical Biography of Arturo Barea*, Michael Eaude's fascinating revaluation of the great Spanish author of *The Forging of a Rebel*.

Our collaboration in 2009 was inaugurated by Gareth Stockey's incisive account of another crucial element in Anglo-Spanish relations, *Gibraltar. A Dagger in the Spine of Spain*. We were especially proud that it was continued by the most distinguished American historian of the Spanish Civil War, Gabriel Jackson. His pioneering work *The Spanish Republic and the Civil War*, first published 1965 and still in print, quickly became a classic. The Sussex Academic Press/Cañada Blanch series was greatly privileged to be associated with Professor Jackson's biography of the great Republican war leader, Juan Negrín.

2011 took the series to new heights. Two remarkable and complementary works, Olivia Muñoz Rojas, *Ashes and Granite: Destruction and Reconstruction in the Spanish Civil War and its Aftermath* and Dacia Viejo-Rose, *Reconstructing Spain: Cultural Heritage and Memory after Civil War*, opened up an entirely new dimension of the study of the early Franco regime and its internal conflicts. They were followed by Richard Purkiss's analysis of the Valencian anarchist movement during the revolutionary period from 1918 to 1923, the military dictatorship of General Primo de Rivera and the Second Republic. It is a fascinating work which sheds entirely new light both on the breakdown of political coexistence during the Republic and on the origins of the violence that was to explode after the military coup of July 1936. The year ended with the publication of *France Divided: The French and the Civil War in Spain* by David Wingeate Pike. It made available in a thoroughly updated edition, and in English for the first time, one of the classics of the historiography of the Spanish Civil War.

An extremely rich programme for 2012 opened with Germà Bel's remarkable *Infrastructure and the Political Economy of Nation Building in Spain*. This startlingly original work exposed the damage done to the Spanish economy by the country's asymmetrical and dysfunctional transport and communications model. It is followed now by Angela Jackson's rich and moving account of an extraordinary life – that of the left-wing nurse Patience Darton. It is the first of a trio of books concerned with the International Brigades and the Republican medical services in the Spanish Civil War. The others are a comprehensive account of the Republican medical services by Linda Palfreeman and a life of Tom Wintringham by Hugh Purcell and Phyl Smith.

Those three books are part of a programme of important titles on the Spanish conflict including *The War and Its Shadow: Spain's Civil War in Europe's Long Twentieth Century* by the distinguished historian Helen Graham. The present volume is another remarkable contribution to the historiography of the civil war. *Skeletons in the Closet, Skeletons in the Ground* by Richard Barker is a painstaking reconstruction of the terror visited upon an Andalusian village as a result of the military coup of 1936 based on interviews with survivors carried out over many years. The work is enriched by a perceptive introduction by Francisco Espinosa Maestre, the doyen of Spanish historians of the right-wing repression. As he points out, Barker's work combines the techniques of anthropology, sociology and oral history. In doing so, Barker also examines the long afterlife of the terror, the years of humiliation and servitude imposed upon the surviving inhabitants of Castilleja del Campo. He has thereby produced a local study that casts its light far beyond the tiny town in the province of Seville in such a way as to illuminate the entire history of the terror unleashed by Franco's military coup.

PAUL PRESTON
Series Editor
London School of Economics

Foreword

Francisco Espinosa Maestre

The first thing that came into my head when I read Richard Barker's work was the word time: when he began to prepare it, how many interviews he had to conduct with each informant before they would allow themselves to be recorded and their testimonies turned into information, how many hours it must have taken him to put the dozens of tapes on paper, how long to put together this impressive oral concerto. We are talking about years, as much for the time span covered in the work as for the little clues that appear throughout the text. For family reasons, Barker, a professor of Spanish from the United States, has spent, over many years, occasional summers in Castilleja del Campo, Seville. Unlike the more recently arrived historians from the so-called "movement for the recovery of historical memory," he began his research in time to collect testimonies from informants who lived through those years. Indeed the majority of the testimonies were collected at the end of the 1980s. Sometime he ought to tell us why instead of dedicating his stays in Spain to the study of the customs, the local celebrations, or the activities of religious fraternities he opted to reconstruct the history of the town from the proclamation of the Second Republic to the first democratic elections after Franco's death, taking as his central focus the fascist repression. Although there is one thing we do know: it was on an afternoon in August 1986, sitting in the shade of a fig tree listening to Antonio Monge Pérez, when the idea of portraying in depth the history of the civil war in Castilleja was born.

There immediately come to mind the names of other English-speaking authors, British and American, who also left evidence of their passing through Spain: Gerald Brenan (Yegen, Granada), Julian Pitt-Rivers (Grazalema, Cádiz), George A. Collier (Linares de la Sierra, Huelva), Margaret Van Epp Salazar (Galorza, Huelva), Jerome R. Mintz (Casas Viejas, Cádiz), and Ronald Fraser (Mijas, Málaga).[1] Anthropology, sociology, ethno-history, and oral history. Richard Barker's work can be placed beside the works of these authors without hesitation. We are in the presence of a laborious work of research of an historical nature, very much in the wake of Fraser, in which oral sources occupy a primordial position but are not the only ones. There is an important difference however from all these works, Barker's book was written in Spanish for a Spanish audience. And something else. In this case, unlike some of the works cited, the transcriptions of the various testimonies capture and reproduce the authentic speech of each informant.

Castilleja del Campo, a small town in the Aljarafe region of the province of Seville with fewer than eight hundred inhabitants, on the highway between Seville and Huelva, becomes a microcosm that faithfully reflects the situation much of the country was experiencing. The greater part of the municipal district, in which there were two estates that totaled 45,200 acres belonging to two noblewomen, one a countess and the other a marchioness, were the property of several large landowners and a group of small and medium proprietors. Then there were the laboring masses, marginalized by the system and dependent on occasional work. The countess's administrator was the Seville military man, landowner and politico, Pedro Parias González, with influential posts in the Andalusian Landowner's Association in those years and civil governor of Seville after the military coup. A personage who was without doubt as important as General Queipo de Llano, barracks companion of his youth. Barker dedicates the first part of his work to the Republic and explains very well the situation after its proclamation. We soon come up against the land problem: the town council demonstrated from the outset an interest in settling peasants in the "Village Meadow," a property that had long ago belonged to the municipality but that had passed into private hands some time in the nineteenth century. We will grasp the importance of the land problem if we bear in mind that the Municipal District comprised 159,700 acres and that the agrarian reform project declared 45,200 acres subject to expropriation, in other words, 28 percent of the total area.

Contrary to the crude revisionist maneuvers that claim to justify the coup of July 18, 1936 by moving the "origins of the civil war" back to October 1934, here we can see what that "October Revolution" really represented in the greater part of the country: the opportunity the Right was waiting for to retake the municipal governments lost in the elections of April 1931. The reactionary policies from that moment until the elections of February 1936 were absolute and remained etched in the people's memory. As everywhere, the months of the Popular Front were employed in reinstating the great reforms, postponed or aborted, of the first Republican biennium, beginning with agrarian reform: thus in Castilleja, beginning on March 5, there were more laborers settled on the "Village Meadow" and shortly thereafter the town council began to take steps to have part of the countess's and marchioness's estates declared "of social utility."

There is no reason to believe that the months of the Popular Front were that pre-Revolutionary chaos imagined by the Right, as claimed by Franco's propagandists and nourished to this day by certain historiographers at the service of "July 18." It happens that the fascist repression was so terrible that everywhere precedents were sought that would justify or explain in some way that wave of terror. In the case of Castilleja del Campo, as in other towns, that precedent was based on a tragic event that took place in May 1936: a young Falangist from the town was shot to death as the result of a confrontation between a group of Castilleja Falangists and a group of outsiders of contrary ideology who were passing by on the highway in a truck on their way back from a rally held in Huelva. Even though we now know from many other cases that even if nothing had occurred, the fascist repression would have followed its course regardless, this incident, in which not a single Castilleja leftist had any involvement, would later be utilized to justify some of the assassinations. The research carried out in this case by Richard Barker demonstrates the limitation of oral history, more useful in tracing the memory that has remained of such events than in determining what really happened. Doubtless the disclosure of the preliminary investigation report into this incident, if in fact it still exists, would open up new perspectives.

Another event utilized to justify the repression were the excesses of the column of miners from Huelva as they passed through Castilleja on July 19, in spite of the fact that they caused no personal injury and that local leftists prevented any outbreak of violence. This event introduces us to a story that we have heard before: the story of a "local pact" between the Left and the Right that would guarantee that whichever forces took the town no one would be harmed. The Left fulfilled their side of the bargain; the Right did not. And this was not because there were no right-wingers in these towns willing to respect the pact but rather because the strategy of terror and the plan for extermination that came from above were unstoppable: those who were not disposed to do *whatever was required*, like that Castilleja mayor who resigned his post when the assassinations began, were sidelined for not being up to the *grand task*.

Richard Barker closes this part of his work with the occupation of the town by the insurgents and immediately plunges into the most laborious part of his research: a wide-ranging and meticulous study of the repressive process that occupies much of the work and constitutes its nucleus. Here is evident the profit the author has known how to derive from the personal testimonies and the appropriate support and contrasting evidence he has found on numerous occasions in the municipal archive. It is probably, along with that of the aforementioned Fraser, the most important work of oral history dealing with the fascist repression in a town. Oral history and choral history, for the many people who collaborated with *Ricardo*; one has the impression of witnessing the town's history from many vantage points. The human gallery of characters is of great richness: those who had survived, like Antonio Monge or Manuel Ramírez (Castilleja's memory) and the dead (assassinated), like José Ramírez Rufino, the Republican mayor shot on August 27, 1936 together with his nephew José María and four other men of the town, or Manuel Tebas Escobar, learned peasant, teacher by night of day laborers. How many of these self-taught educators of day laborers, like Tebas or "Acostita," mayor of nearby Bollullos del Condado, were exterminated by Spanish fascism?

Barker describes in intimate detail, story by story, the terror that takes hold of this small locale in the wake of its occupation, well-aimed terror that snuffs out the lives of the mayor, the schoolteacher, the union leaders, the more outspoken of the peasants . . . at least 17 people, including the one who decides to flee in the middle of the plaza as they are taking him to the firing squad in order to force them to kill him right there so that the gunshots and the blood spatter the conscience of all those who observe and look the other way in the face of the daily terror. And then the terror of the living: the nine women purged with castor oil and, heads shaved, publicly humiliated; the twelve widows and fourteen orphans; the men forced to transport and bury cadavers . . . Horrendous scenes, says Barker. And all this in a town of 800 inhabitants where the Right had been respected. It is self-evident: this was not vengeance for the nonexistent "red terror" nor the purported Bolshevik revolution in progress but simply for the five years of reformist Republic that was about to bring down the Old Order.

The book also reflects the terror in Queipo de Llano's Seville, from the penal odysseys of some of the townspeople (the terrible story of the schoolteacher Joaquín León Trejo) to visits to the all-powerful Pedro Parias for the complicated purpose of saving relatives from the firing squad. Proof that the author has known how to complement the oral testimonies with the standard resources of historical research are two magnificent documents: the list of those "assassinated by the fascists" found by family members among the papers of Eugenio Pozo de la Cueva and the report on "Individuals to whom was applied the War Decree" sent to the Office of the Justice of the Peace by the Civil Guard in February 1939.

Without failing to reflect the repression that continued in the postwar, Richard Barker dedicates the third part of his work to the war, or more accurately, to the war's underside as seen through the experiences of some of the informants. A topic seldom dealt with and which demonstrates how the losers themselves (leftists, family members of those shot) were used as cannon fodder by the insurgents to defeat members of their own class and, by extension, the Republic. One crossed over to their ranks; others were afraid to, so as not to put family members who remained behind in the town in danger. This explains the friendly contacts at the front, of which the book gives testimony. In the final analysis, this was a war and postwar of "the underdogs."

For those who, on occasion, returned from the front, the memory of Castilleja is terrible: a desolated place that reminds us of Rulfo's story of *Pedro Páramo*; a return to a situation that is not the one from before the Republic but rather another that is much worse, in which all rights, even the most basic, had ceased to exist. The research also goes to the heart of the economic repression, a very powerful weapon in the hands of the New Order, especially in a system in which everyone was obliged to bend the rules in order to survive. There is a good portrayal of Spain in the years of hunger, rationing, and the black market, of mere survival, of boys working from a young age, and of girls serving endless days in the houses of the wealthy in exchange for almost nothing. And, above all, the book pays homage as well to the women, the real mainstays of that defeated and humiliated world during the darkest stage of the dictatorship; women like Suceso Rodríguez or Carmen Muñoz, whose terrible hardships are reflected in the narrative.

Barker has also collected testimonies on the changing times after the eternal postwar. His work concludes with Franco's death and the first democratic elections. The epilogue deals of necessity with what was done at that time with the memory of what lay behind. It becomes clear that because of the way the transition was achieved there was no place for the victims of the Franco repression. The only thing that was accomplished in Castilleja, and it is an exceptional case attained with no little effort, was that the street named for the Falangist killed in May 1936 disappeared. If there was not to be a street for all the victims, there should not be a street for any of them. What normally occurred elsewhere was worse: the Franco version of the past remained alive and that of the defeated remained hidden. The case of Castilleja constitutes a good example of what the transition did with the past.

We are in the presence of a great work carried out on-site, one of those research projects that are undertaken only once in a lifetime. At the end the author affirms, correctly, that if there had been a Commission of Truth to examine the crimes of the Franco regime "this book would not exist." He may well have said it thinking of the effort involved and the time devoted to the task, effort and time that under normal circumstances would have fallen to others. For that alone we ought to be profoundly grateful to him.

SEVILLE, December 18, 2006

Note

1 Gerald Brenan, *Al sur de Granada*; Julian Pitt-Rivers, *Los hombres de la sierra*; George A. Collier, *Socialistas de la Andalucía rural*; Margaret Van Epp, *Si yo te dijera . . .*; Jerome R. Mintz, *Los anarquistas de Casas Viejas*; Ronald Fraser, *Escondido* and *Mijas*.

Author's Preface

The telephone man plants a seed

At my back, the sun was setting behind the church steeple in Escacena del Campo. I was walking downhill along the path that descends from Montijena Hill to the Seville - Huelva General Highway. I had been photographing Castilleja del Campo in the reddish evening light. It was August 1986, almost the end of my second summer in the town of my wife, "Carmina." That was Carmen's nickname in Castilleja. When I arrived at the highway, I encountered an older man who was returning to town after working his plot of land. He greeted me as if he knew me, which did not surprise me because, by then, most of the town's six hundred and fifty residents knew who I was. But the familiarity with which he talked to me did seem somewhat strange. We entered the town and turned right, walking uphill to the door where my wife and mother-in-law were waiting for me.

They told me that this was "Antonio the Telephone Man," so called because the telephone exchange was in his house. Until a short while before, it had been one of only a few telephones in the town and, during eight months in 1980, Carmen and I communicated by that telephone as we coordinated our respective bureaucratic odysseys, I through the Department of Immigration and Naturalization and she through the American Consulate in Seville, so they would grant her a visa and we could be married in the United States. That is why Antonio knew me so well. He had been a privileged witness to the frustrating Kafkaesque stage of our courtship. Before saying goodbye, Antonio proposed we get together the following afternoon on his plot of land for a chat.

It was still hot when Carmen and I arrived, and Antonio was resting under the fig tree that provided the only shade on his parcel. He was weaving grass to make traps for the sparrows that were eating his figs. We chatted about many things I no longer remember until the conversation took an unexpectedly dark turn. Antonio described an event he witnessed shortly before the outbreak of the civil war, the murder of a young man from the town at the hands of Communists from Seville who were passing by on the highway. He included many details I omit here, and concluded by saying that later they killed a lot of people here. "What people?" "Leftists."

"Why?" It was getting dark and Antonio wanted to pick some figs for us. The conversation was over.

When we said goodbye at my mother-in-law's door, Carmen and I thanked him for the figs and for a very interesting afternoon. Antonio told me he had many other things to tell me and that he knew other people his age who would like to talk to me about these things. I did not see him again in the short time we had left in Castilleja that summer. Back in the United States where I was teaching Spanish at a small college, I often remembered the event Antonio the Telephone Man had described, and its tantalizing conclusion: "Later they killed a lot of people here." The idea of so much violence did not conform to the image I had of my wife's town, a cheerful, friendly place celebrated in "Sevillanas" sung by Los Rocieros that Carmen used to play on our phonograph when she was homesick, and whose refrain was: "This is Spain. Ay, what joy. Ay, what joy, the example of a simple town of Andalusia."

We returned to Castilleja in the winter of 1989–90. I brought a tape recorder to interview Antonio and the other people his age he had mentioned. I naively thought that interweaving testimonies from several points of view could result in a small book that put a human face on the Spanish civil war. I never suspected that I was embarking on a project that would take almost two decades to bear fruit. I usually describe the seed of this project as the result of a chance encounter, but I have often thought it was not really fortuitous, that Antonio had seen me taking photographs on Montijena Hill and had timed his return to town so we would meet on the Seville – Huelva General Highway. Perhaps this astute Andalusian peasant sitting under his fig tree weaving traps for sparrows was also weaving a trap for me, a trap like the one Scheherazade had woven for the sultan Schahriar in *The Thousand and One Arabian Nights*, telling stories but leaving them unfinished so the sultan would have to come back the next night to hear the rest.

The first interviews and a small book

That winter in 1989–90, during a period of three weeks, I was able to interview sixteen residents of Castilleja, men and women, right-wingers as well as leftists. I did not arrive at the interviews with a list of specific questions because, at first, I was too ignorant to even know what to ask. Gradually I began to know more, but I always gave the person I was interviewing free rein to talk about whatever came into their head. The spontaneous declarations were always the most interesting and the less I talked, the better the interview. To do oral history one must adhere to the saying a colleague of mine from Guiana learned from her mother: "When God gave us two ears but only one mouth, maybe he was trying to tell us something."

There were times during these first interviews that reminded me of the name of a game show that used to be on Spanish television: *Si lo sé, no vengo* (*Had I Known, I Would Not Have Come*). If the killing of "a lot of people" mentioned by Antonio was at odds with the image I had of the town, how much more shocking it was when those I interviewed said that it was townspeople themselves who bore the greatest responsibility for the killings. Manuel García Ramírez, for example, gave the following answer when I asked him who was responsible: *You ask who did it? Well people from the town. Yes. Because those who came from outside did not know anybody. Are we not in agreement about that? Yes. Of course. They took the ones the people here told them to take. For political reasons. And probably from personal hatreds as well.* Equally alarming were declarations about other methods of repression: the public humiliation of women; economic and social marginalization of the widows and orphans of the men who had been shot; economic reprisals against those who had stood out during the Republic; townspeople condemned to prison, labor battalions, internal exile, or supervised liberty.

For two and a half years I listened to the tapes, taking notes, and transcribing passages that could be used in a small book about what had happened in Castilleja. I wrote a rough draft in 1992 during my third summer in the town. I showed part of it to some of those I had interviewed. Their reactions ranged from lukewarm to highly critical. A close friend as well as my brother-in-law read the entire manuscript. The former reacted positively, although I suspect mostly out of politeness, and the latter told me he did not like the style. For reasons I will explain shortly, part of the manuscript also fell into the hands of a few people in the town who were adamantly opposed to "stirring up all this." They reacted with admonitions and even a threat.

In fact, I was not satisfied with the book either. Although there were parts that were dramatic and moving, and I thought I had succeeded in giving a human face to the Spanish civil war, the puzzle was missing too many pieces to form a coherent narrative. In too many places I had had to resort to speculation about the motives and causes of what had happened. I had not even been able to put together a complete list of all the victims of the repression. Above all, I was by then very aware that naming those responsible for the repression carried the risk of wounding the sensibilities of their family members.

I gave serious thought to abandoning the project, but some of my colleagues, professors of sociology, political science, philosophy, and

English, read a translation I had made of the book and were of the opinion that, although obviously a work in progress, the book had "possibilities." But where to go from there? To continue interviewing witnesses would have resulted in more examples of the same perspectives. And the only documentary references I had to events in the town were brief journalistic accounts of the murder of the young man of Castilleja before the war, news items I had encountered in the Municipal Newspaper Library of Seville.

My training is in Spanish literature, not history, so the first step was to educate myself on the Republic, the civil war, and the Franco dictatorship so I could place the events in Castilleja in their national and international context. I became an insatiable reader of histories of the period. During my third summer in the town, in 1996, I bought many works by a new generation of Spanish historians who examine the period from a post-Franco perspective. And I continued reading.

A self-taught historian in the municipal archive

In 2000, my university granted me a one-semester sabbatical which allowed me to be in Castilleja from January to August. Among the new books I found in the Seville bookstores were works about the repression on the provincial and local level, all recently published by Spaniards. The one that most influenced me was *La Guerra Civil en Huelva* by Francisco Espinosa Maestre. It is a detailed study of events in the province of Huelva, with lists of the names of those shot, town by town. It has a section called "Sources for the Study of the Repression," which could be considered an instruction manual on how to undertake research in the municipal archives. I spoke to Luis Goicoechea Roso, municipal secretary of Castilleja del Campo, who was kind enough to allow me to spend as much time as I wanted in the town's archive.

I found it to be unpleasant work. The archive was a room without windows or ventilation and I could not spend more than two hours there without my eyes watering and my nose itching from the dusty old documents. It was also frustrating. The documents were organized by year and by general categories, but it had still not been professionally archived with an index. Sometimes I spent days without finding anything of interest. But whenever I was most discouraged, I would come upon true gems. Among other things, my discoveries enabled me to identify the majority of those who had been shot and their descendants. They also filled in many of the gaps in my understanding of the town's history, especially during the Republic.

More interesting for me were the lines of investigation the new information afforded, such as tracking down the descendants of the men who had been shot, copying photographs of the latter, and recording testimonies about them. I met two of the children of Castilleja's schoolteacher during the Republic, Joaquín León Trejo. Not only did they let me copy photographs of their father, they provided a great deal of information about their three uncles, two of whom had been shot, as their father had been, and another who had gone into exile in the United States after serving as a colonel of Engineers and Aviation in the Republican army. When I returned home after my sabbatical, I believed I had enough material to finish the book, but I was still worried by the repercussions that the publication of so much information about the repression could have in a town as small as Castilleja. Nor was it clear to me that there was an audience whose interest in such a book would compensate the risks of publication.

The project finds an audience

Back in the United States, I postponed the writing of the book, primarily because of my doubts about the advisability of publishing the results of my research, but also because of a fortuitous occurrence that took me in a different direction. Thanks to the internet, in the autumn of 2000 I was able to track down the American descendants of Colonel Francisco León Trejo, brother of the Castilleja schoolteacher. One of his sons and one of his grandsons were enthusiastic about the possibility of a family history in English, centered on the León Trejo brothers. Although I regretted squandering all the work I had invested in the history of Castilleja, it seemed less risky to explore the human dimensions of the civil war by portraying these four brothers who had suffered the tragic consequences of that conflict. The responsibility for their tragedies was much more diffuse than in the case of the victims of the repression in Castilleja and, therefore, there was less danger of wounding sensibilities.

At about the same time, another occurrence attracted my attention, although at the time I did not know how much importance it would have for me. I heard a report on National Public Radio about the exhumation of cadavers from a mass grave in Priaranza del Bierzo. It was thus that I learned of Emilio Silva, the grandson of one of the men whose bodies were exhumed, and the founder of the ARMH (Association for the Recuperation of Historical Memory). I followed the activities of the ARMH with great interest during the following years and continued working on my little history of the León Trejo brothers. In the spring of 2004, I was at home writing when the telephone rang. "I am Noelia Rodríguez, from Castilleja del Campo." "Carmina is not home. Would you like to leave a message?" "Well in fact, I wanted to talk to you." She explained that she was organizing a conference with the local members of AMHyJA (Association for Historical Memory and Justice of Andalusia) and that her mother Otilia had told her I had been investigating the history of Castilleja for many years. As soon as she named Otilia Escobar Muñoz, I realized I was talking to the granddaughter of Manuel Escobar Moreno, one of the men shot in 1936.

On June 4, I found myself before a microphone in the Castilleja Town Meeting Hall presenting lists of the names of the various categories of victims of the repression in the town: the men who had been shot, their widows and orphans, the women who had been publicly humiliated, and the men who had been imprisoned during the war and the Franco dictatorship. My presentation paid homage to the victims of the repression without naming those responsible. More than 10 percent of the residents of the town packed the hall. The presentation was well received and I returned to the United States knowing that my research had found an audience.

This book

The book you are reading goes beyond a tribute to the victims of the repression in Castilleja. It is an exploration of what happened and why, which would be impossible without naming many of those responsible. I am still aware of the risk of wounding the sensibilities of family members. I have spoken to some of these descendants who have accepted what their ancestors did and have assured me that I do not need to apologize for publishing this history. I have met others who know very little about the role of their ancestors in the repression. Their families had never talked to them about what happened in the town, with the laudable intention of protecting them. But this protection has not always worked. During the winter of the first interviews, I was at a party during which a young woman mentioned one of her great-uncles. A boy from a leftist family blurted out, "Your great-uncle was a murderer." The poor girl was speechless. Would she not have been better protected had she known enough to avoid being caught off-guard at such an inappropriate occasion?

The young woman spent the rest of the party in a corner with a young man, great-grandson of the Republican mayor who was shot during the repression. He gently explained to her some of what had taken place fifty-five years before. Two and a half years later she was still troubled by this glimpse of the skeletons in her family's closet and asked my wife if she could read what I was writing. My wife lent her a copy of the part of the manuscript I had written so far and the woman confronted one of her uncles with it. This led to my being threatened by one of her cousins.

This cousin was among the descendants of those responsible who seem to think that the mere act of talking about Castilleja's past is to open old wounds that have already healed. I can assure them that, during my research, I never met a family member of the victims of the repression who had closed wounds. If family members of those responsible are made uncomfortable by the publication of this book, their discomfort cannot be compared to the suffering of the victims' families. If I name some of those who killed, either with firearms or by drawing up the lists of those to be shot, it is not my intention to tarnish their memory. Nor do I believe myself capable of doing so. They themselves took care of that more than seventy years ago. They are all dead by now and, even if they were alive, they were pardoned by the Laws of Amnesty passed after Franco's death.

Neither is it my intention that this book be used as a weapon to be thrown in others' faces. Castilleja del Campo needs to turn the page. If it has still not been able to do so more than seventy years after the repression, perhaps it is because that page cannot be turned without being read.

To readers who are not from Castilleja

As I wrote this book, I imagined the people of Castilleja del Campo as the ideal audience. Nevertheless, I hope this book will be of interest to readers who are not from Castilleja del Campo. Chance led me to write this history of a town I consider neither exceptional nor typical. What happened in Castilleja del Campo from the advent of the Republic until after the postwar period also happened, always with variations, in many towns in Andalusia and the rest of Spain.

A note on quotations

This book includes quotations from the recorded interviews, some quite extensive. I use italics to distinguish them from the rest of the text. I have not corrected lexical or grammatical peculiarities and I have attempted to preserve in translation the flavor of the testimonies. Occasionally I have eliminated repeated phrases or digressions, but without falsifying the intention of the person interviewed. There are also quotations from documents.

They appear as block or run-in quotations. In my translations there are typographical, lexical, grammatical, and orthographic errors or peculiarities, which reflect errors or the style of the original.

Acknowledgments

It would be unforgivable not to recognize the people and institutions that have made this research project possible. In the first place my wife, Carmen Muñoz Luque, without whom I would never have come to know Castilleja del Campo. During almost two decades she put up with my obsession with the Spanish civil war and helped me with the lexical peculiarities of the older generation of her town as I transcribed the interviews. I also thank my late mother-in-law, Ignacia Luque Monge, in whose house many of the interviews took place.

I am grateful to the University of Wisconsin–Stevens Point for the grant that partially covered the expense of my trip to Castilleja in 1989 when I conducted the first interviews and for the semester sabbatical in spring 2000 that made possible my research in the Castilleja Municipal Archive, the Archiepiscopal Archive of Seville, and other archives. Another grant and a one year sabbatical in 2008/2009, gave me the means and time to make additions and corrections to the original book and translate it to English. The kind cooperation of the mayor of Castilleja, Vicente Zaragoza Alcover, the municipal secretary, Luis Goicoechea Roso, the justice of the peace, Raquel Luque Monge, and the secretary Rocío Morera has been indispensable.

The people on both sides of the Atlantic whose help, encouragement, or criticism has enabled me to write this book are so numerous that I fear offending someone by forgetting to include their name on this list that necessarily includes, from among my friends, colleagues and family members in the United States: John Bailiff, Gail Barker, Jesse Barker, Barbara Butler, Peter N. Carroll, Beverley David, Michael Gordon, Lance Grahn, Robert Knowlton, Michael Leander, Marcia Mace, James Missey, Valentina Peguero, Michael Roskin, Richard Ruppel, and Robert Wolensky. And from among my friends in Spain, the list includes: Juan Alonso del Real, José Armenta Vergne, José Antonio Borrego Suárez, Patricio de Blas Zabaleta, Francisco Espinosa Maestre, Juan Álvaro Fernández Luque, José María García Márquez, Antonio Gómez Luque, Cecilio Gordillo Giraldo, José Luis Gutiérrez Molina, Narciso Luque Cabrera, Juan Manuel Muñoz Luque, Almudena Muñoz Rivera, José Porras Sánchez, José María Ramírez Bravo, Isabelo Rebollo Tebas, Francisco

Manuel Rivera Luque, Raúl Rivera Luque, Modesto Rodríguez Escobar, Felipe Rodríguez Fernández, Miguel Ángel Rodríguez Luque, Fernando Sígler Silvera, and Vicente Zaragoza García.

The interest and enthusiasm of the Castilleja del Campo members of the Association for Historical Memory and Justice of Andalusia have been of special importance: Álvaro Fernández Rivera, Antonio García Luque, Sara Rebollo Tebas, and Noelia Rodríguez Escobar.

My greatest debt is to those who agreed to interviews, shared their memories during casual conversations, or allowed me to copy photographs and private documents. Their names appear on the list of oral sources. Without exaggeration I can call them the real authors of this book, relegating myself to the humble role of scribe. It has been a great honor for me to have met them and to have served as the transmitter of their recollections.

The past is never dead. It's not even past.

WILLIAM FAULKNER

Part One

Republic

One

The First Republican Biennium

Regime change

On April 12, 1931, there were municipal elections in Spain. Republican and Socialist candidates won in almost all the large cities and in many towns, including Castilleja del Campo. Two days later, King Alphonse XIII went into exile, never to return, and in Castilleja, as in all Spain, people gathered in the streets to celebrate the end of the monarchy. Miguel Rodríguez Caraballo, a right-winger, was in the doorway of his house next to the church and he remembers that a car from the neighboring town of Carrión de los Céspedes passed by, its loudspeaker proclaiming, *"We won, we won. Long live the Republic!"* Carmen Monge Romero, a leftist, was twenty-four years old and joined the demonstration carrying a flag and shouting, *"The Republic! The Republic!"* She remembers that *everyone was in the street, at least the young people.*

That night the transfer of power took place in the Castilleja town hall. José Ramírez Rufino, president of the Republican Committee, and ten other members of the committee demanded control of the municipal government. The monarchist mayor, Juan Reinoso Padilla, ordered the municipal secretary, Hilario Luque Ramírez, to confer by telephone with the new Republican civil governor of Seville, Ramón González Sicilia de la Corte. The latter made known "that, in fact, the proclamation of the Republic in Spain has taken place" and ordered the transfer of the insignias of command to José Ramírez Rufino.[1] In Madrid, a provisional government was being formed, led by Niceto Alcalá-Zamora and in which Republicans Manuel Azaña, Santiago Casares Quiroga, Marcelino Domingo, Alejandro Lerroux, Diego Martínez Barrio, and Socialists Indalecio Prieto, Francisco Largo Caballero, Julián Besteiro, and others would serve.

On April 30, the new town council of Castilleja del Campo met in the town hall. Mayor José Ramírez Rufino, nicknamed "Joselito the Barber" for his profession, presided. Councilmen Leocadio Ramírez Rufino and Manuel Romero Rodríguez were present. The new mayor of Castilleja marked the regime change by ordering the removal of portraits of the king and of

General Miguel Primo de Rivera from the town meeting room, the municipal court, and the town's schoolrooms. Primo de Rivera, with the approval of the king, had established a dictatorship by coup on September 23, 1923. Paintings of the Sacred Heart of Jesus would also be removed from all public buildings, indicating one of the characteristics of the new regime, which would establish the separation of church and state in a secular, even openly anticlerical, climate. The minutes reflect another characteristic of the new regime: "The Mayor was empowered to acquire for the Meeting Room of this Town Council a painting with the symbolic representation or allegory of the Republic."[2]

Conflicts with the oligarchy

The Second Spanish Republic was born amid great economic difficulties. It had inherited the largest budget deficit in Spanish history. There was severe unemployment, especially in the Andalusian countryside. One of the first measures taken by the provisional government in Madrid was to establish a public works program to provide jobs for unemployed day laborers. Indalecio Prieto, the new Socialist finance minister, announced the distribution of funds to the provincial governments of Andalusia and Estremadura for distribution to the municipalities.[3]

During a town council meeting on May 9, 1931, the Castilleja municipal secretary, Hilario Luque Ramírez, reported on a meeting in Sanlúcar la Mayor at which it had been announced that the government would distribute economic aid "in proportion to the number of inhabitants of each town" for the "general repair of streets and rural roads."[4] At the next meeting, it was announced that in the town of Pilas thirty-five thousand pesetas would be distributed to the district "as economic aid to remedy the labor crisis." Castilleja's share would be 443 pesetas and the council decided it would pay 4.25 pesetas for five hours work.[5] This decision, as innocent as it may seem, was regarded as a threat by those who had previously controlled the economic life of the town: the large landowners, their administrators, and their handpicked representatives on the town councils. This control had depended on the chronic unemployment which permitted landowners to pay between 4 and 5 pesetas for a day's work. With a government independent of the landowners or their administrators paying the same for half a day's work, the landowners lost the absolute control they had enjoyed over the labor force. According to the minutes of subsequent meetings, the employment of day laborers for public works in Castilleja would continue in the future. The town council would spend 516.24 pesetas on public works in May 1932, paying unemployed laborers 4.25 pesetas for five and a half hours work.[6] At a meeting on October 1932, it was agreed to undertake street repairs.[7]

A public works program could alleviate the economic crisis in the countryside, but the real solution would be agrarian reform or, at the very least, a change in the relations between landowners and their workers. Property in Castilleja and the rest of Andalusia was so poorly distributed that a few landowners provided the only source of employment for day laborers, the majority of the population. Much of the land in Castilleja belonged to Doña María Gamero Cívico y de Porres, Countess of the Atalayas, and Doña Elisa de Porres Osborne, Marchioness of Castilleja del Campo. Their families' landholdings went back centuries. The county of the Atalayas was granted to Don Pedro Antonio de Porres y Silva by King Charles III on May 2, 1763. The marquisate of Castilleja del Campo was granted to Don Tomás Francisco Ponce de León y Cueto by King Charles II on June 8, 1682.[8] There were also two large landowners without titles of nobility, José María Cuevas Escobar and Juan Martín Calero Rebollo, and some medium and small landholders.

Like most of the landed gentry of Andalusia, the countess and the marchioness lived in the city and left the management of their property to administrators, managers, foremen, and permanent workers. The marchioness visited Castilleja generally twice a year and owned the largest house in the town. The countess had estates in several other localities and, apparently, had never set foot in Castilleja. Her estates were administered by Don Pedro Parias González, who visited the town frequently. The center of administrative activity for the countess's property in Castilleja was a building called "the palace," which more closely resembled a rustic country house than a palace for the nobility.

Before undertaking agrarian reform, the provisional government in Madrid took measures to change the relations between landowners and their day laborers. The first of these was the Decree of Municipal Boundaries, April 28, 1931, which prohibited the employment of workers from outside each municipality until all the laborers from within the municipality were working. Laborers registered with their local unions. In order to hire them, the landowners' managers had to go to the union, which distributed the work among its members. This law gave the landless agricultural workers and their unions a control over the labor market they had never had before and took from the owners the absolute political and judicial power they had enjoyed in the past. They could no longer use their ability to give or withhold work as a means to reward laborers for their political support or punish them for their political opposition or union activities. This change inverted the relationship between workers and landowners. Day laborers did not have to kowtow to the bosses in order to earn a living. It was the bosses who had to go to the union if they needed workers and they had to accept those workers the union provided.

Antonio Monge Pérez explained how the system functioned in Castilleja del Campo during the Republic. I had asked him about the criteria for selecting the men who were shot during the repression: *It was the people who had been active in the unions, you know? Defending the rights of the workers. Those who said, "We have to distribute work so that everyone gets to eat," the poor, in particular, who were affiliated with the union. It was those who worked in the union, which had its office in the town hall. That was where the workers who were neediest signed up. Those who had a little piece of land or a business or something, they did not get work like the others. So those in charge were there to make sure things worked as fairly as possible.*

And the people who were in the union office distributed work to the poorest workers when the bosses came to say, "Okay, I need three men to reap, or to prune olive trees, or to till the olive groves," like that. Well, the bosses took a great hatred toward those people because often they did not want certain people because they did not work as hard as others. They wanted to hire three or four men, but they wanted only the cream of the crop, the hardest workers, the strongest. And the heads of families who were most needy, and were weaker, well, the bosses did not want them. And then the union leaders would tell them, "Yes, yes, you have to give him work because he has a family and he has to feed his children, and you have to hire him," like that. And the ones who were union leaders, or town councilmen, all these things contributed to the bosses conceiving mortal hatreds toward them, you see? And later, they carried out the massacre here, you could call it, no? That is how it was.

The bosses also had to pay the workers more. On May 7, Francisco Largo Caballero, the Socialist labor minister, introduced mixed juries to negotiate wages and working hours. The effect was that workers earned almost twice what they earned during the monarchy. Many landowners in Andalusia reacted to the new situation by letting their land lie fallow. The government responded to this agricultural lockout on May 7 with the Decree of Obligatory Cultivation, which imposed fines on landowners who refused to cultivate their lands, but the fines were small and the terms of the decree were difficult to enforce. Later, another strategy to pressure landowners to cultivate their lands was to declare their fallow land to be of "social utility," which made it subject to expropriation according to Article 44 of the constitution passed on December 9, 1931. Article 44 would open the door to a kind of agrarian reform in Castilleja.

The municipal government of Castilleja used these legal means to alleviate the miserable lot of the town's laborers. Starting with the town council meeting of January 23, 1932, and continuing until October 14, 1934, when Mayor José Ramírez Rufino was forced from office, the minutes contain references to the approval of land grants to the town's poorer residents, small plots in what the minutes call the "Village Meadow."[9] This part of the town next to the highway is still called "the meadow" even though it is now an urban development. It is not entirely clear who owned this land at the time. The name "Village Meadow" suggests that it belonged to the town, but this name could have been an historical throwback, a reference to municipal property that was disentailed in the nineteenth century and then sold to the countess's ancestors.

I have called the granting of parcels in Castilleja a kind of agrarian reform because its purpose was not only to provide the poor with land to cultivate but also to give them a place to live. In the 1930s, Castilleja was much smaller physically than it is today, even though there were almost one hundred more inhabitants.[10] The poorest were crowded into houses shared by many members of one or more families. The primitive dirt-floored huts built on the parcels of the "Village Meadow" alleviated these overcrowded and unsanitary conditions and provided their owners with small vegetable gardens to supplement their chronically deficient diets.

Those who acquired such plots in "the meadow" needed access to potable water. The mayor took steps to remedy this need at a council meeting on April 9, 1932, during which he demanded "That the area along the old road be immediately expropriated to its rightful owners, in other words the people of this town. . . ." and ". . . That the Well located on the public thoroughfare (highway), be for the people and not continue for even one more moment misappropriated by grandees to whom it does not belong nor who deserve it." The "old road" referred to in the first demand and the well, mentioned in the second demand, were right next to the "Village Meadow," and the mayor clearly saw them as property of the municipality. The bitterness behind these demands is evident in the indignant and even sarcastic language of the motion. The conflict over the "old road" would continue for several more years.

Another measure taken by the town council was symbolic in nature and reflects the confidence of the town's Republican authorities in their confrontation with the Andalusian oligarchy. On August 8, 1931, the council agreed to change the names of the town's streets. One of the changes was to eliminate Pedro Parias Street, renaming it Fermín Galán. Pedro Parias González, besides administering the many estates of the countess, was a large landholder himself. A retired lieutenant colonel in the cavalry, he had been president of the Provincial Council of Seville from 1928 to 1930 and the director of the Economic Federation of Andalusia (FEDA).[11]

He was also a f[illegible] w name given to his street was a del[illegible] him a great deal that his street [illegible] lán Rodríguez, one of two [illegible] against the monarchy in [illegible] ther Republican martyr of [illegible] el García Hernández, also [illegible] named for no less an icon [illegible]

[illegible] he conspirators in an [illegible] ille by the monarchist [illegible] and his son Gonzalo [illegible] days following the c[illegible] e summer of 1932 an[illegible] who participated in thes[illegible] nt of the local Civil Guard barra[illegible] rnor, sent a message to the Castilleja town [illegible] orization to carry out several house searches by night [illegible] by day, since there is evidence of the existence of a great number of small firearms, and by so doing quash the efforts of extremist elements against the present regime."[13] Two days later, the municipal judge and the municipal secretary of Castilleja granted the requested authorization.[14] The results of the searches were negative, if in fact the Civil Guard actually carried them out. This paramilitary body was itself part of the conspiracy.

- A Republic was put in place.
- Made efforts to improve things for the working class such as providing war work & improving living conditions.
- Government became independent of landowners & their administrators; government also now independent of the clergy.
- Attempted but failed coup against the Republic.
- Opponents turn to politics.

General Sanjurjo's coup began in Seville on the morning of August 10, 1932 with the declaration of a state of war and, at five o'clock that afternoon, the commandant of the Civil Guard barracks in Carrión de los Céspedes arrived in Castilleja and removed the Republican mayor from office.[15] The dismissal of the Republican mayor José Ramírez Rufino did not last long because General Sanjurjo's coup failed immediately, demonstrating that it would not be easy to overthrow the Republic by force. Subsequently, those who opposed the Republican-Socialist coalition led by Manuel Azaña began to direct their efforts toward taking power through the ballot box.

Conflicts with the church

The changes in the names of Castilleja del Campo's streets were directed against the church as well as the oligarchy. Venerable Mañara Street, which commemorated the seventeenth-century Seville nobleman who was almost a saint to the province's Catholics, was changed to Pablo Iglesias Street, in honor of the founder of the Spanish Socialist Party and every bit a saint to the nation's Marxists. Conflicts with the church would be more than symbolic. On September 11, 1931, Cardinal Ilundáin, archbishop of Seville, received a letter from the parish priest of Castilleja, Don Felipe Rodríguez Sánchez. The letter is a complaint about one of the public works projects in the town.

> Castilleja del Campo   9/11/31
>
> Most Excellent and Reverend Cardinal Archbishop of Seville= I place before you for the information of Your Roman Excellency that the Mayor of this village without notification, and under the pretext of street expansion, has destroyed the porch of our Church, has carried off half the materials, which had been purchased by my predecessor, and has shared some of these out, refusing now to finance the repairs and all from sectarian motives. = Since all my protests against so many outrages are useless, and with the rainy season's approach it being a danger for the walls of the temple to delay repairs, I communicate it to Your Roman Excellency and await your instructions. = Felipe Rodríguez[16]

This letter is all there is on the conflict between the priest and the mayor over the demolition of the church's porch, which leaves a number of unanswered questions. Was the part of the porch that was destroyed on ecclesiastical or municipal property? Would the conflict have been resolved without rancor if the mayor had consulted Don Felipe before widening the street? Did the mayor return the materials that had been carried off? Two things, however, are clear. The church wall did not collapse, because it is still there today. Nor did the Republican mayor and the town's priest ever make peace. At a council meeting four months later it was "agreed unanimously and as proposed by the Mayor, to demolish the two Crosses erected in the streets of this town."[17] This led to another letter from Don Felipe to Cardinal Ilundáin:

> 1/28/32
>
> Most Excellent and Reverend Cardinal Archbishop of Seville
>
> The Town Council of this village agreed a few days ago to remove the Crosses from the public thoroughfare, demolishing their pedestals. Next to the walls of the temple there is one that belongs to the Parish, whose wrought iron railings and pedestal are on property ceded by the Town Council of –1900– and whose maintenance have since that time been at the expense of the Parish; they are not in the public thoroughfare.

Next Sunday, in spite of my protest, they have decided to repeat this outrage, and at the hour of mass, announcing the same profanations they carried out with another Cross last Sunday.

Since no rights are respected here nor any protests heeded, occupied as this Municipality is by nothing but sectarian plans, I inform Your Excellency and await your instructions.

May God grant Your Roman Excellency many years.

Felipe Rodríguez[18]

The next day, the cardinal wrote the following comment at the bottom of Don Felipe's letter:

Seville, January 29, 1932

Lamenting bitterly the outrage that, according to the information of the Parish Priest of Castilleja del Campo, the Town Council intends to commit demolishing the cross that is installed near the Parish's temple; and this being on the property of the Church itself, we order the aforementioned Priest that if the intended demolition is carried out he direct a formal protest against this outrage that is unjustified and by no means prescribed by the law. This protest should be formulated in writing and sent to the Civil Governor and to the Examining Magistrate of the jurisdiction. – The Parish Priest should ensure that the holy cross not be profaned, after its demolition. The Parish Priest will report to us everything he does and the results of the affair.

Cardinal Archbishop[19]

Four days later Don Felipe wrote another letter in fulfillment of the instructions of the cardinal to inform him of the actions taken and their results:

2/2/32

Most Excellent and Reverend Cardinal Archbishop of Seville

I hereby inform Your Roman Excellency regarding the demolition of the parish Cross decreed by this Town Council.

In order to avoid profanations, incidents and commotion, and considering that the councilmen's intention is to suppress all religious symbols in the streets, I made haste last Saturday to remove the aforementioned Cross, gathering all the materials, and on Sunday I celebrated a mass of atonement for the profanations of the previous Sunday.

Unfortunately, for the time being it is in vain to formulate protests here for these deeds.

B.R.el A.P.de V.E.R. [*I Respectfully Kiss the Pontifical Ring of Your Roman Excellency*]

Felipe Rodríguez[20]

This exchange of letters reveals the legal disposition of the land where the cross was erected. It was on property ceded to the parish by the town council in 1900, but the Republican mayor did not agree with this gift made thirty-two years before. The conclusion to Don Felipe's last letter implies that he did not intend to formulate a written protest to the civil governor and the examining magistrate since, "for the time being," such protests would be "in vain."

The conflict between Castilleja's mayor and parish priest over the demolition of crosses exemplifies what was taking place throughout Spain in 1932. No provision of the new constitution had provoked more heated controversy than Article 26, which severely restricted the historic privileges and activities of the church. In October 1931, during the debate over Article 26, Manuel Azaña, head of the provisional government, had declared that Spain was no longer Catholic in the same way it had been in the sixteenth century.[21] He was describing Spain's new reality. Under the Republic, an increasingly secular society was emerging that was more attractive to the majority of Spaniards than the rigid ideology extolled from the pulpits. In 1932, only 10 percent of the population in the city of Seville attended mass, the number of civil weddings was increasing by the day, and almost half the burials were secular.[22]

There are no further letters from Don Felipe until the end of the year, when he wrote again to Cardinal Ilundáin. It is a letter filled with desperation, reflected in his convoluted syntax, which I have preserved in the following translation:

Castilleja del Campo   12/23/32

Most Excellent and Reverend Cardinal Archbishop of Seville.

Your Roman Excellency has doubtless read in the press of the shooting of which my fellow parish priest in Carrión and others were victims when they came to this town for the conclusion of the cult of the Immaculate Conception.

Although those involved are known, but since the Mayor here is the principal perpetrator of the persecution we suffer against religious practices, with the backing of a communist center and to which are affiliated the majority of the councilmen, a by now personal struggle and a situation so anarchic has been created, that it is impossible to celebrate religious rites, what with the threats and attacks they direct at us and the exposure of my family and my person. Since neither the Civil Guard nor the authorities have attempted to investigate anything and the same can be said each time there are attacks against the Church with such impunity they threaten to burn the temple.

I who have tried to assure that my village be pious, as the majority are, it is so intimidated with so much persecution that I am without parishioners and I find myself obliged to tell Your Roman Excellency, after consulting with the Archdeacon and Rector of the Seminary who advises me to do so, of the impossibility of remaining here, at the risk of some lamentable mishap, because my family cannot consent to be so offended without coming to the defense of our beliefs and with one of my brothers being continually exposed as I am to some serious incident because of the war declared on the Church by the Municipality as well as by the communist center and the more I have protested the greater the persecution.

Since on the other hand I cannot move too far from here because of my father being afflicted with so much suffering and because I have assumed part of the confessions of my fellow priest in Carrión helping him with everything because he is by now old and frail, for the previous need and the latter interest, I take the liberty of requesting of Your Roman Excellency my temporary transfer to Carrión de los Céspedes, little more than a kilometer from here with frequent bus service and to come here only for what is strictly necessary. In this way I attend to my parish, my family finds peace, and I am near my father, serving as well my fellow priest as I have been doing for many years as Your Roman Excellency knows well.

With tears in my eyes I write these lines to Your Roman Excellency, tears that are not motivated by the persecution, which comforts and cheers me as a priest, they are the effect of seeing my town in the clutches of anarchy.

B.R.el A.P.de V.E.R. [*I Respectfully Kiss the Pontifical Ring of Your Roman Excellency*]

Felipe Rodríguez[23]

The shooting that motivated this letter is a serious matter. Nevertheless, Don Felipe dispenses with it in a sentence and a half. Apparently, the frail old priest in Carrión and those who accompanied him escaped the incident unharmed. If there had been fatalities or injuries, Don Felipe would certainly have mentioned them. The perpetrators were either very bad marksmen or their intention was only to frighten the victims. The shooting incident is just a pretext to launch into a diatribe against the Republican authorities and the workers' center, and to request a transfer to Carrión.

OIIGARCHY = when power vests with a small number of people.

The church had been the historic ally of the oligarchy and the measures taken by the Republic had strengthened this alliance. The church was as dismayed by Article 26 of the new constitution as the landowners were with the Decree of Municipal Boundaries, the labor agreements established by mixed juries, and the Decree of Obligatory Cultivation. Furthermore, just as the Decree of Municipal Boundaries had wrested control of the labor market from the bosses, it had also taken away the control the priests had enjoyed over their parishioners. While the bosses could no longer deny work to politically recalcitrant laborers, the parish priests could no longer withhold character references from laborers for not attending mass. Workers no longer needed such references. By signing up with the local labor union they could find work without having to feign a piousness they perhaps did not feel.

Don Felipe wrote of ". . . the threats and attacks they direct at us and the exposure of my family and my person." In a town the size of Castilleja, all conflicts are personal and involve families. And all alliances as well. The brother described as "being continually exposed as I am to some serious incident" was part of the Castilleja del Campo oligarchy. Don José Rodríguez Sánchez was the manager of the countess's estates in Castilleja and, in the spring of 1936, would replace Pedro Parias as administrator of all her landholdings. The way he handled these posts would earn him the nickname "*El Topamí*" ("All for me"). The fear expressed by Don Felipe was a premonition, but would need two corrections. It would not be his brother José who would suffer a "serious incident" but rather the family of his other brother, Don Julio Rodríguez Sánchez, a retired captain and veteran of the Moroccan War. Don Julio's son Manuel Rodríguez Mantero would be the mortal victim of a shooting at the hands of leftists in the spring of 1936. The other correction is that the perpetrators of the shooting in which one of Don Felipe's family members was to meet his death would not be leftists from Castilleja, as Don Felipe feared, but members of *Juventudes Comunistas* (Communist Youth) from Seville who were passing through town on the highway.

As far as the request for a transfer to Carrión de los Céspedes is concerned, Cardinal Ilundáin's response was blunt:

Dec. 26

In these times all of us who have the salvation of souls in our hands must remain steadfast at our posts. Bonus pastor animam suam dat pro ovibus suis. [*The good shepherd gives his soul for his sheep.*] It is necessary for our families to fathom well the gravity of our duty to remain at the side of our faithful. In my judgment you would run a greater risk coming and going

from Carrión to Castilleja than you would living in your parish. Your most
affectionate Prelate blesses and commends you . . .
Cardinal Archbishop[24]

The cardinal's judgment had perceived the contradiction between the
pretext of the letter, the shooting incident on the road between Castilleja
and Carrión, and the request for a transfer to Carrión, which would require
Don Felipe to travel often along the same kilometer of road.

What could have been the real motive of the Castilleja priest's request
for a transfer to Carrión de los Céspedes? In the summer of 2000, I read this
letter to Marina Luque Reinoso, from a right-wing family. She asked me
when the letter was written. I told her it was from 1932, and she burst out
laughing. According to Marina, and her opinion has been seconded by
others, the true motive of the request was that Don Felipe's mistress lived
there. Without commenting on this explanation, I turn to another topic.

Educational reform

One of the Republic's most ambitious programs was to reform the country's education system, combat illiteracy, and create a population capable
of emerging from poverty and participating in a democracy. Between
1930 and 1934, the number of state schools in the province of Seville
increased from sixty-six to one hundred and ninety-two. The oligarchy
opposed educational reform. Extending literacy to landless peasants
threatened the landowners' control of the rural labor force. The church
opposed the state-run secular schools also. They were a threat to its
monopoly on education.

In the spring of 1932, the Castilleja del Campo town council announced
an opening for a state schoolteacher at a competitive convocation held in
Seville. One of those who attended was Joaquín León Trejo, from a Seville
family with Republican sympathies. His son José León García told me the
story of how his father became the Castilleja schoolteacher. Joaquín had
taught in the city of Seville and, since 1926, in the town of Pruna, province
of Seville. During the convocation, he filled out applications for openings
in Carabanchel, outside Madrid, and in Bilbao. He also saw the post in
Castilleja del Campo and asked one of his friends where that was. His friend,
confusing it with Castilleja de Guzmán, said it was just outside Seville, and
Joaquín filled out an application for that opening as well. With his experience, he could have won a post wherever he wanted, but he was assigned to
Castilleja because he was the only applicant. He ended up being the

Castilleja del Campo schoolteacher by mistake. During his four years in the town, Don Joaquín created a generation of Castilleja residents well-instructed in science, mathematics, and reading. Many of those I interviewed had passed through his classes and the literacy rate among them was much higher than that of subsequent generations and, needless to say, of the generations that had preceded them.

Some of those in the town were offended by the new schoolteacher's lack of respect for traditional values. Eduardo Rodríguez Mantero described his first encounter with Don Joaquín. Eduardo was seven years old and introduced himself on the first day of class saying he was the priest's nephew. As Eduardo recalled, Don Joaquín had responded by saying, *"Tropezamos de la Iglesia"* ("We trip over the church"). Since this makes no more sense in Spanish than it does in English, I imagine the teacher had actually said, *"Hemos topado con la Iglesia"* ("We have come up against the church"). Joaquín León Trejo was making a joke, quoting a passage from *Don Quixote*, but giving to Cervantes's work an anticlerical interpretation that may not have been the great novelist's intention.

In the novel (Part Two, Chapter Nine), Don Quixote and Sancho are in Toboso at night, looking for Dulcinea's castle. They approach a large building that turns out to be the town church and the following dialogue takes place:

> *"Con la iglesia hemos dado, Sancho."* ("We have come upon the church, Sancho.")
> "I see that," Sancho replied. "And I pray to God we have not come upon our grave, . . ."

Cervantes wrote "church" without capitalization, so that Don Quixote was referring to the building and not the institution. Furthermore, he uses the expression *dar con* (come upon) rather than *topar con* (come up against). And Sancho's reply continues with ". . . for it is not a good sign to walk past a cemetery at such an hour as this . . ." In short, if there is anticlericalism in this passage from Cervantes's novel, it is well disguised. Nevertheless, it has been misquoted to this day as an anticlerical reference to the inquisition.

Eduardo was surprised that his usual way of introducing himself to adults had not garnered him the respect that it always had. It is easy to imagine Don Felipe's reaction when his nephew told him the story of his first encounter with the new schoolteacher. One of Joaquín León Trejo's sons, Antonio León García, told me he had never seen his father argue with the town's priest, but neither had he ever seen them exchange greetings when their paths crossed in the streets of Castilleja.

Besides the government's program to combat illiteracy, the new freedom of expression brought by the Republic afforded other educational options in Castilleja del Campo. Adults who knew how to read, like Manuel Tebas Escobar, gave night classes in reading and arithmetic to laborers, according to his daughter Sara Tebas Rodríguez. One of Manuel Tebas's former students, Aurelio Monge Romero, told me the night classes were also attended by children unable to attend school because they had to work during the day to help their families. This type of activity had an economic side. When contracting laborers, or paying them, it was more difficult for the landowners' managers to deceive those who knew how to read and do arithmetic. The workers' center, which was in Manuel Tebas Escobar's house, was also a place for raising the political consciousness of laborers. It had a library with newspapers and books. According to Feliciano Monge Pérez, there was an anarchist named Lucrecio Paz Delgado who lived in the town and who used to go to the workers' center to read newspapers, like the anarchist *Land and liberty*, to illiterate laborers.

The end of the first Republican biennium

During 1933, the Republican-Socialist coalition became strained and the Right saw an opportunity to retake power through the ballot box, having failed to do so by force during General Sanjurjo's attempted coup in August 1932. President Niceto Alcalá-Zamora called for new elections for November 19, 1933. Although no group had enough seats to govern on its own, a Center-Right coalition was formed with Alejandro Lerroux as head. The principal reasons for the right-wing victory were the Left's lack of unity in the face of a united Right, and the abstention of the members of the anarcho-syndicalist union, the CNT. Another factor was women's suffrage, one of the progressive provisions of the new constitution. During the election, many women believed their priests' admonitions that voting for Socialist or left-leaning Republican candidates was a mortal sin.[25] Since the change of government would bring a suspension of the reforms undertaken by the Republic during its first biennium, this is a good time to summarize the changes in Castilleja del Campo from 1931 to 1933.

The town's laborers, especially the neediest among them, saw a perceptible improvement in their living standard due to measures taken at the national level and the implementation of these initiatives by the town council and local labor union. The program of public works introduced by the Socialist finance minister Indalecio Prieto provided funds for the employment of jobless workers. The fair distribution of these funds by the labor union and town council guaranteed that the jobs went to the poorest workers. The decrees and labor laws implemented in Madrid nearly doubled the wages of day laborers. The union, in collaboration with the town council, saw to it that day labor was distributed fairly. The settlement of families in the "Village Meadow" initiated by the mayor alleviated over-crowding and improved the town's diet.

Other changes were more subtle. Union control of the labor market, a result of the Decree of Municipal Boundaries, gave labor a dignity it had not had before and made workers politically independent from the landowners. They could now express their opinions openly and vote according to their interests and consciences without fear of reprisals. This freedom produced an atmosphere of solidarity among the town's workers, a confidence in their own importance, and hope for the future. The new freedom of expression also extended to religion. With the separation of church and state, and the diminished power of the parish priest in the economic life of day laborers, these workers felt free to express secular, anti-clerical, and even anti-religious ideas that in the past would have marked them as antisocial, blasphemous, or heretical, all motives for marginalizing them from the labor force. The educational reforms in the town, with the arrival of a progressive schoolteacher, reduced illiteracy among the young, and night classes in the workers' center provided opportunities for adults to learn to read and do arithmetic, important skills for defending them-selves against the exploitation of their labor.

These changes had a dark side as well. The advent of the Republic had caught the Right off guard, and its attempt to take back power by force had failed during General Sanjurjo's attempted coup, but the elections of November 1933 showed that the Right had not lost its desire to rule the country. For the time being, the Right would settle for a peaceful recovery of the privileges it had lost to the reforms of the first Republican biennium. But the conflicts with the oligarchy and the church had sown seeds of hatred that would eventually yield an exceedingly bitter harvest for Castilleja's leftists, as it would for the leftists of the entire nation.

Notes

1 Certificate of Destitution, 14 April 1931, Castilleja del Campo Municipal Archive.
2 Minutes, 30 April 1931, Castilleja del Campo Municipal Archive.
3 George A. Collier, *Socialistas de la Andalucía rural*, 96.
4 Minutes, 9 May 1931, Castilleja del Campo Municipal Archive.
5 Minutes, 16 May 1931, Castilleja del Campo Municipal Archive.
6 Minutes, 14 May 1932, Castilleja del Campo Municipal Archive.

7 Minutes, 21 October 1932, Castilleja del Campo Municipal Archive.

8 Juan Carmelo Luque Varela, *Crónica de una fiesta viva*, 28.

9 Minutes, 23 January 1932, and subsequent minutes, Castilleja del Campo Municipal Archive.

10 According to the census of 1935 there were 744 inhabitants while, in the year 2000, there were approximately 650. Municipal Census, 31 December 1935, Castilleja del Campo Municipal Archive.

11 Juan Ortiz Villalba, *Sevilla 1936*, 57.

12 Ibid.

13 Correspondence, Castilleja del Campo Municipal Archive.

14 Ibid.

15 Certificate of Destitution, 10 August 1932, Castilleja del Campo Municipal Archive.

16 Correspondence, 1931, Archiepiscopal Archive of Seville.

17 Minutes, 23 January 1932, Castilleja del Campo Municipal Archive.

18 Correspondence, 1932, Archiepiscopal Archive of Seville.

19 Ibid.

20 Ibid.

21 Gabriel Jackson, *The Spanish Republic and the Civil War*, 48.

22 José María Macarro Vera, *La Sevilla republicana*, 88.

23 Correspondence, 1932, Archiepiscopal Archive of Seville.

24 Ibid.

25 Gerald Brenan, *El laberinto español*, 201–2.

Two

The Black Biennium

Biennium :- a period of 2 years.

Another regime change

The period from November 19, 1933 to the victory of the Popular Front on February 16, 1936, is referred to as the "black biennium." National politics were dominated by the conservative Republican Alejandro Lerroux and by José María Gil Robles, who opposed the Republic. The labor reforms of 1931 – 1933, when not suspended or modified, were not enforced. Landowners regained control of the rural labor market, employing whomever they wanted and locking out workers who had been active in the unions.[1] Wages fell 40 or 50 percent, to what they had been under the monarchy. Legislation curtailing the privileges of the church was ignored and educational reform came to a halt.[2] Funds for public works were no longer distributed to the towns to provide work for the unemployed.

Along with the reverses brought by the black biennium, there were events that foreshadowed an even blacker future. In October 1933, one month before the electoral victory of the Right, José Antonio Primo de Rivera, son of the ex-dictator Miguel Primo de Rivera, had founded the Spanish Falange, inspired by Italian Fascism and German National-Socialism. In February 1934, a Falange headquarters opened in Seville with approximately one hundred and fifty members. It was closed by the Seville municipal government when its members provoked an altercation on April 14 during the celebration of the third anniversary of the birth of the Republic, but it reopened a year later.[3]

In Castilleja del Campo the black biennium was not exactly a biennium, although it certainly was black for the town's leftists. The national elections that brought an end to the reforms of 1931 – 1933 had not affected the composition of the municipal government. The same Republican mayor, José Ramírez Rufino, and the same councilmen would remain in office for almost a year, but they did not have the power they had before and there is a notable lack of activity on their part. There is no evidence of their conflict with the oligarchy until a meeting on June 30, 1934, when the minutes announced the expropriation of the land known as the "old road," the same land the town council had demanded during the meeting of April 9, 1932.[4] The announcement had little effect and had to be repeated at the following meeting: "This mayor's office hereby makes known to Doña María Gamero Cívico y de Porres that the parcel of land that she has plowed and which is called 'Old Road' is the property of this Municipality."[5] This would be the last we would hear from José Ramírez's town council in its struggle with the oligarchy. He would be removed from office three months later.

An administrative commission

The change of government in Castilleja del Campo on October 14, 1934 was due to events on the national level. Since before the elections of November 1933, the PSOE (Spanish Socialist Workers' Party) had become increasingly radicalized. It abandoned the reformism that had always characterized its policies and adopted revolutionary methods and rhetoric.[6] During the summer and early autumn of 1934, the Socialists made preparations for an insurrection to bring down the Center-Right government. Residents of Castilleja were suspected of participating in these preparations. On September 20, 1934, the municipal judge received a request from the Civil Guard barracks ". . . to practice searches of the residences of those living in that Locality whose names I express in the margin as well as of the Workers' Center . . ." The names of three leftists appear, with the nicknames of two of them, and the office held by the other: "José Escobar Moreno (alias) Regular, Lucrecio Paz Delgado (alias) Cuartano, Manuel Tebas Escobar President Workers' Center."[7] There is no documentary indication of the results of the searches.

The so-called October Revolution was a disaster. There was an uprising only in Barcelona, where it was crushed in two days, and in Asturias where, during two weeks, armed miners resisted legionnaires and Moroccan mercenaries commanded by General Francisco Franco. The executions by firing squad, mass arrests, torture, and purges that followed were foretastes of the repression during the civil war.[8] Important figures from the first Republican biennium, including the former head of government Manuel Azaña and the former labor minister Francisco Largo Caballero, were arrested.

Another result of the insurrection was the dismissal of left-leaning town councils. On October 14, 1934, without having held municipal elections, Castilleja del Campo found itself with a new municipal government. The town's mayor and councilmen from the first Republican biennium did not even attend the Act of Destitution. The new mayor, Manuel Romero

Rodríguez, and the new councilmen were designated by the civil governor, José Manuel Nogales y Camacho. This administrative commission, so named to distinguish it from an elected town council, soon showed its political sympathies, changing the names of several streets on October 26. The founder of the Socialist Party, Pablo Iglesias, lost his street, which was renamed Gil Robles Street, for the leader of the CEDA (Spanish Coalition of Autonomous Right-wing Parties). The street of the Socialist and former labor minister Largo Caballero became Alejandro Lerroux Street, honoring the new head of the Spanish government and leader of the Radical Party which, despite its name, was a conservative Republican party. The street of the anarchist educator Francisco Ferrer was given to Martínez de Velasco, leader of the Agrarian Party, which represented the interests of large landowners. Two new streets were baptized: General Franco Street, for the hero of the campaign against the Asturian miners; and Salazar Alonso Street, for the new interior minister whose idea it had been to dismiss left-leaning town councils.

The administrative commission cooperated with the oligarchy. On November 16, 1934, the countess requested the resolution of her conflict with the previous town council, and the new authorities ruled in her favor: ". . . with respect to the adjudication of the parcel denominated 'Old Road' the commission awards it to her."[9] As far as the granting of parcels in the "Village Meadow" is concerned, during the mandate of the commission, there is not a single one, although a request for a parcel presented by Antonio Luque Romero was discussed during a meeting on May 10, 1935. The discussion was tabled indefinitely.[10] Coincidentally, this request was made on the same date that the Madrid government suspended the Law of Agrarian Reform.[11]

Conditions also favored the parish. On May 31, 1935, the town's priest, Don Felipe, wrote Cardinal Ilundáin a report on the success of the Holy Mission and Eucharistic Procession celebrated that month and attributed that success to the changed atmosphere in Castilleja: "Thanks be to God the traditional religious spirit here, somewhat in decline due to the propaganda of recent years, has been lifted, with more than two thirds fulfilling their obligations to the Church . . . Copious, thanks be to God, have been the fruits."[12]

Things had improved for the oligarchy and the parish, but not for the workers. The union, which had been part of the anarcho-syndicalist CNT, declared itself autonomous *so that it would not be so confrontational, so that it would not be part of any political party*, according to Celedonio Escobar Reinoso. For the town's leftists, it was a time to dissimulate ideologies, but not to forget them. While they awaited more favorable conditions to recover the freedoms and the progress lost during the black biennium, another ideology was making inroads in the town. In 1935 there began to be Falangists in Castilleja del Campo. By 1936 there were between twelve and fourteen residents affiliated with the Falange, according to Conrado Rufino Romero. Manuel García Ramírez remembered the names of eleven of them.[13]

The end of the black biennium

During the autumn of 1935, the Center-Right government in Madrid began to unravel and lose the confidence of the country as a result of the personal ambitions of the anti-Republican José María Gil Robles, leader of the CEDA, and the financial scandals of Alejandro Lerroux's Radicals. Meanwhile, Republicans and Socialists were putting aside their differences. The October Revolution of 1934 had been a disaster, but the heroism of the Asturian miners had inspired the Left. The insurrection in Asturias had been able to hold out for two weeks because only there had all the workers' organizations been united. The UGT (socialist union), the CNT (anarcho-syndicalist union), and the Communists had united in Asturias under the acronym UHP (Union of Proletarian Brothers). The Asturian miners had shown the various factions of the Left that if they wanted to return to power, they must unite. Republicans, Socialists, and anarchists had all suffered the arrests and purges of the repression following the events of October 1934. The final blow for the Center-Right was a series of scandals involving bribes taken by associates and family members of the head of government, Alejandro Lerroux, demonstrating that the Radicals were not very different from the old Liberal and Conservative Parties under the monarchy in their willingness to use power for personal gain.[14]

President Alcalá-Zamora dissolved the Cortes and called for elections to be held on February 16, 1936. In January, Manuel Azaña's Republicans, who had adopted the name Republican Left party, formed a Popular Front coalition with the majority of left-wing groups and organizations and with the Republican Union party of Diego Martínez Barrio, from Seville. The Republican Union had split from the Radicals two years before and would be the most moderate party in the Popular Front. During the campaign, the Popular Front promised amnesty for all those still in prison for political reasons since the October Revolution and promised the restoration of the reforms of the first Republican biennium. The Right, represented by Gil Robles's CEDA and various monarchist parties, ran on a promise to combat "the revolution."[15]

There was much at stake for agricultural regions like Andalusia in these elections. A victory for the Right would ensure the continuation of a system that benefited landowners at the expense of rural laborers. A Popular Front victory would give the Left the opportunity to restore and extend the reforms of the first biennium. Castilleja del Campo took the elections very seriously. José María Ramírez Mauricio, a twenty year old laborer in the town, wrote a letter to his grandmother, Ana Monge Romero, who lived in Seville. The purpose of the letter was to counter the pressure exerted by the oligarchy as the election neared. One of the reasons for the Right's victory in November 1933 had been the newly enfranchised women who had voted according to the instructions of their priests. The oligarchy was also seeking the women's vote:

"To give to grandmother"
Castilleja del Campo on 1/28/1936

Dear grandmother: I hope that upon receiving this you enjoy the most complete health: like the whole family, we are all well.

Grandmother, the object of this letter is to inform you that yesterday a daughter of the Porres family and another daughter of Rosario Romero [*Moreno*] came asking for you and the first time they refused to state the purpose of their visit but the second time they began to state their purpose little by little and eventually said they had brought a letter for you, it is doubtless to ask you to vote their way.

It surprises me a great deal that for many years the marchioness has not remembered you until now on the eve of elections but she did not remember you when grandfather died and she did not go to give you her condolences, she does not remember at all except on these occasions only because they benefit from this person or that person's vote and you must understand that when they benefit it is at our expense, and I also tell you that when uncle Manolito [*Manuel Mauricio Monge*] went months and months without work and uncle Antonio [*Mauricio Monge*] as well they have not remembered you or them at all.

I think you are old enough to understand what is good and what is bad, by which I mean that you also know that during the whole time that the Right has been in power one of your sons even went hungry on account of she who now asks you to vote for her class and furthermore you understand since you have already told me that you would be for a government that knows how to govern Spain and there would be work and money to earn and you must understand that I and your sons fight for that kind of government because it is in the interest of those of us who work only with our arms and it is clear that what is in our interest also has to be in your interest because it is in the interest of your grandchildren and your children. The mother who votes for a government that benefits her children it is because she loves them and the one who does not vote for that kind of government it is without doubt because she does not love them, before the elections I will go see you so that all this may be resolved.

In reference to the wires I gave you before you left I say that I do not need them anymore because I am not going to build the radio.
Answer me about all this soon, even though it is only a few words.
Give regards from all to all your grandson who loves you says goodbye
Answer me soon[16]   José Ramírez Mauricio

José María Ramírez Mauricio was the nephew of José Ramírez Rufino, the mayor during the first biennium. He was also one of Joaquín León Trejo's most diligent students, according to Joaquín's son José León García. The influence of the schoolteacher on this young day laborer is apparent in his ability to write and in the scientific knowledge that led him to dream of building a radio. José María would be shot eight months after writing this letter, the youngest of the men killed during the repression in Castilleja del Campo.

The election was a victory for the Popular Front. One of the first measures of the new government, led once again by Manuel Azaña, was to restore the town councils dismissed in October 1934. Even before the election, the former mayor and councilmen of Castilleja del Campo had anticipated this eventuality. On January 6, 1936, they wrote a letter to Mayor Manuel Romero Rodríguez requesting they be reinstated.[17] On February 20, 1936, four days after the Popular Front victory, José Ramírez Rufino was again the mayor of Castilleja del Campo, according to the Certificate of Reinstatement. The outgoing mayor was not present, but one of his councilmen, Francisco Rodríguez Luque, signed the certificate.[18]

The Left returned to power in Castilleja del Campo thanks to the Popular Front victory, but the town did not contribute to this victory. An incident there caused the suspension of the elections. A document in the Office of the Justice of the Peace provides a glimpse of what happened:

In Castilleja del Campo on February 16, 1936
The undersigned individuals who constitute the electoral board of the only precinct of this village in virtue of having been thrown to the ground the ballots contained in the urn have proceeded to gather the ballots and resulting from the recount of the same that more ballots appear than the number of electors who have voted according to the respective voting lists agree unanimously to suspend the Election.

> In testimony of which the present document is filed which is signed by the
> three who constitute the board.
>
> Assistant,   President,   Assistant
> Juan Calero Cuevas   Manuel Tebas   Juan [*Martín*] Calero [*Rebollo*][19]

The decision to suspend the election was no doubt arrived at with great difficulty by the board president, Manuel Tebas Escobar, a leftist, and the two assistants, Juan Calero Cuevas and Juan Martín Calero Rebollo, both right-wingers. The document does not give a complete account of what took place at the Castilleja polling place on February 16, 1936, but there is another document that allows speculation regarding the incident.

On February 27, 1939, the commandant of the Civil Guard barracks in Carrión sent the Castilleja municipal judge a document entitled "Account of the individuals of Castilleja del Campo to whom was applied The War Decree of the Most Excellent General in Chief of the Army of the South for their anarchic actions and extremist ideas."[20] It is a list of the names of thirteen of the seventeen men in the town who were shot. Next to the names there appears "Causes why they were applied the Decree." For Manuel Tebas Escobar and Enrique Monge Escobar the cause is "Communist, broke the Urn in elections and wounded . . ." In both cases, the phrase is cut short for lack of space. Apparently, the president of the electoral board, Manuel Tebas, and his cousin Enrique Monge suspected that right-wing voters were putting more than one ballot per person in the urn. To test their suspicion, they broke the urn, causing some type of injury to someone who was present. The ballot recount confirmed their suspicion and the right-wing assistants had no alternative but to accept the suspension of the election.

The incident is significant because, in addition to being the motive for suspending the election in Castilleja, and the alleged justification for shooting two of the town's residents, it illustrates the type of electoral manipulation practiced at the time in small towns. One of the justifications for the military coup on July 18, 1936, was that the Popular Front was an illegitimate government that had come to power in a fraudulent election. In the case of Castilleja del Campo, electoral fraud was a tactic of the Right, not the Left.

Notes

1 Manuel Tuñón de Lara, "Orígenes lejanos y próximos," in Manuel Tuñón de Lara and others, *La guerra civil española: 50 años después*, 29.
2 Gerald Brenan, *El laberinto español*, 204.
3 Juan Ortiz Villalba, *Sevilla 1936*, 60.
4 Minutes, 30 June 1934, Castilleja del Campo Municipal Archive.

5 Ibid., 7 July 1934.

6 Gerald Brenan, *El laberinto español*, 206.

7 Correspondence, Castilleja del Campo Municipal Archive.

8 Manuel Tuñón de Lara, "Orígenes lejanos y próximos," in Manuel Tuñón de Lara and others, *La guerra civil española: 50 años después*, 30.

9 Minutes, 28 December 1934, Castilleja del Campo Municipal Archive.

10 Minutes, 10 May 1935, Castilleja del Campo Municipal Archive.

11 Manuel Tuñón de Lara, "Orígenes lejanos y próximos," in Manuel Tuñón de Lara and others, *La guerra civil española: 50 años después*, 30.

12 Correspondence, 1935, Archiepiscopal Archive of Seville.

13 Antonio Calero Cuevas; José Calero Cuevas; José Cuevas Reinoso "Pepe Pechuga" ("Joe Chicken-breast"); Casildo Escobar Reinoso, armed guard on the countess's estate; José María Fernández Rodríguez "El Niño Guapo" ("Pretty Boy"); Álvaro García Carranza "El Algabeño" ("The Man from La Algaba"); Antonio Luque Cuevas "El Cotorro" ("The Chatterbox"); Francisco Luque Cuevas "El Solano" ("The Ill Wind"); Manuel Luque Cuevas "El Solanillo" ("The Little Ill Wind"); Antonio Rodríguez Mantero, "Antoñín," nephew of the priest Felipe Rodríguez Sánchez; José Rodríguez Sánchez "El Topamí" ("All for me"), brother of Felipe Rodríguez Sánchez.

14 Gerald Brenan, *El laberinto español*, 221–3; Manuel Tuñón de Lara, "Orígenes lejanos y próximos," in Manuel Tuñón de Lara and others, *La guerra civil española: 50 años después*, 31.

15 Manuel Tuñón de Lara, "Orígenes lejanos y próximos," in Manuel Tuñón de Lara and others, *La guerra civil española: 50 años después*, 31–2.

16 I thank Noelia Rodríguez Escobar and José María Ramírez Bravo for providing me a copy of this letter.

17 Correspondence, Castilleja del Campo Municipal Archive.

18 Certificate of Reinstatement, 20 February 1936, Castilleja del Campo Municipal Archive.

19 Dossier 28, Office of the Justice of the Peace, Castilleja del Campo.

20 Dossier 24, Office of the Justice of the Peace, Castilleja del Campo.

Three

The Popular Front

The Left returns to power

On February 22, 1936, José Ramírez Rufino celebrated his return to power with the obligatory change of street names. Some were a reversion to the names the streets had during the first biennium: Gil Robles Street was again Pablo Iglesias Street, Alejandro Lerroux Street reverted to Largo Caballero Street, Martínez de Velasco Street was again Francisco Ferrer Street, etc. Had the administrative commission saved the street signs to avoid unnecessary expenditures? The new streets named for General Franco and Salazar Alonso by the administrative commission would become Doctor del Campo Street and José Nakens Street, and the Town Hall Square, which had remained the same through the two previous modifications, was changed to Martínez Barrio Square, in honor of the native of Seville who had founded the Republican Union party, to which Mayor Ramírez now belonged.[1] Soon the town council would address more consequential issues.

More land grants in the "Village Meadow"

On March 5, the mayor proposed granting more parcels in the "Village Meadow" for "the most needy and humble classes of this locale." The council approved the proposal over the municipal secretary's protest.[2] This protest is somewhat surprising because during the first Republican biennium there are no such protests on the part of the secretary over similar grants. Hilario Luque Ramírez had been Castilleja's secretary since the monarchy. He remained at this post during the Republic, the civil war, and for many years after the war. He was a man of the Right but, in theory, his work as secretary required neutrality. In practice, the administrative experience of municipal secretaries allowed them to influence the functioning of municipal governments in subtle or, at times, not so subtle ways. They could, for example, observe unwitting infractions of regulations by mayors and councilmen with less legal training than they had, and then inform the following administration of their predecessors' infractions.[3]

Hilario Luque's protest on March 5 was not a serious attempt to influence the town council's decision. It was probably to show the landowners, the previous authorities, or some future administration, that he had expressed his opposition. It is also possible that at this meeting Hilario Luque observed a greater militancy toward the oligarchy than he had seen in the same mayor and councilmen two years before. In subsequent meetings there is an unprecedented enthusiasm for populating the meadow, reflected in the rhythm at which parcels were distributed: on March 24, five parcels were granted; on April 15, seven parcels; and on June 5, six members of the "most needy and humble classes" received parcels in the "Village Meadow."[4]

José Ramírez Rufino's division of the meadow into small plots was changing the town's urban contour to such an extent that some of the residents who lived on the west side of what is now December Fourth Street had to adapt their habits to the new situation. On June 25, the mayor was empowered to prevent the residents "of the houses located along the western sidewalk of Castelar Street in this Village from entering the corrals of said houses from the rear, thereby trespassing on properties of this Municipality in the 'Village Meadow,' as well as preventing said residents from utilizing the aforementioned properties for depositing garbage or storing manure."[5]

Agrarian reform

Mayor José Ramírez's granting of parcels in the meadow reflected the more aggressive agrarian reform policies of the government in Madrid in 1936. The landowners had reacted to the election of the Popular Front with a lockout, aggravating the unemployment crisis of agricultural workers. The situation of the latter was becoming desperate with the approach of the planting season. On March 20, the Institute for Agrarian Reform was authorized to occupy provisionally any estate left uncultivated if it were deemed to be of "social utility."

Castilleja's authorities took steps to occupy the estates of the countess and the marchioness. On May 5, they approved a payment "to the agent of this Town Council Don Santiago Gutiérrez Vidal in the amount of fifty pesetas for two land registry certificates respectively of the rural estates that in this municipality are owned by Doña María Gamero Cívico and Doña Elisa de Porres y Osborne, by this council, for the purpose of studying the possible application of the Agrarian Reform Law to said estates."[6] They needed to prove that the land was being left fallow and was therefore subject to the Law of Obligatory Cultivation. On May 15, the mayor and councilmen agreed to "credit to the accounts of Don Francisco Rufino Pérez and Don José Fernández Luque the amount of ten pesetas in payment of two days spent in investigations carried out toward the application of obligatory cultivation."[7]

The local union, which had affiliated itself with the Socialist UGT during the Popular Front, was also involved. On June 5, the union president, José Escobar Moreno, and the union secretary, Manuel García Ramírez, sent a letter to the general director of Agrarian Reform in Madrid requesting that the countess's estate be declared of social utility and "turned over to this Society for collective cultivation." The letter begins with a description of the labor crisis in Castilleja where "owing to the lack of work in this locale 60 out of 90 workers are unemployed and lack even the necessities to live." Handwritten at the bottom of the letter are the calculations of the number of workers registered with the union, one hundred and fifty, and the number of unemployed, one hundred, and a note on the property of the marchioness: "Señora Doña Elisa de Porres's estate is parceled among 14 small land workers who, with their families, work the plots themselves."[8] The letter also describes the political motives behind the neglect of the countess's estates, ". . . that are not cultivated appropriately nor according to their possibilities, it being the manifest purpose of this proprietor to restrict work as fully as possible with the sole purpose of obstructing the labor the Popular Front has undertaken and, through hunger, break the necks of the workers of this town."[9]

On June 9, the local union also sent a letter to the town council, requesting that the properties of the countess and the marchioness be declared of social utility.[10] The council met the following day and, "deeming that the favorable resolution of this matter would amount to a complete resolution of the unemployment problem . . . agreed unanimously to grant ample authority to the Mayor so that in the name and in representation of this Council he direct a petition to the Most Excellent Director of the Institute of Agrarian Reform to the effect that the three Estates in question be declared of social utility and turned over for their collective exploitation to the Union of agricultural Workers of this Town."[11]

The mayor took action at once. Five days later, the town council paid one hundred pesetas to the mayor, two councilmen, and the municipal secretary, Hilario Luque, "for a trip taken to Seville in representation of this Council to submit a request that several estates of this district be declared of social utility."[12] The mayor and the two councilmen were pursuing an impossible dream, a town where they had achieved "a complete resolution of the unemployment problem," and where day laborers would collectively work the estates of proprietors who had exploited them for centuries and who were now leaving the land fallow in an attempt to crush them and "through hunger, break the necks of the workers of this town." In a month and a half this dream would turn into an unimaginable nightmare.

Violence during the Popular Front

While the Castilleja town council and the local union sought to remedy the labor crisis through the legal means established by the Popular Front government, the climate of violence in the country was growing. The level of violence has been exaggerated by the Franco regime's propaganda, which also minimized the responsibility of the Far Right. In Madrid, the city of Seville, and several towns in the province of Seville, there were confrontations between left-wing extremists and Falangist gunmen. They often had fatal consequences.

The Falange made its presence felt in Castilleja as well. On March 27, Corporal José Martínez Pascual, commandant of the Civil Guard barracks in Carrión de los Céspedes, arrived in Castilleja and wrote a request to the municipal judge: "Clandestine leaflets having been distributed in this town and suspecting they could have been distributed by individuals affiliated with the society known as La Patronal [*the Landowners' Center, which was also Falange headquarters*], I beg your service in expediting the appropriate judicial warrant to practice a search of the aforementioned locale."[13] The search was carried out immediately. In another letter the same day, Corporal Martínez reported that the search had "yielded no positive result whatsoever."[14]

The failure to find clandestine leaflets in "la patronal," which was in the house of the Falangist José María Fernández Rodríguez "El Niño Guapo" ("Pretty Boy"), does not necessarily mean there were none. Advised of the arrival in town of the Civil Guard, the individuals affiliated with the "patronal" could have hidden them. Or, considering its political sympathies, the Civil Guard may have turned a blind eye during the search. It is also possible the leaflets had come from outside Castilleja. Nor do we know what the leaflets were. They could have been what are called "black propaganda." Since early April, pamphlets had appeared in Spain, prepared by members of the Far Right, but purporting to have their origin in anarchist or Communist organizations. They contained detailed but spurious plans for a revolution. Sometimes they included blacklists with the names of right-wingers to be eliminated. The Falange was eager to foment polarization.

Elements of the extreme Left also contributed to the polarization, even attacking leaders of the Popular Front government. On May 31, the moderate Socialist leaders Indalecio Prieto and Juan Negrín had to escape by car from a rally in Écija when members of the revolutionary JSU (United Socialist Youths) began shooting at them. The same day there was another violent incident, this one in Castilleja del Campo. Unlike Prieto and Negrín, the victim of this shooting, a twenty year old Falangist named Manuel Rodríguez Mantero, would not escape.

A tragedy in the town

A death engraved in the town's memory

The death of Manuel Rodríguez Mantero was the first event in this history that would form part of the town's collective memory. Everyone I interviewed spoke of it. Isidora Mistral remembers that it was a Sunday and that the festival of El Rocío was coming to an end.[15] Isidora and her family worked for one of the wealthy families without a title of nobility and, like their bosses, she and her family were Falangists. She had just turned seventeen. Instead of going home after mass, she and eight or ten of her girlfriends headed west along the highway to a hill known as "La Casilla la Dura." They all belonged to the "Feminine Section," the Falangist women's organization. They were hoping to see the pilgrims returning from El Rocío. Or at least that is what Isidora told me. Their intention may have been less innocent. That day, young Communists from Seville would be attending a rally in Huelva to celebrate the unification of the Communist and Socialist Youth organizations.

From among the olive trees on the side of the highway Isidora and her friends saw the open trucks full of young men go by and they raised their right hands in the fascist salute. *Quite a few of them tried to get out of the trucks, and had a leg thrown over the sideboards. "Stop, stop!" they were telling the driver. "Stop, there are Falangist girls over there!" The driver did not stop, but one of the men said, "Alright, on the way back we will settle this. On the way back." We said, "On the way back? We will not be here. Eh? We are going the other way, to Carrión."*

That morning, Antonio Monge and his father Leovigildo also saw the fourteen or fifteen trucks go by. They were east of town working a small plot the family owned. Leovigildo Monge belonged to the Republican Left party and was one of the town's most outspoken leftists. In the evening, when Antonio and Leovigildo Monge were returning to Castilleja, they saw four of the town's Falangists waiting on the side of the highway two or three hundred meters east of town. One of them was Casildo Escobar, the countess's armed guard. Another was Manuel Rodríguez Mantero, a twenty year old boy affectionately called Manolín by the people of Castilleja. The other two were Manuel Luque Cuevas "El Solanillo" (The Little Ill Wind), also twenty years old, and Gustavo Luque Romero, fifteen. Casildo Escobar was armed with the short rifle he used when he patrolled the countess's property. He also had a pistol. As Antonio and his father approached from the east, a truck full of young Communists emerged from the town and approached from the other direction. The four Falangists raised their right hand in the fascist salute.

Antonio Monge described what happened next: *Then those in the truck began to shout, and they began to shout back, "Sons of bitches, cuckolds, this, that, and the other!" Then the ones in the truck were yelling to the driver, "Stop, stop!" But the man did not stop because he was probably thinking, by not stopping nothing will come of it. It will all remain just words. And the man drove on. But with all the hand gestures of "Cuckolds, sons of bitches, this, that, and the other!" they dropped a flag. They were carrying red flags. One of them dropped a flag and then they yelled to the driver, "Stop! We dropped a flag!" And now the man stopped.*

Then four or six of them came back and confronted them and my father got between them so that nothing would happen. And he could not prevent it. Manolín was shot in the chest and I, when I saw they had shot the boy . . . the blood . . . he was wearing a navy blue uniform and the blood was spurting from his chest, I said, "This one [Casildo Escobar, with the rifle and pistol] is going to mix it up with these people and they with them," and I was telling my father, "Come here and leave them be!" And then my father stayed put because they wanted to finish the boy off there on the ground, and he was telling them, "But, man, this is a fine boy but the others who brought him . . ."

The ones who had come with Manolín took off running and I crouched down in the ditch there watching my father because I did not want to leave him alone. But of course, if I stayed up there on the highway, well, in a cross-fire they were going to get me, and I had nothing to do with it. I say, "Let them deal with it." But my father, since that is how the poor man is, he was afraid of nothing . . . and so, he stayed to hold them back so they would not finish him off there. And, finally, one of the Falangists that passed by me running, because I was in the ditch, took off in the direction of the mountains and the one that shot Manolín, thinking that I was one of those who were there with him, took aim at me. And my father said to him, "Hey, that is my son. That is not the one." He almost shot me. My father stopped a car that was headed for Seville and they brought Manolín here to the house of an aunt of his [Nicolasa Rodríguez Sánchez]. And later they took him to Seville and I do not know if he got to Seville alive or if he died on the way. I do not remember what happened.

Doubts about Antonio Monge's version: the problem of oral testimonies

Conrado Rufino Romero, a right-winger, told me in 1992 after reading a draft of this part of the story that he did not remember Antonio's being there with his father, that it was Juan Antonio Tebas Rodríguez, Castilleja's municipal policeman, who had gone to help Leovigildo bring the wounded Falangist back to town. Conrado contradicted Antonio's version in other details as well. According to Conrado, the other Falangists abandoned Manuel Rodríguez before the truck arrived, the Communists' truck had stopped at once, and one of the Communists shot Manuel when he saw him taking his hand out of his pocket, as if fearing the Falangist was drawing a gun.

The contradictions between Antonio's version and Conrado's made me doubt whether Antonio had been present during the shooting. This doubt would last until I met Antonio's younger brother Feliciano in 2005. He assured me that Antonio had indeed been there with their father Leovigildo. Nevertheless, the contradictions in different testimonies underscore the difficulties inherent in any attempt to reconstruct the past from the accounts of witnesses. It will be important to bear in mind the problematic nature of oral history from here on. Heretofore, the primary sources have been the documentation in the municipal archive, which is abundant for the era of the Republic, whereas the witnesses who remembered that period were already scarce when the first interviews were recorded. When dealing with the repression and the war, the opposite is the case. The documentation is sparse, but the recollections of witnesses are, if anything, too abundant. The problem will be to weigh contradictory accounts of events. At times, the only thing I can guarantee is that on a particular day of a particular year, someone who was alive during those times pronounced these words and I recorded them.

May 31, 1936: other versions

In 2005, when Feliciano Monge Pérez confirmed his brother Antonio's presence at the shooting, he also specified the time it took place, saying that it was growing dark, with *the sun well set*. That could explain why there are so many versions. It would be difficult to see what was happening from a distance. Feliciano also added details that differ from his older brother's account, details Feliciano could have heard from his father Leovigildo or from his brother Antonio but which the latter subsequently modified. According to Feliciano, the one who shot Manolín had not been a young

Communist in the trucks but rather a Communist leader who got out of a car that was accompanying the trucks and who fired from behind the car's hood. Feliciano also said that his father Leovigildo came running to the scene after hearing the gunshot. Other details described by Feliciano coincide with Antonio's version. He said that when his father got to the wounded Falangist, Manolín said to him, *"Leovigildo, do not leave me,"* and that Leovigildo told the Communists, *"This is a very good boy, the bad ones are those others,"* referring to the Falangists who had fled.

Antonio Monge Pérez ends his eyewitness account of the shooting and of the transport of the young Falangist to his aunt's house rather succinctly. *And later they took him to Seville and I do not know if he got to Seville alive or if he died on the way. I do not remember what happened.* There are several versions of the shooting's aftermath. Feliciano said it was a man from Carrión on his way home from Seville who stopped his car to help Leovigildo and that the two of them put Manolín in the car to take him to the house of his aunt Nicolasa. According to Feliciano, Leovigildo had not wanted to take the boy to his mother's house because she would have been too upset seeing her son, whose chest was spurting blood. Isidora Mistral said that when she and her friends returned from Carrión, they saw people remove Manolín, already dead, from the car and carry him into his aunt's house.

Some said that Manuel Rodríguez Mantero died en route to Seville. Others said he died after arriving in Seville. Among the latter is Manolín's brother Eduardo. In fact, Manolín died two days after the shooting. His death was announced on June 3, in *ABC, Andalusian Edition*, and *La Unión*. The item in *La Unión* bears the title "Demise of a wounded man":

> In the Central Hospital yesterday Manuel Rodríguez Mantero, 20 years of age, born in Melilla and resident of Castilleja del Campo, Castelar Street Number 6, passed away.
>
> The deceased young man was wounded when he was shot last Sunday by the occupants of a truck at the intersection of the Huelva highway and the highway of the town where he lived, and where he was with some friends.[16]

Unanswered questions

The day after the shooting, the governor of Seville, José María Varela Rendueles, gave a press conference that dealt with various topics. The newspaper *El Liberal* entitled one of these topics "Concerning an assault on a truck occupied by young communists":

The journalists asked the governor if he had news of an assault committed yesterday against some communists who were returning from a rally that took place in Huelva.

Mr. Varela answered that the Civil Guard of Castilleja del Campo had communicated the news to him, adding that it had arrested several fascists who had perpetrated the deed.

The governor did not have further details, and said that upon receiving the statement from the Civil Guard he would proceed accordingly.[17]

An article on the press conference appeared the same day in *La Unión*, but there is a blank space where the governor's declaration concerning the shooting in Castilleja would have appeared according to the chronological order of the topics discussed.[18] That part had been censored. During the Popular Front, the government had declared a "state of alarm" in accordance with the Law of Public Order. The "state of alarm" allowed press censorship, and it was common to censor news concerning disturbances in order to avoid their inspiring more violence. This censorship did not work perfectly, as in this case in which the news of the shooting in Castilleja was censored in only one newspaper.

The article presents certain complications. For example, how to explain the description of the shooting as an "assault committed yesterday against some communists"? This phrase suggests that the Falangists had gone beyond merely giving the fascist salute. Perhaps the journalists had spoken to some of the Communists, who described it that way to justify having shot the boy. Or the Communists really believed they were in danger, which would agree with Conrado Rufino's version in which the shooting occurred when Manolín was taking his hand out of his pocket. If that is what happened, it is not logical that Manuel Rodríguez would have left his hand in his pocket until the last moment if his only intention was to give the fascist salute, nor is it logical that four Falangists would have gone to the highway to confront trucks full of Communists and that only one of them was armed.

And what are we to make of the reference in the press conference to the arrest of "several fascists who had perpetrated the deed"? I asked several people, both leftists and right-wingers, if there had been any arrests as a result of the shooting. They all said they had no recollection of arrests. But on June 5, 1936, the town council agreed to pay the town's doctor, Juan Luis Vergne Herrero, twenty pesetas "for rental of his car for trip to Sanlúcar to transport three prisoners."[19] The same day, the town council agreed to pay "to the Municipal Policeman of this City Don Juan Antonio Tebas Rodríguez, compensation for two trips to Sanlúcar la Mayor, one to testify in the Court of Inquiry and another to negotiate various matters, by order of the Town Council."[20]

On Wednesday, June 3, there was a censored article in *El Correo de Andalucía*. The text is so poorly erased that it is possible to read some fragments, but not the article's title. In transcribing the passage I have used brackets to indicate long illegible passages, ellipsis points to indicate short illegible passages, and periods to indicate illegible letters:

> . . . on ..nday . . . [   ] . . . eriously wounded . . . [   ] . . . munist . . . [   ]
> . . . viduals salu..d . . . [   ] . . . saying . . . . . . the . . [   ] . . . C.sil.. E.cob . . .
> armed gua.. [   ] . . . n the h.ghw.y . . . . . . sildo . . . . . . n.el Luq.., 20 years
> o..; . . . q.e, . . .15; and Man... .....gu.. Ma.t.ro, 19; . . . [   ] . . . Manuel
> Ro.....ez ....ero, who was driv.n . . . . . .tral in Seville, where . . .[21]

The longest fragmentary passage, ". . .n the h.ghw.y . . . . . . sildo . . . . . .n.el Luq.., 20 years o..; . . . ..q.e, . . .15, and Man... .....gu.. Ma.t.ro, 19; . . ." would be ". . .on the highway . . . . . Casildo . . . . . . Manuel Luque, 20 years old; . . . q.e, . . . 15; and Manuel Rodríguez Mantero, 19; . . ." The information in the censored article had no doubt come from the investigation of the shooting carried out by the court of inquiry in Sanlúcar la Mayor, where the Castilleja municipal policeman had testified. It took me twelve years to ascertain that " . . . ..q.e., . . . 15," was Gustavo Luque Romero.

After the censored article in *El Correo de Andalucía* on June 3, the incident is mentioned two more times in the press. On June 15 a notice from the civil governor was published in *El Liberal* prohibiting the transport of persons to political meetings in open trucks in order to avoid "the unfortunate events that have occurred."[22] And on June 25 an article was published in *ABC* entitled "Concerning the assault on a young man in Castilleja del Campo." The complete text is as follows:

> Don José Rodríguez Sánchez, residing in Castilleja del Campo, reported yesterday in the Jáuregui police station that last May 31, while a truck was returning from a rally, his nephew, Manuel Rodríguez Mantero, was assaulted and shot, and a few days later passed away in the Central Hospital of Seville.
>
> The complainant says that by his own investigations he learned that the license plate of the truck in which his nephew's assailants were traveling is 11748, owned by don José Delgado Romero, residing at 66 Pagés del Corro Street.
>
> Agents of the Social Brigade, Messrs. Seisdedos and Santos arrested Mr. Delgado Romero and the driver José Martín Cubero.

During interrogation the persons under arrest said that on the day in question the truck was rented to transport some forty individuals to Huelva and that, upon their return, they heard a gunshot and saw a man fall, and that the man was taken into a car, but they could not say for certain if the shot was fired from the truck.

The detainees have been placed at the disposition of the Sanlúcar Court of Inquiry, which is conducting the preliminary investigation.[23]

The same day this article appeared, the Castilleja del Campo town council met. The minutes of that meeting give an idea of how chaotic May 31 was in Castilleja del Campo:

The mayor made known that as the result of an incident that developed days ago near this town and due to which the corresponding investigation is still pending; the pistol belonging to the Town Council that was used by the Municipal Policeman Don Juan Antonio Tebas Rodríguez has been misplaced and in consequence and for his use the aforementioned policemen has acquired a new pistol and a box of bullets.[24]

A motion was passed to compensate the municipal policemen in the sum of seventy-nine pesetas.

Consequences

Manuel Rodríguez's death was at the hands of outsiders and none of the town's leftists had anything to do with it. In fact it was an outspoken leftist, Leovigildo Monge, who had attempted to save the young Falangist. Leovigildo would become every bit a historical figure in the town's collective memory. For leftists he was evidence of the good will of the local Left and the injustice of the repression. Right-wingers, the same as leftists, emphasized the irony that it was a man of the Left who had brought the wounded boy home after his Falangist companions had abandoned him.

Nevertheless, some of Castilleja's leftists reacted to the shooting in ways that would have serious consequences. Marina Luque Reinoso said she had heard that some local leftists stopped the car that was taking Manuel Rodríguez to Seville so that the boy would bleed to death before arriving at the hospital. Her testimony is corroborated by Manuel's brother, who added more details. Eduardo Rodríguez Mantero said that four local leftists stopped the car but then let it pass out of pity for the boy's mother, who was also in the car. The mother later refused to identify these leftists and, according to Eduardo, *that is why they were not all shot*. But two local leftists would be shot for something else that happened the same night. According to Conrado Rufino Romero, a group of leftists marched through the streets of the town chanting slogans such as *"Death to Falangists!"* and *"The first has already fallen!"*

In the document sent by the commandant of the Civil Guard to the Castilleja municipal judge on February 27, 1939 with the title "Account of the individuals of Castilleja del Campo to whom was applied The War Decree of the Most Excellent General in Chief of the Army of the South for their anarchic actions and extremist ideas," next to Alfredo Reinoso Monge's name the cause is "Instigator demonstration against dead Falangist," and next to Cándido Nieves Perea's name there appears "Extremist, distinguishing himself death Falangist."[25] Only two of the names on the list include a reference to the demonstration. Apparently, none of the other men who would be shot had participated. But even if the demonstration did not represent the attitude of the majority of the town's leftists, it was profoundly offensive to the boy's family and other right-wingers, strengthening their mortal hatred of the Left, a hatred whose true causes were the conflicts between the town council and the local union on the one hand, and the oligarchy and the church on the other.

These were causes that would explain the violence of the civil war in the country as a whole, but they were too abstract, too general. The residents of a town as small as Castilleja del Campo in which *everyone is family*, as many said, would need a more concrete, a more personal explanation, one more specifically related to Castilleja: the revenge of the victim's family members and fellow Falangists for a murder that was never solved. The true culprit, an anonymous Communist from Seville, had escaped. Castilleja del Campo would soon be under the control of the oligarchy, the church, and the Falange, all frustrated during the Popular Front. When the Right regained control of the town, the oligarchy would be represented by, among others, the new administrator of the countess's estates, José Rodríguez Sánchez, who was Manuel Rodríguez Mantero's uncle. The church would be repre-sented by the parish priest, Don Felipe Rodríguez Sánchez, the other uncle of the victim. And the Falange would be represented by the dozen or more Falangist comrades of Manuel Rodríguez.

For the parish priest Don Felipe, the shooting of his nephew justified the concern expressed in his letter to Cardinal Ilundáin on December 23, 1932, that "some serious incident" would occur to one of his family members. The victim was not, as he had feared, his brother José, nor did this family tragedy occur "because of the war declared on the Church by the Municipality as well as by the communist center," as he had written to the cardinal. But it would give him a personal justification to take revenge on any leftist, whether responsible for his nephew's death or not.

Civil Guard = Spanish gendarme : a military force charged with police duties among civilian population .

The Impending cataclysm

Preparations for a military coup: February 16 to July 11, 1936

After the Popular Front victory in the February 16 elections, José Antonio Primo de Rivera contacted the provisional head of government, Manuel Portela Valladares, and offered the services of the Falange to prevent the Popular Front from forming a government. General Franco asked Portela Valladares to declare a "state of war" in accordance with the Law of Public Order, which would have been tantamount to a military coup. The monarchists asked the leader of the CEDA, José María Gil Robles, to stage a coup d'état. Neither Portela Valladares nor Gil Robles accepted these proposals, but several military men and their civilian accomplices began to conspire against the new regime.

Pedro Parias, the countess's administrator, was so busy with the conspiracy that he had to give up this post, which was taken up by José Rodríguez Sánchez, brother of Castilleja's priest, Don Felipe. Feliciano Monge Pérez told the story: *I heard this told by the brother* [of Don Felipe], *he says, "In those times before the Movement, when things began to heat up . . ." . . . well it turns out that Don Pedro Parias, who was the administrator in the count's hacienda with Miss María, well he had a lot of influence in the town and he said to Pepe, Pepe the priest's brother, he says, "Look here Pepe, I am going to have to give up this post." And then he went and offered it to Pepito, the priest's brother.*

And then there in Castilleja "El Regular" [José Escobar Moreno] *and three or four more said to Pepe, they say, "Look here, Pepe, the post you have taken on, if you do not give it up, you are going to lose the thing you love most in your life." Which was the daughter, who is still alive. What's her name? "Mariquita. Mariquita"* [María Francisca Calero Rebollo]. *She had already been born. When the Movement began she was already born. She was still a baby. And they slid a letter under his door and that is what it said: "If you do not give up the post they have given you, you will lose that which you love most in your life." He says, "I have given her my name and she is going to be my daughter."*

The leftists' letter telling José Rodríguez Sánchez he would lose his daughter if he continued as the countess's administrator sounds like a threat, but it is not. José Rodríguez Sánchez lived out of wedlock with a woman who had his daughter, whom he loved and recognized as his own. Meanwhile, there were rumors, related to me by Manuel García Ramírez and Feliciano Monge Pérez, that Pedro Parias's relationship with the countess was not only professional but intimate as well. The letter implies that if José Rodríguez did not give up the post, he too would have to be involved sexually with the countess, jeopardizing his relationship with his daughter and his daughter's mother.

Feliciano's account continues: *Then he* [José Rodríguez] *took the letter to Seville and he showed it to Don Pedro Parias and to the colonel of the Civil Guard, a certain* [Santiago] *Garrigós* [Bernabéu]*, and to one other guy. I do not know who he was, another fat cat. They were examining the letter and they say, "Look here, this letter you take it home and you save it." They say, "Because things are coming to a head. We do not know how it will go, whether for their side or for ours. If it turns out for our side, now you know what you have to do." And since that is the way it went, the first eight men they killed, since it was him and the priest who did it, they locked them up to kill them.* This story shows Pedro Parias deeply involved in the conspiracy and, together with Colonel Santiago Garrigós Bernabéu of the Civil Guard, recommending to José Rodríguez Sánchez that he take revenge on Castilleja's leftists if the military coup succeeded.

Meanwhile, the conspiracy was going forward at the national level. In March, there were meetings of military men attended by Generals Francisco Franco and Emilio Mola. On April 13, General Gonzalo Queipo de Llano y Serra, who had distinguished himself until then as a Republican general, had his first meeting with Mola and expressed interest in joining the conspiracy. On June 23, Queipo de Llano received the order to take charge of the uprising in Seville. His reputation as a Republican and his post as inspector general of Customs Guards would allow him to move about freely without arousing suspicions. Furthermore, he could count on a good friend in Seville, his classmate at the Valladolid Cavalry Academy, Pedro Parias González.

In Castilleja: July 12 to July 18, 1936

Despite the recent loss of his nephew Manuel, Castilleja's priest found a reason to be of good cheer. On July 12, he wrote his last letter to Cardinal Ilundáin:

> 7-12-936
> Most Excellent and Reverend Cardinal Archbishop of Seville,
> I have received the official letter of V.E.R. [*Your Roman Excellency*] naming me Councilor of the Executive Board of the Feminine Organization for Catholic Action in Carrión de los Céspedes, expressing my gratitude to V.E.R. for said nomination and declaring that I will endeavor to fulfill my obligations, putting into practice a prudent labor of a formative nature.
>   Felipe Rodríguez, the least of your parish priests, respectfully kisses the A.P. de V.E.R. [*Pontifical Ring of Your Roman Excellency*][26]

The same day, dramatic events were taking place in Madrid. On July 13, the inhabitants of Castilleja heard the news on the radio or read it in the newspapers. The previous afternoon, four Falangists had shot José Castillo, lieutenant of the Republican Assault Guard and a Socialist militant. His companions in the Assault Guard decided to take revenge by assassinating a prominent right-winger. They went to the apartment of José Calvo Sotelo, monarchist deputy, arrested him and, after shooting him, left his body in the morgue at the Almudena Cemetery, where it was identified on July 13. Although the residents of Castilleja would not know it, these events led General Mola to give the definitive order to initiate the coup at five o'clock in the morning on July 18.

The town's schoolteacher Joaquín León Trejo, was aware of the seriousness of the situation. His son remembers his father's mood at the time. According to José León García, he and his brother Antonio were once singing a Republican song and his father told them, *"Sing! Sing now! Because soon, who knows?"* José also remembers his father's reaction to the news of Calvo Sotelo's assassination. *"This is a catastrophe,"* he had said. Joaquín León Trejo had three older brothers: José, Francisco, and Manuel. José and Manuel were members of the Republican Union party like Joaquín and, like him, would be assassinated during the repression. Francisco was a lieutenant colonel of Engineers and Aviation. He would never belong to any political party because he believed it inappropriate for military men to involve themselves in politics, but Francisco León Trejo took seriously his oath to defend the regime in power. He would remain loyal to the Republic just as he had remained loyal to the monarchy during the Jaca insurrection in December 1930. Francisco León Trejo was named military commander of the Cuatro Vientos airdrome in Madrid on July 14, 1936. There he would defend the Republic, contributing substantially to the defeat of the military coup in Madrid.[27]

According to José León García, during the week between the assassination of Calvo Sotelo and the military coup, Castilleja's schoolteacher spoke by telephone with his brother Francisco, who told him that things were as serious as they appeared and encouraged him to go to Seville, where he could join the resistance. There was little he could do in Castilleja whose fate would depend on the outcome of events in Seville. The true drama would unfold in the cities and on the military bases. Joaquín went to Seville on his bicycle and got in touch with a friend, Captain Justo Pérez Fernández of the Republican Assault Guard. That is where he was when the war broke out.

On the night of July 17, a large automobile built by the Hispano Suiza Company passed through Castilleja traveling west. It had left Seville at nightfall and was heading to Huelva. The street along which the highway passed was then named for the Republican ex-president, Niceto

Alcalá-Zamora. In less than two months this street would have another name, that of the man whose daughter was married to the son of Alcalá-Zamora, the man who was the passenger in the Hispano Suiza motorcar, General Gonzalo Queipo de Llano y Serra. He had arrived in Seville that morning after traveling all night from Madrid and had spent the day in the Hotel Simón where, after a nap, he met with military and civilian conspirators. Then, as he himself would later write, "I left for Huelva on the pretext of visiting the Customs Guards who were stationed there, but the real purpose of the journey was so that my presence in Seville would not arouse suspicions."[28]

On the morning of July 18, Queipo de Llano returned to Seville, passing once more through Castilleja in his Hispano Suiza. Shortly before, he had had an alarming experience. Apprized of the uprising of the Army of Africa in Morocco, the government in Madrid had issued orders for the arrest of military men who were not at their assigned garrison. Consequently, two civil guards had stopped the Hispano Suiza in La Palma del Condado but, convinced that the inspector general of Border Guards did not have a fixed garrison, they let him continue on his journey. They then called the Civil Guard barracks in Sanlúcar la Mayor where the duty officer spoke by telephone with Governor Varela Rendueles. The governor, thinking that this "Republican" general was loyal to the government, told the Civil Guard in Sanlúcar not to intercept him.[29]

At noon, Queipo de Llano was again in the Hotel Simón where his first visitor was the Falangist José García Carranza "El Algabeño II." García Carranza called his companions, among them Pedro Parias and his sons.[30] A little after one o'clock, Queipo went to the army headquarters and arrested General José Fernández de Villa-Abrille, commander of the Second Division.[31] Between two thirty and three o'clock, troops from army headquarters and other barracks, members of the Civil Guard, and armed Falangists, among them Pedro Parias's sons, converged on downtown Seville.[32] After a battle with Republican assault guards, the insurgent forces controlled an ample sector of the downtown. Queipo de Llano arrested Governor Varela Rendueles and named his old friend Pedro Parias González governor.[33]

Shortly before ten in the evening, the residents of Castilleja del Campo heard the first of Queipo de Llano's many radio "chats":[34]

> People of Seville: To arms! The Fatherland is in danger and in order to save
> it a few men of courage, a few Generals, have assumed the responsibility
> of placing ourselves at the forefront of a Movement of National Salvation
> that is triumphing everywhere.

The Army of Africa hastens to cross to Spain to join in the task of crushing that unworthy Government that had taken upon itself to destroy Spain in order to convert it into a colony of Moscow.

By order of the Junta of Generals, I have assumed command of the Second Organic Division, since General Villa-Abrille has proven himself insensible to the dangers that menace the Fatherland and to the exhortations of his fellow officers. All the troops of Andalusia, with whom I have communicated by telephone, obey my orders and are now in the streets.

General Villa-Abrille, all the authorities of Seville, and all who sympathize with them and with the so-called Government in Madrid, are under arrest and at my disposal. . . .

[*Here there is an exaggerated description of the coup's successes in the rest of Spain.*]

People of Seville! The die is cast and decided in our favor and it is useless for the rabble to resist and produce that racket of shouts and gunshots that you hear everywhere. Troops of Legionnaires and Moroccans are now en route to Seville, and as soon as they arrive, those troublemakers will be hunted down like vermin. Long live Spain! Long live the Republic![35]

It is surprising that Queipo ended his first radio chat with "Long Live the Republic." This confused many of those who listened to the broadcast. During the first days of the war, this "Republican" general would continue to insist that the military coup was not against the Republic but against the Popular Front government and that the goal of the coup was to establish an "honorable Republic." While the General was speaking, the new civil governor of Seville, Pedro Parias, was calling the towns of the province instructing his associates in the oligarchy to take over the town halls with the help of the Civil Guard.[36] But the coup was not going to be so easy. The Left in Andalusia was not going to be defeated by telephone.

Notes

1 Minutes, 22 February 1936, Castilleja del Campo Municipal Archive.
2 Minutes, 5 March 1936, Castilleja del Campo Municipal Archive.
3 George A. Collier, *Socialistas de la Andalucía rural*, 134–5, 153–4.
4 Minutes, 24 March 1936, 15 April 1936, and 5 June 1936, Castilleja del Campo Municipal Archive.
5 Minutes, 25 June 1936, Castilleja del Campo Municipal Archive.
6 Minutes, 5 May 1936, Castilleja del Campo Municipal Archive.
7 Minutes, 15 May 1936, Castilleja del Campo Municipal Archive.
8 Correspondence, Castilleja del Campo Municipal Archive.
9 Ibid.

10 Ibid.

11 Minutes, 10 June 1936, Castilleja del Campo Municipal Archive.

12 Minutes, 15 June 1936, Castilleja del Campo Municipal Archive.

13 Correspondence, Castilleja del Campo Municipal Archive.

14 Ibid.

15 Isidora Mistral is not her real name. She and her husband allowed me to record an interview with them on the condition that their real names not appear in the book.

16 "Fallecimiento de un herido," *La Unión*, 3 June 1936.

17 "De una agresion á un camión ocupado por jóvenes comunistas," *El Liberal, Afternoon Edition*, 1 June 1936.

18 *La Unión*, 1 June 1936.

19 Minutes, 5 June 1936, Castilleja del Campo Municipal Archive.

20 Ibid.

21 *El Correo de Andalucía*, 3 June 1936.

22 *El Liberal, Afternoon Edition*, 15 June 1936.

23 *ABC, Edición de Andalucía,* 25 June 1936, p. 36.

24 Minutes, 25 June 1936, Castilleja del Campo Municipal Archive.

25 Dossier 24, Office of the Justice of the Peace, Castilleja del Campo.

26 Correspondence, 1936, Archiepiscopal Archive of Seville.

27 Fernando León Saenz, "En Cuatro Vientos no se sublevó nadie" (unpublished manuscript); Telephone conversations from 2001 to 2004 with Alejandro León Saenz, the colonel's son.

28 Gonzalo Queipo de Llano, "Carta a Franco . . . ," in *Estampas de la guerra*, 5:8.

29 Juan Ortiz Villalba, *Sevilla 1936*, 79.

30 Ibid., 95.

31 Francisco Espinosa Maestre, "Sevilla, 1936: Sublevación y represión," 187–8.

32 Ibid., 191–5.

33 Juan Ortiz Villalba, *Sevilla 1936*, 107–8.

34 Ibid., 114.

35 Ian Gibson, *Queipo de Llano*, 131–2.

36 Juan Ortiz Villalba, *Sevilla 1936*, 115.

Four

July 19 to July 24, 1936

The "pact"

By nightfall on July 18, General Queipo de Llano controlled only part of Seville, and the coup had failed in Huelva. Castilleja, halfway between these two cities, attempted to prepare for all eventualities. Residents from across the political spectrum met in the office of Juan Luis Vergne Herrero, Castilleja's doctor. He was the ideal person to mediate a mutual protection pact. Everyone I interviewed said Don Juan was a right-winger, except for Conrado Rufino Romero, who said he was apolitical. María Vergne Graciani went into more detail, saying her father was from a right-wing family and shared his family's convictions, but he was married to a woman from a Republican family and got along well with his father-in-law. According to María, her father believed that a small town doctor should not discuss politics because he needed the confidence of all his patients: *I remember the staunchest Communist or a card-carrying Falangist come to my house and my father treated them exactly the same, with the same affection.* Residents who wanted peace in Castilleja all felt comfortable at the doctor's house, whatever their ideology.

Those I interviewed who spoke of the pact described it in different ways, but its contents were always essentially the same. Aniceto Luque Luque said it was *the agreement that whichever side took the town, no one was to be killed.* María Vergne Graciani described it as a promise that *we who are Republicans, if the Republican forces from Huelva take the town, we defend you and you who are Falangists or right-wingers, if those forces take the town, then you defend us.* Carmen Monge Romero said that *here at the meeting the leftists told the people on the Right not to worry because nothing would happen to them.*

According to María Vergne, there were at least three meetings attended by right-wingers and leftists in her father's office, but the testimonies are unclear about when the meetings took place. Celedonio Escobar Reinoso gives the impression that the meetings began before July 18. It is only logical there would be such conversations. Six weeks before, when Communists from Seville killed Manuel Rodríguez Mantero, the town had lost a young man whom everyone described as *a very fine boy*. The collective hope for a mutual protection pact could have originated at any moment during June or early July. It would have seemed especially urgent to come to an agreement after the assassination of the monarchist deputy José Calvo Sotelo, and there certainly would have been an emergency meeting the night of the coup.

More important than when the meetings took place is the question of who attended and who did not. The doctor's daughter remembers there were more than twenty people involved. Among them were many of those who would later be shot. She named Lutgardo García Ramírez, a member of Manuel Azaña's Republican Left party. María Vergne had a special affection for him because of his talent for telling stories. José León García said the Republican mayor had meetings at the doctor's house with many right-wingers: the Cuevas, the Luques, and José Calero, owner of "La Gasolinera," a combination gas station and café, located on the highway. Two men who did not attend were the uncles of the young Falangist who had been assassinated, the priest Felipe Rodríguez Sánchez and his brother José, the countess's new administrator. According to María Verge, *Don Felipe did not go nor did his brother Pepe. Neither of the two.*

A question about the pact evoked the following dialogue with the right-wing couple who did not want me to use their real names:

> Richard Barker: *Was there an agreement between leftists and right-wingers to the effect that no one was to be killed here, no matter what happened?*
> Isidora Mistral: *But it was not to be.*
> Leopoldo Rubio: *It was not to be.*
> Richard: *Why not?*
> Isidora: *Because the main obstacle was the . . .* (Long pause.)
> Leopoldo: (In a very low voice.) *. . . priest. They say the priest was the one who put his foot in it because, just like everywhere, in those days they were in charge.*

The majority of those I interviewed, whatever their ideology, said much the same thing. Leftists generally expressed this opinion with less delicacy than Isidora and Leopoldo.

The pact is put to the test

The miners' column from Río Tinto

In the wee hours of the morning of Sunday, July 19, a column of civil guards and customs guards from the city of Huelva passed through Castilleja del

Campo en route to Seville. It was under the command of Gregorio Haro Lumbreras, commandant of the Civil Guard in the province of Huelva. He was operating under orders from General Sebastián Pozas Perea, director of the Civil Guard in Madrid, lieutenant colonel Julio Orts Flor, stationed in Huelva, and Diego Jiménez Castellano, the civil governor of Huelva.

The plan was to join up with a column of miners that was forming in the Río Tinto mining region. Haro Lumbreras was to wait for the miners in La Pañoleta, a town just west of Seville, and march through the working-class suburb of Triana to reinforce those who were resisting Queipo de Llano. But, unbeknownst to his superiors, Haro Lumbreras was part of the conspiracy to overthrow the Republic. Instead of waiting for the miners, he passed through Triana, pretending to go confront Queipo de Llano's forces. He then placed his column under the command of the insurgent general, who ordered him to make a roundabout march through the towns of La Algaba, Santiponce, and Camas, and return to La Pañoleta. This circuitous route was because Haro Lumbreras would not have been able to deceive the working-class residents of Triana twice. Arriving back in La Pañoleta the following morning, Haro Lumbreras's column was deployed around the Seville–Huelva highway to ambush the miners' column.

Meanwhile, the miners had requisitioned automobiles, trucks, and dynamite from the Río Tinto Mining Company. When they began their march in the pre-dawn hours of July 19, they also had a small number of arms captured in raids on the local Civil Guard barracks.[1] The civil governor of Huelva, Diego Jiménez Castellano, had recently ordered the confiscation of privately owned weapons in the province. Huelva's Civil Guard barracks were veritable arsenals, but the province's civilians were unarmed.[2] The miners had neither the time nor the means to attack other barracks as they passed through the province. Castilleja del Campo, on the border of the provinces of Seville and Huelva, would be the first town where they would search for arms.

The town is disarmed

Upon their arrival in Castilleja, the miners stopped in "the meadow" at "La Gasolinera," the café owned by José Calero. A few trucks climbed the hill to the the town hall. Local leftists joined them, some out of curiosity, like Antonio Monge Pérez, then nineteen years old, who remembers that it was difficult for him to walk that day because one of his feet was swollen from an infected tick bite. Others went to the town hall to prevent the miners from causing damage in the town. These included Mayor Ramírez, who was sixty-one years old, and José Pérez Rodríguez, who was thirty-seven.

According to Isidora Mistral, when some of the miners on the town hall porch aimed their rifles at the marchioness's house across the street, José Pérez Rodríguez interceded so they would not shoot. Nevertheless, in the document of February 27, 1939, entitled "Account of the individuals of Castilleja del Campo to whom was applied the War Decree . . . ," next to José Pérez's name, the reason he was shot is: "Coadjutor of the disarming of the population by the miners Río Tinto."[3]

Castilleja's leftists offered to help the miners requisition arms on the condition they not burn the church or the houses of right-wingers, nor harm anyone. Groups of miners, accompanied by local men, spread out through the town searching houses. Naturally, the town's right-wingers were terrified. Carmen Moreno Romero's family lived in the marchioness's house, where her father was the foreman. Carmen remembers that, when the miners took aim at the house, one of her sisters fell ill from the scare and did not recover for several days. Later eight or ten men, miners and Castilleja leftists, entered the marchioness's house and searched it. They threatened those who lived there, but there were no arms. According to Miguel Rodríguez Caraballo, one local leftist, Lucrecio Paz Delgado "El Cuartano," put his pistol to the chest of Severo Moreno Monge, the marchioness's foreman. "El Cuartano" would later pay dearly for this act. The motive for applying the war decree to him, as it appears in the document of February 27, 1939, was "Anarchist, collaborated with the miners from Río Tinto."[4] He would be brutally tortured before being shot.

According to Antonio Delgado Luque, twelve or fourteen miners searched the countess's "palace." Other miners searched the house of José María Cuevas Escobar. He was an older man, the richest in town besides the countess and the marchioness. His house was near the town hall in the Plaza de Martínez Barrio. It had a flour mill and a storeroom for wheat. Isidora Mistral and her mother were working there. When José María Cuevas looked out his window and saw the miners on the town hall porch, he fled, climbing over his patio wall after leaving instructions with Isidora's mother to open the door for the miners. She was so nervous that she dropped the house key in the wheat that filled the storeroom and the miners had to break down the door. They searched the room shared by two of José María Cuevas's sons, Manuel and Rogelio, and took a pistol and a watch. In another room they found an image of the virgin which they took out to the plaza and destroyed by firing four shots into it. From there they went to the house of José María's other son, José Cuevas Reinoso, whose watch they also took.

In total, the miners searched between twenty and thirty houses, according to Conrado Rufino Romero. Conrado said they searched the house of his father, Francisco Rufino Pérez, and took two shotguns as well as gunpowder and shot for loading shells. Later, Conrado's father recovered the guns, one that the miners left in Castilleja because it was old and unusable, and the other in Sanlúcar la Mayor. According to Conrado, because the Castilleja leftists restrained the miners, the only damage done during the disarming of the town, other than the destruction of the image of the virgin, was the *ransacking of dwellings during the search of rooms, furniture, and attics.* The Republican authorities prevented the miners from entering at least one house. Knowing that Aniceto Luque Luque was a hunter, they called him to the town hall so he could hand over his shotgun there.

The Republican authorities also protected the church. After agreeing to help in the requisition of arms, Mayor Ramírez, several councilmen, and José Pérez Rodríguez, who would later be shot as "Coadjutor of the disarming of the population by the miners Río Tinto," went to the church to prevent the miners from burning it. Modesto Escobar Moreno, president of the local union, also protected the church, according to Marina Luque Reinoso. One private home was saved from burning. It belonged to Manuel Rodríguez Mantero's family. He was the young Falangist assassinated on May 31. The house was near "La Gasolinera" where most of the miners' trucks had parked. According to Manuel's brother Eduardo, one miner tried to buy gasoline to burn the house, but they refused to sell it to him. Then, according to Eduardo, a local leftist told the miner to leave that family alone, that it had already suffered enough.

It is not entirely clear how long the miners stayed in Castilleja. The majority of those I interviewed said they were in town very briefly because they were in a hurry to get to Seville. Celedonio Escobar Reinoso said they stayed a couple of hours. It is possible that the column went on toward Seville without those who were searching houses and that the latter were to rejoin their companions at the top of La Cuesta del Caracol (Snail Hill) above La Pañoleta. One truck left Castilleja del Campo too late to fall into the ambush. Modesto Escobar Moreno, president of Castilleja's union, went along in this truck. According to his cousin Celedonio Escobar Reinoso, the truck with Modesto in it was approaching La Cuesta del Caracol when the battle was already over. It turned around and escaped.

After the "miners' invasion," the inhabitants of the town were unarmed, leftists as well as right-wingers, according to Miguel Rodríguez Caraballo. It is possible more arms remained in the hands of Falangists than of leftists. Celedonio Escobar Reinoso said there had only been shotguns for union members who stood guard around the town before the miners' invasion, but all these arms had been confiscated. Manuel Ramírez Mauricio said there were still a lot of weapons in town. *They were hidden in houses, or wherever, or under the roof tiles, or in the forage, or wherever.* Significantly, the testimonies of Castilleja's residents, whether leftists or right-wingers, contradict the propaganda of the Franco regime, which would justify the assassination of leftists in towns where no right-wingers had been killed by claiming that, in such towns, no right-wingers were shot because the leftists "did not have enough time." July 19, 1936, provided Castilleja's leftists time and opportunity to do as they wished. What they did was protect the lives of their right-wing neighbors, and the property of the church and the oligarchy. More than fifty years later, many leftists in the town would remember this with great bitterness saying, as did Manuel García Ramírez, that *the miners wanted to burn the church and the leftists here did not allow it. As a reward they killed almost twenty of them.*

The "battle" of La Pañoleta

Gregorio Haro Lumbreras's column completed its circuitous route through La Algaba, Santiponce, and Camas in time to take up concealed positions around the Seville – Huelva highway. When the miners' column descended Caracol Hill, civil guards opened fire with machine guns, detonating the dynamite in the first trucks and setting off an explosion that could be heard from Seville. Some of the following vehicles managed to turn around and flee. Other miners escaped on foot, leaving behind twenty-five dead and scores of wounded. Seventy-one prisoners were taken to Seville. Two of them would be released in mid-August because they had not been with the miners. They had been having a drink at an inn where some miners took refuge. One of the prisoners was condemned to military confinement because he was underage. The other sixty-eight were publicly executed by firing squad at dawn on August 31 in the working class neighborhoods of La Macarena, Triana, Amate, and Ciudad Jardín. Some were shot in La Pañoleta, where the "battle" had taken place. The bodies were left for several hours where they had fallen, as a warning to passersby.[5]

The descriptions of the "battle" of La Pañoleta in General Queipo de Llano's subsequent radio "chats" give the impression that Seville had been saved from a grave danger because divine providence was on his side. The rumor even spread that the virgin, dressed in white, had appeared in the sky over La Pañoleta. During an interview in 2004, María Vergne, eldest daughter of Castilleja's doctor, repeated this story. In fact, what had appeared in the sky was a column of white smoke, evidence not of divine intervention but of the logical consequences when desperate workers transporting dynamite in open trucks are ambushed by a professional paramilitary force armed with machine guns and led by a commander prepared to disobey the orders of his superiors.

National, provincial, international, and local events

During the first days after the coup, things were not going as well for the rebel generals as Queipo de Llano was claiming during the "chats" he broadcast over Unión Radio de Sevilla. In the pre-dawn hours of July 19, when the miners' column began its march, one could listen to the following declarations:

> People of Seville! The National Movement is emerging triumphant everywhere and even Barcelona and Madrid hurry to defend the Holy Cause of the Fatherland in its struggle against the rabble. . . .
>
> The first Moroccan troops have already left Ceuta for Algeciras and Cádiz, where they will disembark in the first hours of the day. . . .
>
> The news received from all parts is increasingly encouraging and I hope that, in a few days, Spain will free itself of all the knaves and perverts that had taken over the reins of Power. . . .
>
> Soon, very soon, there will be a rebirth in Spain of the tranquility that is indispensable to her greatness! People of Seville: Long live the Republic![6]

Antonio Delgado Luque was partly right when he described the "chats" of the man who would come to be known as the "Radiophonic General": *half of what he said was a lie.* In this chat on the day after the coup, Queipo de Llano gets everything wrong. Barcelona and Madrid would take almost three years before involuntarily joining the "Holy Cause." The coup's failures in Catalonia and Madrid must be added to those in Biscay and Guipúzcoa, which left General Emilio Mola in Navarre with a war on two fronts, one in Madrid and another in the Basque country. Franco's army was trapped in Africa because the coup had failed in the navy and Republican ships patrolled the Strait of Gibraltar. As to the the imminent rebirth of a Spain that was tranquil and free of "knaves and perverts," it is better to hold back one's laughter, although not one's tears.

The rebel generals turned to Mussolini and Hitler for help. Under cover of Italian aviation and the German navy, small contingents of Franco's troops managed to get to Spain, arriving in Seville on July 20, where they joined up with legionnaires transported from Tetouan in a few Fokker and Dorniers airplanes. Under the command of Antonio Castejón Espinosa, these forces and those of Queipo de Llano occupied the working-class neighborhood of Triana by one o'clock in the afternoon on July 21. A massacre of the defenders followed. On July 22, Castejón's legionnaires, troops from Seville's garrisons, Falangists, and others attacked the working class neighborhoods of Seville's old quarter, where workers with rudimentary weapons defended improvised barricades. The attackers divided into three groups and entered simultaneously through the Arch of the Macarena, Sol Street, and the Córdoba Gate, converging on the Plaza San Marcos after fierce fighting. Captured defenders were immediately shot.

One of those who took part in the defense of this part of the city was Joaquín León Trejo, Castilleja del Campo's schoolteacher, who, in the week prior to the coup, had gone to Seville on his bicycle after talking to his brother Francisco, military commander of the Cuatro Vientos airdrome. According to his son José, Joaquín escaped the trap and found refuge at the house of friends, an older couple who lived on Puente y Pellón Street. The man's name was Francisco Jiménez, but he was called "Paco Pelotas" (Frank Balls) because he owned a toyshop. There, Joaquín León Trejo was safe, but only for a short time. His friend, Captain Justo Pérez Fernández of the Republican Assault Guards, was less fortunate. At dawn on July 23, he was executed by firing squad near the Pavilion of Castilla and León in María Luisa Park, together with Commander José Loureiro Sellés and Lieutenant Pedro Cangas Prieto, also of the Assault Guard, and with Rafael Carrasco Martínez, president of the Pyrotechnic Workers' Union.[7]

News of their punishment reached Castilleja the same day during Queipo de Llano's "chat" at ten o'clock in the morning:

> Carrying out the disposition of the war decree, this morning the artillery commander Mr. Loureiro has been shot for having given orders to turn over two hundred rifles and as many pistols to the Marxists, so they could assassinate our valiant soldiers. Captain Justo Pérez, coadjutor of a similar crime, has suffered the same punishment, and so has Lieutenant Manuel [*the General calls him "Manuel," but his name was Pedro*] Cangas who, driving an armor-plated car, fired at us, causing numerous casualties to the outnumbered Seville garrison.
>
> The president of the Pyrotechnic Workers' Union has also been shot for having called a strike and for coercing workers.
>
> Absolutely everyone who falls into our hands for coercion of workers will suffer the same punishment.[8]

Castilleja's union leaders and Republican authorities no doubt began to suspect that the pact with local right-wingers would not protect them if Queipo de Llano's forces took their town. Besides the radiophonic general's menacing "chats," they heard eyewitness accounts. As Antonio Monge Pérez recalled: *People from Seville fled in all directions. Many of them came here. At the house of one of my sisters they took in a family because they said, "It is all*

out of proportion there. They are killing everyone on the Left." The family stayed
quite a few days until things calmed down a little. According to Antonio Monge,
the fugitives from Seville admonished Castilleja's leftists for their pacific
attitude: *Then those people who fled, naturally, they talked about what was
happening. They said, "You are respecting the life of right-wing people and afterwards they do not respect your lives."*

The Town Council surrenders

Shortly before Castilleja was occupied, a sixteen year old boy and a forty
year old man left the town on bicycles. They were going to Sanlúcar la
Mayor, thirteen kilometers to the east, toward Seville. The boy, who told
me this story sixty-four years later, was José León García, eldest son of the
schoolteacher Joaquín León Trejo. The man with him was Manuel Feijóo,
known by his nickname "El Portugués." They were carrying a letter from
Castilleja's Republican mayor, José Ramírez Rufino, to the Socialist mayor
of Sanlúcar, Manuel Gutiérrez Mateos. When they delivered the letter, the
mayor of Sanlúcar opened it and read it to them. It was a request that if
military forces passed through Sanlúcar, the mayor there should tell them
that in Castilleja del Campo everyone was family, that there were no
conflicts. As it turned out, the forces that would occupy the town did not
pass through Sanlúcar la Mayor. They came from the south, through Pilas.

With the city of Seville subdued, Queipo de Llano set his sights west-
ward, toward Huelva. That province was of great strategic importance. If
it remained in Republican hands, the port of Huelva would be a base for
the Republican navy, which could control the Atlantic Coast and the
estuary of the Guadalquiver River. Huelva could also serve as a bridgehead
for Republican forces. In rebel hands, the southern part of Huelva province
would open a route to Portugal, whose government supported the coup.[9]
On July 23, a column of volunteers commanded by Captain Ramón de
Carranza left Seville on the highway that is now A-474. They took Bollullos
de la Mitación, Aznalcázar, Pilas, and Hinojos. On the afternoon of July 24,
a detachment of the Carranza column headed north from Pilas and took
Carrión de los Céspedes and Castilleja del Campo.[10] They established their
headquarters in the countess's palace, according to Conrado Rufino
Romero. The town, having been disarmed by the miners' column, offered
no resistance. The majority of leftists took off running in all directions.

Some were arrested the same evening, among them Mayor Ramírez, who
was taken to the town hall at nine thirty to hand over power. The municipal secretary Hilario Luque Ramírez was sick that day and the Certificate
of Surrender was typewritten by Lieutenant Ramón Jiménez Martínez of

the Civil Guard, who presided over the event. Castilleja's municipal policeman Juan Antonio Tebas Rodríguez was also present. Lieutenant Jiménez appointed Antonio Rodríguez Fernández mayor of Castilleja and head of an "administrative commission."[11] Antonio Rodríguez, known as "Antoñito el de Aurora," would hold this post for only eleven days. He would be replaced on August 4 because, in accordance with the mutual protection pact, he refused to collaborate in the repression.[12]

Notes

1 Francisco Espinosa Maestre, *La Guerra Civil en Huelva*, 93–102; and *La justicia de Queipo*, 116–17.
2 Francisco Espinosa Maestre, *La Guerra Civil en Huelva*, 88.
3 Dossier 24, Office of the Justice of the Peace, Castilleja del Campo.
4 Ibid.
5 Francisco Espinosa Maestre, *La justicia de Queipo*, 117–22.
6 Ian Gibson, *Queipo de Llano*, 133.
7 Juan Ortiz Villalba, *Sevilla 1936*, 181.
8 Ian Gibson, *Queipo de Llano*, 164–5.
9 Francisco Espinosa Maestre, *La Guerra Civil en Huelva*, 103–4; José Manuel Martínez Bande, *La campaña de Andalucía*, 27.
10 José Manuel Martínez Bande, *La campaña de Andalucía*, 135.
11 Certificate of Surrender, 24 July 1936, Castilleja del Campo Municipal Archive.
12 Minutes, 4 August 1936, Castilleja del Campo Municipal Archive.

Part Two

Repression

Five

July 25 to August 27, 1936

Persecution of the Left

Fugitives and men in hiding

Some of the leftists who escaped returned fairly soon. With Antonio Fernández Rodríguez as mayor, they thought they could trust the mutual protection pact. Manuel García Ramírez was home the next day and Manuel Ramírez Mauricio returned two days later. Celedonio Escobar Reinoso also returned, following a close call. On the morning of July 26, he rode his bicycle into La Palma del Condado, which had still not been taken. Militiamen arrested him because they thought he was a spy. He was saved from being shot because there was an anarchist there named Adolfo, from Villalba del Alcor, who said, *"No, slow down. I can respond for this one. This one I know."* Manuel García, Manuel Ramírez, and Celedonio Escobar lived to tell their stories. Others did not.

Manuel Monge Romero also fled, but he turned himself in at the urging of his mother, Aurelia Romero Rodríguez. According to Manuel's sister Carmen, *As soon as my mother told him, "Ay Manuel, don't run away, they say that if you turn yourself in, they will not kill you," he says, "Mother, I am going to turn myself in but they will slaughter me like a lamb." And that is what happened, because my mother said she did not want him to be out there like that.* For the rest of her life, Aurelia Romero would regret having trusted the new authorities in Castilleja as well as General Queipo de Llano, who made the following declaration during his radio chat on July 27:

> Many towns in the province of Seville have been punished by the troops, with a severity proportionate to the resistance offered and the excesses committed. And now, many inhabitants of these towns wander terrified through the countryside, not daring to return. Nevertheless, let them know that I am prepared to pardon them, with one single condition: that they turn themselves in to the Commandant of Police in their respective towns, and upon turning themselves in, hand over a weapon: the same weapon with which they resisted us. With this, a veil will be drawn over the past.[1]

Two days later, Queipo de Llano qualified his promise:

> In accordance with my warnings, fugitives who were wandering about the countryside are beginning to return and turn themselves in to the authorities; but they do it without weapons, and that is inadmissible. Whoever, upon turning themselves in, does not turn over a firearm, will be incarcerated.[2]

The General did not explain where fugitives like Manuel Monge Romero, who had fled without weapons, would obtain this firearm.

Some of Castilleja's leftists hid in the town. Severo Luque Rodríguez went to the house of his neighbors, a right-wing family, saying to the woman of the house, *"Ay, María* [Reinoso Trigo], *where can I go? Hide me in your house! Hide me in your house!"* María told him, *"Hide wherever you want!"* The family had an oven for baking bread and María's husband, José Luque López, hid Severo there. He would not be among those shot. The source for this incident was Marina Luque Reinoso, one of the couple's children. José María Ramírez Mauricio, the young man who had written a letter to his grandmother before the election of the Popular Front, hid in the attic of his own house. His brother Manuel told how he was captured: *A friend of his along with his own godfather came searching the attic. The friend saw him but said nothing. He kept his mouth shut. Then, since the godfather did not see anything, they left. And when they got to the town hall, they said, "There is no one there." And another came later with the godfather and found him. And they took him away to kill him.* José María would be one of the men shot on August 27.

Men held in the town hall and their family members in the school

Besides Mayor Ramírez, other prisoners were filling the town hall. The doctor, Don Juan Luis Vergne Herrero, in whose house the mutual protection pact had been negotiated, visited the prisoners regularly. His daughter María remembered a conversation her father had with the Republican mayor: *I was fourteen years old then, which was not all that young and these things have great impact and I remember. My father used to take me to visit the prisoners because there was absolutely no one bad there. And that gentleman the mayor used to say to him, "Don Juan, they are not going to do anything to me, are they? Because I have done nothing." And it was true. He had not done anything. He was a very good person, the poor thing. And my father used to tell him, "No, my boy, no. Why would they do anything to you? No, they will not do anything to you." Naturally, we went quite a few nights.*

While these men were under arrest in the town hall, some of their family members were detained in the school. Aurelia Romero, who had urged her son Manuel to turn himself in, was there. Her daughter Carmen explained the motive for incarcerating the prisoners' family members: *what was happening is that they were thinking that she is going to look for her son, you know? And so there would not be a commotion, well, they put them in the school, arrested.* Aurelia Romero had many children and the authorities made a special arrangement for her, according to her son Aurelio, who sometimes served as a hostage: *Since there were six or eight children in the family, well, my mother had to go home to cook and do the chores because we had younger siblings six and eight years old. And so I had to go to the school and be locked up instead of my mother so she could go to the house and take care of things. What do you think of that?*

The first victim in Castilleja del Campo

The first man with ties to the town to be shot was not a native of Castilleja. Antonio Cruz Cruz "Adelino" was from Carrión de los Céspedes. A year before the coup, he married Dionisia Monge Romero, from Castilleja. "Adelino" and Dionisia lived in Espartinas, where he worked for the municipal government. The couple fled to Castilleja when Espartinas was taken and were staying in the house of Antonio's in-laws, Francisco Monge Rodríguez and Aurelia Romero Rodríguez.

One day toward the end of July, at sunset, "Adelino" and Dionisia were sitting by the front doorway taking advantage of a refreshing breeze. Dionisia was pregnant with the son who would be baptized Adelino, for his father's nickname. A thirteen year old boy named Narciso Luque Romero was across the plaza playing marbles with his friend Juan Pérez. He saw Dionisia go into her parents' house for two glasses of water for herself and her husband. Then Narciso noticed civil guards and Falangists walking up the street. They were from Espartinas. Feliciano Monge Pérez saw them too. He said they were *three guys* who had parked their car down the street and that, when they got to the doorway where "Adelino" was, the following dialogue ensued: *"Is your name Adelino?" "Yes." "Then come with us." "Why?"*

José "Pepe" Pérez, the father of Narciso's friend Juan, and José's mother-in-law, Felisa, came out to see what was happening. The civil guards and Falangists handcuffed Adelino and, according to Narciso Luque, as they were taking him away, Felisa asked her son-in-law, *"Pepe, are they going to kill him?"* He replied, *"You cannot really believe they would kill someone just like that, can you?"* Less than two months later, José Pérez Rodríguez would himself be killed. When Dionisia came out of the house with the two glasses of water, her husband was gone. Feliciano Monge said they killed

Antonio Cruz Cruz the same night *somewhere near Seville in I do not know what town. Espartinas or near there.* He also said that Adelino had been captured because of a denunciation by a resident of Castilleja, *Enriquillo* [Enrique Luque Ramírez] *and four bandits like him.* Feliciano said the motive for the denunciation was Enrique Luque's desire to possess Dionisia sexually.

The first group's final journey

The send-off

According to Carmen Monge Romero's calculations, the men detained in Castilleja's town hall were there eight or nine days before being taken to Sanlúcar la Mayor. In that case, the transfer occurred on Sunday, August 1, or Monday, August 2, which is supported by documentary evidence. On August 8, the administrative commission agreed to pay seventy-five pesetas for "food for and transport of prisoners."[3] Carmen Monge says that on the evening of their send-off, one of Castilleja's Falangists told the men to eat their supper early because at nightfall they were going to the Sanlúcar jail.

Many townspeople were out in the streets or at their windows to say goodbye. Celedonio Escobar was still going into the countryside at night for fear he would be arrested at his home. He saw the prisoners from a hillside vineyard. The doctor, Don Juan, also saw them, along with his eldest daughter María. They watched from their balcony and, when the truck went by, they waved to the prisoners and the prisoners waved back, some of them seated calmly in the open truck, naively believing they were going to Sanlúcar for only a while and would then be released. After the truck passed, the doctor entered the house and his daughter saw that he was crying. *"They are not coming back, Maruja, they are not coming back,"* he told her.

Family members come to the prisoners' aid

Most of these prisoners were more than three weeks in Sanlúcar before they were shot. Family members took turns bringing them clean clothes and returning with their dirty laundry. According to Otilia Escobar Muñoz, sometimes they went in the car of a man named Victorio Luque Rodríguez, who ran the town's tobacco store, and other times they went *however they could*, because they did not have money for the bus. The men and their families communicated by letters. For the rest of her life Carmen Muñoz Caraballo saved those of her husband, Manuel Escobar Moreno. This couple's daughter, Otilia, was thirteen months old when her father was shot.

As she recalls, the letters said, *"take care of the little girl, give this to my father, my watch for my father, my boots for my brother, and this . . ."* . . . *he was giving away his things because, naturally, he knew what was coming.*

On one occasion, a group of family members went to Seville to ask the new governor Pedro Parias to save their sons. Since he had been the countess's administrator, Pedro Parias knew the detained men and their families. One member of the group was Leocadio Ramírez Rufino, brother of Mayor José Ramírez, and father of the prisoner José María Ramírez Mauricio. Another was Manuel García Romero, the father of Lutgardo García Ramírez. Aurelia Romero Rodríguez had gone as well, with the hope of saving her son Manuel, whom she had told to turn himself in. Her husband, Francisco Monge, also went. This couple had already lost their son-in-law "Adelino" Cruz Cruz. There were other family members too, but my sources could not remember their names.

As they climbed the staircase to Pedro Parias's office, civil guards struck them with pistol butts, shoving them down the stairs. Manuel García Romero who, according to Feliciano Monge, was *the most eloquent*, managed to talk with the governor who asked him, *"What is the matter?"* He replied, *"Look here, Don Pedro, downstairs there are people and we have family locked up and they are in danger."* Pedro Parias's response was to ask him, *"That is what you are all here for?"* Then the governor *grabbed him and turned him around and shoved him with his foot and he went tumbling down the stairs and when he got to the bottom he was half-dead.* According to Manuel García Ramírez, the experience created such an impression on his father that by the time he got home he had suffered a stroke and later he had another stroke that caused his death. Manuel García Romero died January 28, 1937, at the age of fifty-nine, of a "Cerebral Hemorrhage," according to his death certificate.[4] Manuel García Ramírez would always hold Pedro Parias responsible for the death of his father as well as for that of his brother Lutgardo.

On August 11, about the same time as this incident, Governor Parias published a notice in the press for those who attempted to intercede on behalf of prisoners:

> This Government finds itself obliged to call the attention of Organizations and individuals to the necessity of abstaining from making recommendations and exerting influence in favor of persons submitted to the authorities, and to be mindful that, at all times, the collective interests must prevail over individual interests, for which reason not only those who oppose our cause will be regarded as belligerent enemies, but also those who succor or intercede for them . . .[5]

Those desperate parents from Castilleja could expect little help from Pedro Parias.

The second and third applications of the war decree on men of Castilleja del Campo

From among the group of eight men taken from Castilleja to Sanlúcar, the first to die were Alfredo Reinoso Monge and Cándido Nieves Perea. There are different versions of Alfredo's death. He was a small man with great strength and courage who had served in the cavalry during the Republic. According to his nephew Guillermo Reinoso Muñoz, before he was transported to Sanlúcar, Alfredo had said, *"these fascists, I am going to eat them alive."* Guillermo also said his uncle was not shot. He was beaten to death in jail. The guards had ordered the prisoners to line up, give the fascist salute, and sing "Cara al Sol," the Falangist anthem. Instead, Alfredo raised his fist and began singing the Communist "International." According to the document "Individuals of Castilleja del Campo to whom was applied the War Decree," he died on August 10, 1936.[6]

The same date is given for Cándido Nieves Perea's death. Perhaps he joined Alfredo in his suicidal protest. Or perhaps both their deaths had been less spontaneous, that this story of Alfredo's bravura was a myth to highlight his courage. According to Feliciano Monge Pérez, Alfredo did not die from a beating: *Alfredo, a cousin of mine. What a good person he was! And a guy with a pair of balls like you have never seen! A human being with nerves of steel is what he was! That guy, they kept shooting him and they could not kill him. They had to shoot him twice point-blank in the chest before he would fall.* But Feliciano believed Alfredo was shot with the rest of the group, on August 27, so this testimony is also suspect.

Killed by firing squad or from a beating, in some ditch or in the Sanlúcar jail, Alfredo Reinoso and Cándido Nieves had something else in common besides the date of their deaths. According to the document "Individuals of Castilleja del Campo to whom were applied the War Decree . . . ," both men's assassinations had to do with Manuel Rodríguez Mantero. For Alfredo it was "Instigator demonstration against dead Falangist" and for Cándido it was "Extremist, distinguishing himself death Falangist."[7] The fact that both men died seventeen days before the others lends credence to the testimonies that identify Manuel Rodríguez's death as an important motive for the repression in Castilleja.

Six more victims

On August 27, Manuel Escobar Moreno, Lutgardo García Ramírez, Enrique Monge Escobar, Manuel Monge Romero, José María Ramírez Mauricio, and José Ramírez Rufino were taken from the Sanlúcar jail to a dirt road that joins the Seville - Huelva General Highway at the site of the Repudio Inn in the municipal district of Espartinas. There they were shot. It is said that the mayor, José Ramírez, received the discharge bound to his nephew, José María. According to Feliciano Monge Pérez, *José María and his uncle, when they killed them, they died embracing each other. They died in each other's embrace. People who saw it and told me and I know.* The cadavers were buried in a common grave in the Espartinas cemetery.

When news of the executions reached Castilleja, the lights were turned off and Falangists stood guard at the houses of the victims' families to prevent public mourning. There was nothing about the deaths in the newspapers. But there was a transcription of Queipo de Llano's radio chat from the previous day:

> While in the territory still dominated by the Government of criminals there is no security or respect for anyone, in our territory it is just the opposite. The laws are enforced rigorously, and no one is punished without being judged and heard.[8]

Besides being entirely false, given that there were no legal proceedings whatever for the Castilleja men who were shot, it is interesting to observe Queipo de Llano's confused idea of justice. Did he really mean that prisoners were not allowed to speak in their defense until after being judged?

Responsibilities

At the provincial, regional, and national level

Generals Franco, Mola, and Queipo de Llano created the conditions that allowed sending a neighbor to his death without worrying about the consequences. They also set the example to be followed when there was a conflict between loyalty to friends and family, and loyalty to the "Movement." In the first days of the war, Franco approved the execution of his first cousin, Major Ricardo de la Puente Bahamonde.[9] And Mola's declaration is famous: "If I see my father in the opposing ranks I will shoot him."[10] Queipo de Llano declared that the words pity and clemency should be erased from the Spanish dictionary.[11] He certainly erased them from his own dictionary. Queipo had arrested General Miguel Campins Aura for remaining loyal to the Republic. But Campins had served with Franco at the Zaragoza General Military Academy and the two were friends. When Franco sent letters on Campins's behalf, Queipo tore them up. Campins was shot on August 16, 1936. Later, Queipo asked Franco to pardon his friend General Domingo Batet Mestres. He was shot early in 1937.[12]

The civil authorities appointed by the generals were equally ruthless. On one occasion, Seville's new governor, Pedro Parias, looked the other way when he had family ties to the victim. His half sister, Angustias Parias, was the mother-in-law of Blas Infante Pérez, shot on August 11. When she reproached Pedro for the death of her son-in-law, he made excuses, saying that he could not control all the groups that operated on their own in the repression. Angustias replied that in that case he should relinquish the governorship. In fact, Pedro Parias never intended to control the groups carrying out the mass executions. On the contrary, he encouraged them. As early as July 20, before Seville was subdued, he had published a declaration that ". . . victory must not stop the task of purification that the country needs."[13]

His friend General Queipo de Llano was doing the same, as in the following conclusion to his radio chat on July 26:

> People of Seville! I do not have to spur you on, because I am already well acquainted with your courage. To conclude, I tell you that if any effeminate pervert makes defamatory remarks or spreads alarmist false rumors about this glorious national movement, kill him like a dog. Long live Spain!![14]

The generals and civilian authorities in the Nationalist zone wanted to involve as many citizens as possible in the repression in order to win followers who would know that if the Movement failed, it would cost them their lives. In Castilleja del Campo, those in charge were ready to collaborate, some with a deplorable enthusiasm.

At the local level: the administrative commission

The man who succeeded José Ramírez Rufino as mayor of Castilleja was Antonio Rodríguez Fernández "Antoñito el de Aurora," but he served only eleven days, tendering his resignation on August 4. Five of those I interviewed spoke of this man and his motives for stepping down. He was a right-winger who opposed the repression. He may have been a party to the mutual protection pact. In any event, his intention was to respect the spirit of the pact. He was pressured to sign "death sentences," according to everyone who spoke of him, and his resignation was an act of protest. According to Carmen Monge Romero, Antoñito el de Aurora *said that as long as he was in possession of the staff of office that here no one would be killed and they told him there was no other alternative but to kill and he says, "Well I am relinquishing the staff." And he set the staff down and that Pepe Cuevas* [José Cuevas Reinoso] *picked it up.*

The meeting was presided by Corporal José Martínez Pascual, commandant of the Civil Guard barracks in Carrión de los Céspedes, who, "authorized by the Most Excellent Civil Governor of this province [*Pedro Parias*] and by powers conferred by the Most Excellent General in Chief of the Second Division [*Queipo de Llano*], designated the posts" to José Cuevas Reinoso as mayor and to Francisco Luque Cuevas, José María Fernández Rodríguez, Casildo Escobar Reinoso, and Antonio Calero Cuevas as councilmen.[15] They had all joined the Falange before the July 18 coup. Their designation meant the town was in the hands of those most willing to avenge the death of their fellow Falangist Manuel Rodríguez Mantero.

By his own declaration, Corporal Martínez of the Civil Guard had received his authority to name Castilleja's mayor and councilmen from "powers conferred by" General Queipo de Llano to civil governor Pedro Parias. As the countess's ex-administrator, Pedro Parias knew who could be counted on in the elimination of leftists. But these authorities did not act alone. When speaking of Pedro Parias's power, Leopoldo Rubio also mentioned the role of parish priests in the selection of mayors after the coup: *Do you not know how it went in those days with things like that? A delegate from the governor would come* [the Civil Guard corporal] *to change the mayor. First the priest stops by, you know? The priest stops by and consults with the delegate. Mayor So and So, without elections or anything, whatever the priest said.*

Other testimonies confirm the power of priests, even if we limit ourselves to right-wingers. Aniceto Luque Luque spoke of two nearby towns whose experience of the repression was different from that of Castilleja: *There are towns where no one was killed. Here if the priest says, "No one is to be killed," no one would be killed. That I can guarantee. Because then the priests were the boss. There were towns like Hinojos, Chucena, towns here where the priest said, "Here no one is to be killed." Here no one said, "No one is to be killed." That was the end of it.* Conrado Rufino Romero also spoke of the role of Castilleja's priest: *Here the priest did not intervene. And if I did not . . . whoever tries to delve into that, falls from grace at once, no? Some right-winger would say, "Alright, so and so, let us see if he cannot be killed." Well, he would take it up with the priest.* These testimonies, both from right-wingers, depict Don Felipe as an active participant in the repression.

The responsibility for the repression was shared by several groups and individuals: the political authorities, represented by Governor Pedro Parias and Mayor José Cuevas Reinoso; the Falange, represented by Castilleja's mayor and councilmen; the forces of public order, represented by Corporal Martínez Pascual of the Civil Guard; and the church, represented by the parish priest Felipe Rodríguez Sánchez. The oligarchy was also involved, in the person of José Rodríguez Sánchez, the countess's new administrator and, like his brother Felipe, uncle of the slain Falangist Manuel Rodríguez Mantero. This shared responsibility allowed each group or individual to evade criticism by shunting responsibility to other members of the repressive labyrinth. Isidora Mistral spoke of the Castilleja parents who had gone to ask Pedro Parias to save their sons: *Pedro Parias told the people, "How do you expect me to favor them if just today the man who rules the town came here? Who is he?" He said that when he met with the parents who were pleading for their sons. He said, "How can it be if I have just met with the one who rules the town? And that man is the priest."*

Speaking of José Cuevas Reinoso's responsibility in the repression, Antonio Monge Pérez accepted this mayor's explanations but compared his complicity in the killings with his predecessor's behavior: *Pepe Cuevas said no, that he had not been to blame for those things, that it was others. Perhaps he was right, that the people around him . . . But he should have done what the other did who was the first mayor during the Movement, who said, he says, "Look here! No one is to be killed here! Because these people have done nothing and if they are to be killed, I lay down the staff of office here in the town hall, and I tender my resignation and no one is killed under . . . I will sign no death sentences." But Pepe took charge of that, and then they killed all those people here.* Feliciano, Antonio's younger brother, did not completely accept José Cuevas Reinoso's explanations either: *He said to me, out in the fields, "The first two membership cards in the Falange that arrived here in Castilleja were mine and El Niño Guapo's* [Pretty Boy's, councilman José María Fernández Rodríguez], *but neither El Niño Guapo nor I killed anyone." But of course I should have told him, "Maybe you did not kill anyone pistol in hand but you took up the staff so they could kill everyone they had to kill."*

Notes

1 Ian Gibson, *Queipo de Llano*, 214.
2 Ibid., 234.
3 Minutes, 8 August 1936, Castilleja del Campo Municipal Archive.
4 Civil Death Registry, Office of the Justice of the Peace, Castilleja del Campo.
5 *El Correo de Andalucía*, 11 August 1936.
6 Dossier 24, Office of the Justice of the Peace, Castilleja del Campo.
7 Ibid.

8   *La Unión*, 27 August 1936.
9   Juan Ortiz Villalba, *Sevilla 1936*, 121–2.
10 Julián Casanova, "Rebelión y revolución," 81.
11 Ibid., 60.
12 Juan Ortiz Villalba, *Sevilla 1936*, 192–5.
13 Ibid., 147.
14 *ABC, Andalusian Edition*, 27 July 1936.
15 Minutes, 4 August 1936, Castilleja del Campo Municipal Archive.

Six

August 28 to September 14, 1936

The administrative commission in action
New names for Castilleja's streets

It must have seemed odd when the first prisoners were taken away in early August. They began their journey in the plaza named for Diego Martínez Barrio. He was the founder of the Republican Union party to which the prisoner Mayor Ramírez belonged. Then they traveled along a street named for the Socialist leader Francisco Largo Caballero and descended a street named for Emilio Castelar, a president during the First Republic in the 1870s. The truck left town on an avenue named for Niceto Alcalá-Zamora, president during the Second Republic. On September 5, the new authorities renamed the streets. The next group of prisoners would leave the Plaza Calvo Sotelo, named for the monarchist deputy, travel along José Antonio Primo de Rivera Street, for the founder of the Falange, and descend Manuel Rodríguez Mantero Street, named for the local Falangist boy killed on May 31. The truck would leave town along Queipo de Llano Avenue, for the general who had taken Seville. Generals Mola, Sanjurjo, and Franco also got their own streets.

Other changes paid homage to the Andalusian oligarchy. Governor Pedro Parias, former administrator of the countess, recovered the street he had lost to the Republican martyr Fermín Galán. The countess's father also got a street. And there were changes in recognition of the church. Pablo Iglesias Street and Marcelino Domingo Street no longer honored the founder of the Socialist Party and the Republican education minister. They reverted to Venerable Mañara Street and San Miguel Street. The Plaza Ramón y Cajal was again Plaza de la Iglesia.[1] These new names would remain for forty-five years.

Budgetary affairs

The administrative commission also contributed to the war effort. On September 12, 1936, it examined invoices from José Calero Cuevas, owner of the bar La Gasolinera. They were for "food and drinks provided . . . to forces of the Army and Civil Guard and Spanish Falange in the taking of this town." The invoices amounted to two hundred and eighty-four pesetas and five centimos. The municipality agreed unanimously to pay that amount.[2]

The celebration of the town's "liberation" on July 24 was not the only time the owner of La Gasolinera would render services on credit in the war effort. On August 22, Mayor José Cuevas Reinoso remitted a voucher to José Calero Cuevas "for one hundred and five liters of gasoline and thirteen liters of oil . . . employed in the transport of elements of Spanish Falange and Forces of the Civil Guard from the Carrion de los Cespedes barracks, to lend various services in combination with the Army and also independently of the same in the taking of Aznalcollar and investigations in Sanlucar, Escacena del Campo and trips to Seville to carry out searches for fugitives and other affairs related to public order."[3]

Aznalcóllar is a mining town about fifteen kilometers northeast of Castilleja. It was taken on August 17 by a column under the command of Antonio Álvarez Rementería.[4] Falangists from Castilleja del Campo participated. They also took part in the sacking and harsh repression that followed.[5] The "various services" referred to in the voucher would be the taking of Aznalcóllar, services "in combination with the Army," and also the sacking and repression, services lent "independently of the same."

The "searches for fugitives" mentioned in the voucher would be for the leftists who had fled Castilleja del Campo as well as leftists from other towns. Many of the latter were hiding in the mountains to the north. They often carried out raids on isolated country estates and fields in search of food.[6] For personal or family reasons, the fugitives from Castilleja did not go as far as the mountains. They remained close to the town, but did not dare turn themselves in. Their fear was due to the "other affairs related to public order," the assassinations by firing squad.

Men of the town still hiding in the countryside in September

Celedonio Escobar Reinoso and José Escobar Moreno

These two men were semi-fugitives. Their special situations allowed them to return to the town during the day but required them to hide in the countryside at night. In both cases, they had powerful enemies among the new authorities, but they also had someone on the Right who could protect them. Celedonio Escobar was a man of anticlerical ideas because, in his words, *the church was always on the side of the rich, of the Right*. During the Republic he had had two or three run-ins, one quite serious, with Don Felipe and, according to Celedonio, the priest *wanted me killed first of all*. But Celedonio was the brother of Casildo Escobar Reinoso, Falangist and councilman on the administrative commission. Casildo was also the countess's armed guard and the oldest of those who had gone to the highway on May 31, 1936, the day of the confrontation with Communists from Seville. As the countess's armed guard, he was well known by Governor Pedro Parias, who had been the countess's administrator, and he used his influence with the new governor to protect his leftist brother Celedonio.

José Escobar Moreno "El Regular," was one of the town's most outspoken leftists and had many enemies on the Right. But he was also Celedonio and Casildo Escobar Reinoso's cousin and brother-in-law, and Casildo used his influence with Pedro Parias to protect him as well. Nevertheless, Casildo's influence had limits, according to Celedonio. *Then my brother told me and my brother-in-law, "Do not stay at home when I go to bed or they will come for you at night, take you out, and shoot you." We used to go sleep in the olive groves at night. We could come back during the day. It was at night that my brother told us to get out of town because when he was asleep, they could come grab us and take us wherever they wanted and shoot us.* Celedonio Escobar Reinoso and José Escobar Moreno had to sleep in the countryside a couple of months until José was drafted into the legion and Celedonio joined a Falangist militia.

Leovigildo Monge and his sons

Leovigildo Monge Pérez Sr. had to hide in the countryside until early September, along with his eldest sons Leovigildo and Antonio Monge Pérez, despite the fact that he had tried to help the young Falangist Manuel Rodríguez Mantero during the confrontation with Communists on May 31. A younger brother, Feliciano, accompanied his father and his brothers, out of solidarity and to escape the atmosphere of terror in the town.

Like Celedonio Escobar Reinoso and José Escobar Moreno, Leovigildo and his sons had someone to defend them, Juana Mantero Marmor, the mother of the slain Falangist Manuel Rodríguez. According to Feliciano, *Then, well, it turns out that that woman, out of gratitude, when the Movement broke out and they began to . . . the mother of the dead boy . . . when they gave carte blanche for anyone in the town to do as they pleased, on the list of those to be killed, the first four were my father, my brother Leovigildo, my brother Antoñito, and my brother-in-law Pepe* [José Pérez Rodríguez]. *The first four on the list. And that woman, out of gratitude for what my father had done for her son, she found out and went to the town hall and told them, "Leovigildo and his two sons, erase them and take them off the list and leave the son-in-law." And my brother-in-law they killed there in the town.*

Also like Celedonio and José, Leovigildo Sr. had enemies. He was a staunch supporter of the Republic, a small landholder with his own draught animals and a five acre parcel that he worked between other jobs. He was also an avid reader with a substantial collection of books. This was the type of leftist that many right-wingers regarded as especially dangerous. Feliciano described his family's relationship with the family of the Luque Cuevas brothers, Francisco "The Ill Wind," Antonio "The Chatterbox," Manuel "The Little Ill Wind," and José, all Falangists. Feliciano's description sounds like one of those family feuds in the Andalusian countryside so well portrayed in the play *Blood Wedding* by Lorca. *There was a mortal hatred, a mortal hatred, between that family and ours. A mortal hatred. It went back many years. I had not even been born when all that began.* The new regime gave the Luque Cuevas brothers the opportunity to take revenge for whatever it was that had happened in the past. The best course for Leovigildo and his older sons was to hide.

Feliciano describes their life on the lam: *We were in a place they call "El Perpiñá." We were there, well, through the months of July and August in the heat of the sun until they* [his older brothers, Leovigildo and Antonio] *were taken off to war. That year they did not harvest and the whole countryside was nothing but forage. I was thirteen years old then. And in my house there were nine or ten bovine creatures and I had to take care of them all by myself. Because when the day was dawning or before, they* [my father and brothers] *would take off and hide out there. And none of them told me where he was going so if someone showed up I could not say where they were. And I had to spend the whole day by myself. I had to pump the water for the cattle. And around two in the afternoon or thereabouts my father, the poor thing, would come and we would eat together and as soon as we finished eating he would take off and leave me alone again.*

At night we would get together, but one over here, another over there, another over there. And we were like that at least a month and a half or more. I came down with a headache. The sun got to my head and I could not even walk with the pain, it was so great. And my father, the poor thing, would say to me, he says, "Child, go home man and let the doctor see you. Do you not understand that here there is not even an aspirin or anything?" But the fear one had was so great, I say, "Papa, I would die before I would go to Castilleja." "Why?" I say, "Because I would." When it got to be eleven or twelve at night, you could hear nothing but gunshots everywhere killing men who were tied up. Ay, madre mía! Ay, madre mía! When that time of night arrived, over here, over there, over there, over here. Now they are killing, poor things, those men who are tied up. What a shame! I mean, I am going to tell you something that . . . What a shame! What a shame! We went through a lot. After this monologue, Feliciano took a few moments to recuperate before continuing the interview.

Manuel Tebas Escobar

Everyone I interviewed spoke highly of Manuel Tebas Escobar, a laborer who taught reading, writing, and arithmetic at night to other laborers and to children who had to work in the fields during the day. He had been a councilman during the first Republican biennium and the Popular Front. During the elections of February 16, 1936, he presided over the electoral table and broke the ballot urn when he suspected the Right was perpetrating fraud. He knew perfectly well what awaited him if captured and did not hesitate to escape when the town was occupied.

Conrado Rufino Romero, a right-winger, described Manuel Tebas's character and also mentioned a favor his own father, Francisco Rufino Pérez, did for Manuel when he fled the town: *Another* [of those shot] *was a neighbor of mine, Sara's father, Manolito. He taught classes for the boys. He was a teacher by night. It paid little. And he was a man who taught the boys at night, how to read and write and things like that. He was a good man. He lived in the house where the workers' center was. And when he left, he told my father he was going. My father gave him a packet of tobacco. "Here, take this. Take the packet of tobacco."*

Manuel Tebas Escobar left town in such a hurry he did not have time to arrange a meeting place with family members so they could bring him food. Eventually he approached José Luque López, a medium landholder who used to employ a few day laborers, the same right-winger who had hidden a leftist in his bread oven. Just as with that incident, it was the man's daughter Marina who described what happened. In both cases, Marina depicted her father as a courageous and honorable man who got on well with everyone in the town, regardless of their ideology. *No one would dare oppose my father. My father could go anywhere with his head held high.*

My father took food every day to Sara's father, who was in some bramble bushes out there. He was hiding and he did not dare approach anyone and when my father was going out to some land he had, at least ten kilometers from here, or eleven, because no one wanted to harvest his "escaña" [a prickly variety of wheat] *because there were so many fugitives in the countryside, the name they gave the poor things who were in hiding, they called them fugitives, so no one wanted to go out and harvest his lands. And my father, since he was very courageous, because he was, then he had to bind his legs in sacks so the "escaña" would not tear his legs and he had to go out to reap.*

Well, when it was getting to be midday with the sun beating down, then Sara's father showed up where my father was and my father said, "What is the matter, old friend?" He says, "It is that I do not dare approach anyone." He says, "It is alright, tell me what you want." He says, "Take this message to my mother. Tell her that I am alright, that I am hiding in some bramble bushes over there." Then his mother prepared a meal for him every day and every day my father would take it out to him.

Manuel Tebas Escobar surely heard the same gunshots that Leovigildo Monge and his sons heard at night and knew what they meant but, like them, he did not flee the area because of the family ties that bound him to Castilleja. His mother, Rosario Escobar Rufino, lived there, as did his sister, Esmoralda Tebas Escobar, and his wife, Suceso Rodríguez Luque, and their three children, Rosario, Elías, and Sara Tebas Rodríguez, eleven, seven, and four years old respectively. In the year 2000, Sara was the only one still alive. She did not remember her father because she was too young when he was shot, but she said she was very proud of her father for the things she had heard about him. Manuel Tebas's widow, Suceso, would never speak of him to her children because she was always too afraid, but Rosario, Sara's grandmother, and even more so her aunt Esmoralda, used to talk about him to his children.

According to Sara, while her father was in hiding, *he used to come in to some olive groves down there. They used to put on the news through a loudspeaker in the bar La Gasolinera. And they say he used to come close enough to listen to the news, the poor thing. Then my aunt used to say that he spent quite a while out there and that, naturally, "He wanted so much to see all of you." And then, since they used to take food out to him, they gave him a piece of paper with writing on it so he would come see us. They arranged it with him for nighttime, we came down to sleep at my aunt's house, and at midnight he crossed the highway and he was kissing us. That was shortly before he died, before they killed him.*

Lucrecio Paz Delgado "El Cuartano"

Lucrecio Paz Delgado, nicknamed "El Cuartano," participated in the disarming of the town on July 19, 1936, during the "invasion" of the Río Tinto miners. That day, he entered the marchioness's house with the miners and, pistol in hand, menaced the marchioness's foreman, Severo Moreno Monge. Miguel Rodríguez Caraballo, son-in-law of this foreman, described "El Cuartano" in the following terms: *He was an "infeliz." Besides being a revolutionary, he was an "infeliz."* The word "infeliz" could mean either "malcontent" or "ill-fated." The former meaning would describe his politics and the latter meaning would refer to his death, which Antonio Monge Pérez called *the most repugnant that ever happened here.* Feliciano

Monge Pérez said that *the death they inflicted on that man was the most horrific of all.*

According to Antonio Monge, "El Cuartano" *was a very noble and good man. Yes. He was not a believer. He used to say that he did not believe in anything, that he was an anarchist or something, I do not know, but that he did not believe in anything. But he was a person who never harmed anyone. All he did was speak at the workers' center where he used to talk of the interests of the workers, the working conditions, and so on, things like that.* According to Antonio's brother Feliciano, *Lucrecio was one of the best men there was in Castilleja, a man who knew how to read and write, because he enjoyed those things, and he used to go to the workers' center and there he used to read the* [anarchist] *newpaper "Land and Liberty." Two or three newspapers like that he used to read to the people. And he was the one who set the people straight about things.*

His death would indeed be horrific, but even before his capture he survived a frightful experience. There are several versions of the story. The most coherent is that of Feliciano Monge Pérez. *The poor thing, when the Movement took the town, he had to take off and go out into the countryside on his own. Back then, they were looking for him everywhere. He carried a pistol in his pocket and a blanket. And one day quite a few men from Carrión and Castilleja showed up at a country estate that was . . . they had not harvested, they had planted it with wheat, but it was not harvested. Forage everywhere. And they say, "Well, who knows? He may be hiding in there. Let us set it on fire so if he is in there, he will burn." And he was there. And he got into, poor thing, a drainage ditch, one of those they used to have in order to drain the land. And there he wrapped himself in his blanket and the fire passed over him and he did not get up because he knew that as soon as he raised his head, they would be there. And he suffered through that. He got burned, the poor thing. But thinking he was not there they took off and left him. And then he got up and went to a stream there near Chichina. And there he probably washed himself off because in those days there was water in all the streams.* Afterwards, "El Cuartano" approached Antonio Luque Tebas, a leftist who was guarding a melon patch. He asked him for a melon and told him what had occurred.

Like the other fugitives from Castilleja, Lucrecio Paz Delgado hid in the countryside near the town. He was forty-eight years old and did not have the strength for life in the mountains. Celedonio Escobar described him this way: *He could have taken off but no. He was a man of little spirit. He did not have the capacity to escape into the mountains and join up with the guerillas that were up there.* Feliciano Monge described El Cuartano's condition when he was captured: *They caught him, a man who was completely broken, a man who, poor thing, could not even speak after so many calamities.*

Harassment of leftists in the town

Obligatory participation in the "cleansing" of the surrounding area

While Lucrecio Paz Delgado, Manuel Tebas Escobar, and Leovigildo Monge and his sons held out for months in the countryside, leftists living in the town also suffered the repression's terror. The highway and country estates near Castilleja were favorite places for shooting leftists from other towns. Conrado Rufino, a right-winger, spoke of a dreadful task imposed on leftists and the silence that, in 1990, still enveloped the whole sad affair: *If someone was shot out there, well, the leftists here had to go out and get them and bring them here to the cemetery. They called them at night, "Come on. Get up. You have to go get one or two dead men out there." They would pick up two or three and bring them in with a pair of oxen, to the cemetery. They used to call them after midnight and, naturally, many of them would think that it was to shoot them. And they were frightened. Of course.*

Because at that time it did not depend on the town, expressly on the authorities from here, because there were concentrations of civil guards, who were the ones in charge of all that. Although there were also people from the town. Ringleaders. But, of course, all that . . . things that are hushed up, that everyone knows but do not . . . some talk about them, but not others. In a small town, nobody wants to name anyone.

Narciso Luque Romero also spoke of this obligation and related a specific incident involving his father, Antonio Luque Tebas, and his older brother Juan Antonio: *Here when they would kill someone out there on the highway, from Villalba, from Manzanilla, from La Palma, and all those places, well, they would bring them here to the cemetery. And they killed them anywhere, there along the highway. And then they would send carts with oxen from the* [countess's] *palace, which was an estate, the palace, and they used to bring in all those they had killed, two or three or four or however many there were. And they sent leftists out to suffer that, so they would see that they had killed their companions. They called my father many, many times. "Go out there, because in such and such a place there are four that you have to bring in with the carts." At two or three in the morning, which is when they used to kill them. And they would go to the palace, which was their headquarters, and they would go out with the carts and get them and bury them in the cemetery. And the gravedigger would cover them up.*

And by then my mother had a bad heart. My mother was alive then, of course. And not satisfied to call my father to go gather the poor things, one who lived here and was a bandit . . . one night that David [Muñoz Luque] *guy comes to my house. He was my brother Juan Antonio's godfather. And my father says, "What do you want?" "Go to the palace and your son Antonio along with you too." He says, "But man, my son too? Not just me?" He says, "That is the message they sent me with."*

Well my father went over there. And there was a corporal there, "Pirrichi" they called him, Corporal "Pirrichi" [José Martínez Pascual]. *He was a corporal in Carrión. He says, "And your son?" He says, "My son is not coming. You will excuse me but my son . . . you are going to kill my wife." "Why?" "It has been ten or fifteen years now that my wife has heart trouble and now it is bad enough that I have to go, but my son too? So she will die of a heart attack? I cannot consent to your killing her like that."*

The execution of women from the surrounding area

Manuel García Ramírez described the atrocities witnessed by leftists in the area: *Out along the highway the morning light would reveal the cadavers of pregnant women whose bellies were still moving. Right there along the highway. And how did we leftists of Castilleja know about that? They used to call us before the sun came up to go bury the people they killed. I do not wish on anyone to have to live through a thing like that.* This seems like a Dantesque exaggeration, but it is not. Of the more than four thousand leftists who were shot in the province of Huelva, one hundred and sixty-eight were women.[7] And approximately six hundred women were shot in the province of Seville.[8]

Narciso Luque Romero described an incident that took place near Castilleja del Campo after the taking of Aznalcóllar: *The biggest thing, because they themselves talked about it, they brought quite a few to some poplars that were there near the Characena estate. Black poplars we used to call them, thick poplars, and they used to put them there, the poor things, tied to the trunks to kill them during the war. Well near there they used to kill the poor things. And they were from Aznalcóllar. In a truck from Aznalcóllar they brought them to kill them against the poplar trees. And they would come tied two by two.*

And a mother and her daughter came, tied together, from Aznalcóllar. And it turns out the poor thing was almost due to give birth, the mother. They themselves talked about it. The ones who killed them talked about it. When they put them there, then they gave the order. "Fire!" And they went to give them the coup de grâce and they saw that the baby had come out of the poor thing. Alive. That thing of that moment when they aimed, pum, well the poor thing, from the effort . . . and then one of them says, "What the hell! What do you make of that? This one gave birth right here." Imagine! Imagine the stomach one has to have for something like that! He says, "Well this one here, we have to kill it. What else can we do?" And right there with his rifle butt he killed it. Imagine the stomach you have to have for something like that!

The source of Narciso Luque's testimony is shocking. He insists twice that those who told the story were the assassins themselves, Falangists or civil guards. The repression dehumanized the executioners, causing them to lose all sense of shame. They could commit an atrocity such as this and then talk about it as if it were of no great importance, even bragging about it. Of course, to dominate by terror one must prove oneself terrible. The climate of violence fomented from the highest military and civil authorities gave the gunmen an unlimited sense of impunity. They knew they would never have to answer for their actions before the law. They would not even have to answer before the court of public opinion. Who would dare tell them to their faces what one thought of them?

No women from Castilleja del Campo were shot, but knowing that Falangists and civil guards from the area had shot women was enough to strike terror in the female population. One woman in Castilleja was jailed and threatened with death to pressure her fugitive husband to turn himself in. Nine women in Castilleja were forced to ingest castor oil and march through the town with their heads shaved. The humiliation of two of these women was to pressure one of the fugitives to give himself up. And Felisa Pérez Vera, Leovigildo Monge's wife, was jailed, forcing her husband and sons to return to the town.

Leovigildo Monge and his sons turn themselves in

During the first half of September several events took place, events that I present in the most probable chronological order. The first would be the incarceration of Leovigildo Monge's wife while he and his eldest sons were still in hiding, accompanied by thirteen year old Feliciano. The purpose of Felisa Pérez Vera's imprisonment was to leave Leovigildo and his sons without support, according to Feliciano. *When we were hiding in the country-side, well, my brother Alfonsito, who was then nine years old, used to bring us food at midday with a beast of burden we had at our house, the food for our evening meal. And my mother, the poor thing, well she did the laundry for us, she sent us clean clothes, and my brother returned with the dirty clothes on our draught animal.*

But then the bandits went and put my mother in the jail so she could do nothing. So she could not prepare meals or wash or anything. And they write a note and they give it to my brother Alfonsito to bring out to us there. And the note said to him, "Leovigildo, we have your wife locked up, which means that if you do not turn your-self in, she can no longer wash or prepare meals or do anything for any of you anymore." Then my father, the poor thing, says, "Look here, we have to put ourselves in God's hands. What else can we do?" Then we all came back. And when my father got there, they put him there in the jail and they released my mother. They threw her out.

According to Feliciano, his mother had been in the jail only a few days because his father and brothers turned themselves in as soon as they received the message. His father, Leovigildo, did not spend very long in jail either, probably because of the influence of Juana Mantero Marmor, in gratitude for Leovigildo's attempt to save her son, the Falangist Manuel Rodríguez Mantero. Feliciano's older brothers were saved because they left town. His brother Leovigildo was drafted into the army and his brother Antonio into a Falangist militia.

A humiliating parade

The second event in early September was the public humiliation of nine of the town's women. It almost certainly happened after Leovigildo Monge and his sons turned themselves in, because one of the women victimized was Leovigildo's wife, Felisa Pérez. Incarcerated women did not suffer this humiliation. And it is also almost certain that it occurred before the fugitive Manuel Tebas Escobar turned himself in because his wife, incarcerated to pressure him into giving himself up, did not suffer this humiliation.

The man who officiated at this spectacle was Corporal José Martínez Pascual of the Civil Guard barracks in Carrión de los Céspedes. Isidora Mistral lived on the Plaza Calvo Sotelo where the town hall was and she saw it. *A corporal in the Civil Guard came and they gave him the names of those whose heads were to be shaved. He was in the Carrión jurisdiction. Corporal Martínez. He was from Córdoba. What I know is that he came here for the information and they told him "So and so, and what's her face, those are the ones whose heads you must shave."* Dulcenombre Ramírez Mauricio said her next door neighbor, Rosario Luque Cuevas, had played a role: (Whispering.) *This one over here. This one who lives here whose well is next to my wall . . . there is a well that goes to the house of a woman who made a list to shave all the women of Castilleja, the ones who were on the Left. They shaved their heads and they marched them around the town. She is evil.* (In a loud voice.) *Evil.* (Whispering again.) *She is very evil.*

According to Marina Luque Reinoso, Falangists and civil guards went to the houses of the women on the list and took them to the town hall. First they were given bread soaked in castor oil. Then their heads were shaved. Finally, they were paraded through the whole town while a snare drum played to attract spectators. María Vergne Graciani, daughter of the doctor, Don Juan, said the barber who shaved these women's heads was Aniceto Luque Luque. He never mentioned this when I interviewed him. According to María, Aniceto suffered for what he had to do. His hands trembled as he carried out the task. He was only twenty years old then and he had known these women all his life. They were all older than he, some much older. For a long time later, when the doctor went to Aniceto's house, Aniceto would cut his hair, but he told the doctor that he did not give shaves anymore.

Isidora Mistral described the beginning of the parade: *They put them there and made them line up on the town hall porch and told them to raise their hand and sing the Falangist anthem "Cara al Sol." Then they took them on a walk through the whole town. Mothers and daughters and all who went, completely bald. It was a sad thing to see. It was a sad thing, of course, because the women had not done anything. Only that they were leftists.* Carmen Moreno Romero also saw it. Her family worked at the marchioness's house across from the town hall: *They walked them around the whole town with a corporal from the Civil Guard. Also with a snare drum playing, and people came out to see. And the poor things suffered quite a bit of embarrassment.* According to Narciso Luque Romero, the embarrassment of these women was *a big joke to them* [the spectators], and he hummed for me the rhythm of the snare drum, which he still remembered. Manuel Ramírez Mauricio described the spectators, *taking delight in it,* and added a repugnant detail. *They gave them a purgative and, of course, many of them, walking and walking around the whole town, emptied themselves. The fear, the maliciousness, and on top of that, what they had in their bodies.*

Guillermo Reinoso Muñoz, an eight year old boy, was in his doorway with his father, Urbano Reinoso Luque. One of the women in the parade was his mother, Elvira Muñoz Rufino. She was so transformed that Guillermo did not recognize her and told his father, *"Mama is not there, mama is not there, mama is not there."* His father told him, *"Yes she is."* When Elvira Muñoz got home after the parade, she asked her son, *"Guillermo, do you not recognize me?"* Guillermo has told me this story many times, never without tears coming to his eyes as he recalls the shock of hearing his mother's voice come from that woman without hair and with her face contorted with anguish.

Others in town, leftists but also right-wingers, knew what was happening but did not want to see it. One was Manuel García Ramírez: *I did not see it because I did not look out the window to see that. I did not want to see those things.* Carmen Monge Romero did not see it either. *I did not see them because it would pain me to look out and see those women, already of advanced age, with their heads shorn.* Nor did Marina Luque Reinoso, from a right-wing family. She and her sister Herminia were at the schoolmistress's house, where they went for their lessons because there were still women incarcerated in the school: *And then my mother came and the teacher says, "What is happening María? What is going on? Your face is all exaggerated." My mother says, "I have come for my daughters because something is happening right now in Castilleja and I do not want my daughters to see it and I am taking them home." And then the schoolmistress says, "But María, tell me what is going on." My mother says, "They are shaving the women's heads in the town hall. They are shaving their heads. And I do not want my daughters to look out and see that spectacle."*

Marina remembered a conversation with Isabela González Garrido "La Belenda" after this humiliation: *They shaved the head of the poor thing that lived next door named Isabela, more precious than bread, and her husband an excellent man. Nothing happened to that man because my father had hidden him in the bread oven we had in my house. And she, well, she came to my house crying, "Ay, Marina, look at what they have done to me." I say to her, "Isabela, do not cry about that. You will soon see how beautiful you are when your hair grows back."* Carmen Monge Romero remembers the long-term effect this humiliation had on one couple: *One of them lived next door to me and they shaved her head. And I ran errands for the poor thing because it pained me how she cried so much. And that woman became very nervous. And that man, her husband, as long as the Movement lasted, never ate dinner at home. All he used to do was take his dinner plate and go up the alley to hide because he was always frightened. And he and that poor thing moved away from here. After a little while they left here for Seville. Because they could not live tranquilly here, because she was always afraid.*

In some cases, this outrage was inflicted on women in mourning. Rosario Escobar Moreno "La Crespa" was Manuel Escobar Moreno's sister. He had been shot a week or two before, on August 27. Carmen Nieves Perea "La Pomporita" was the sister of Cándido Nieves Perea, shot about a month before, on August 10. Francisca Luque Rodríguez "La Pelusa" and Elvira Muñoz Rufino were sisters-in-law of Alfredo Reinoso Monge, also shot on August 10. For a list of the women who suffered this humiliation, see Appendix A.

According to one of Felisa Pérez Vera's sons, Antonio Monge Pérez, the motive for this punishment was purely political: *My mother was from a very religious family. Her family was right-wing and everything, but we were leftists. We went out when the Republic was declared saying, "La República!" And for the women who went out in the celebration saying "La República! Viva la República!" that was enough for them to take them and shave their heads and walk them through the town.* According to Isidora Mistral and her husband, Leopoldo Rubio, the principal motive was personal vengeance. The selection of most of the victims probably depended on a combination of both motives. They were all leftists, of course, but there were many leftist women in the town who were not humiliated that day. The selection was undoubtedly influenced by personal hatreds, the quarrels between women in a small town. But for two of the women who suffered this humiliation, there was a very specific motive.

The second group's final journey

Manuel Tebas Escobar turns himself in

The oldest woman publicly humiliated was Rosario Escobar Rufino, sixty-four years of age. She was Manuel Tebas Escobar's mother. His sister Esmoralda was also in the parade. These women were punished to convince Manuel that to remain in hiding was a danger to his family members. The authorities had also arrested his wife, Suceso Rodríguez Luque, probably about the middle of August. When the Civil Guard came for her, Suceso was at the house of Concepción García Baquero, wife of the schoolteacher Joaquín León Trejo, who was under arrest in Seville.

Sara Tebas Rodríguez tells the story: [My father] *spent quite a while out there in the countryside. My mother was one month in jail, which is why they did not shave her head. Because she was in the jail. On top of that, she had me in her arms, when she was at the teacher's house, when she used to go there to work, and she had me in her arms. And a corporal from the Civil Guard arrived and told her, "Well, come with me!" And she let me go there on the floor of that lady's house, and a month went by until she came out. She was there in the jail. My grandmother and my aunt took care of me.*

My mother spent a month in jail and then he turned himself in and they threw her out. And he turned himself in because of that, because my mother sent him a message saying, "Look, they have told me that if you do not turn yourself in they are going to kill me." Of course, she should not have said that. Maybe they would not have killed her, or maybe they would, because it did not matter to them to kill women, whether they had children or not. But, of course, he must have thought, "My children are going to be better off with her than with me. What would I do with three children?" And then he turned himself in and they killed him. He was only a short while in jail. A few days before the night when they came with those trucks to take the prisoners away.

They killed my father without his having harmed anyone. My grandmother, the poor thing, they shaved her head, when she was the best there was in the world. My aunt Esmoralda, the same thing, a very complete woman. Only for being my father's mother or for being on the Left. My aunt the same. They were complete women like I say. Good women, homebodies, hardworking. And so. If Sara was right that her father was in the jail only a few days before he was shot, it means he turned himself in at about the same time Lucrecio Paz Delgado "El Cuartano" was captured.

"El Cuartano": the agony of an anarchist

The other man from Castilleja who held out longest in the countryside was

Castilleja del Campo in June 2007.

Repudio Inn, Espartinas, site of the assassinations on August 27, 1936. Seville–Huelva General Highway.

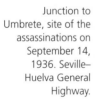

Junction to Umbrete, site of the assassinations on September 14, 1936. Seville–Huelva General Highway.

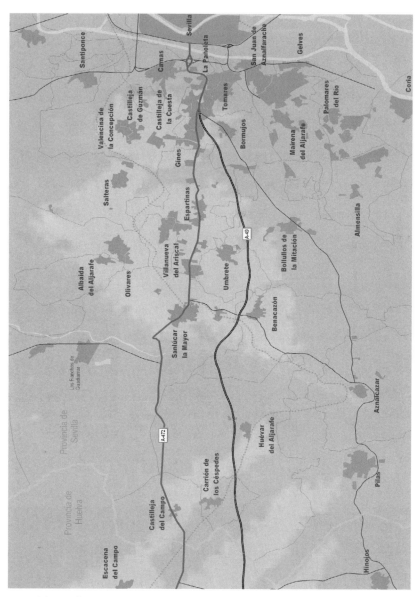

Map of the Seville–Huelva General Highway (now National Highway A-472).

Wall of the Castilblanco de los Arroyos Cemetery where Joaquín León Trejo was shot on August 22, 1936.

Antonio Cruz Cruz.

Joaquín León Trejo in the patio of his house, Castilleja del Campo, 1935.

José Fernández Luque.

Lutgardo García Ramírez.

Oil Portrait of José Pérez Rodríguez.

José Luis López Moreno.

Alfredo Reinoso Monge.

Braulio Ramírez García.

Manuel Monge Romero.

Newpaper clipping with photograph of José Ramírez Rufino.

José María Ramírez Mauricio.

Manuel Tebas Escobar.

Manuel Escobar Moreno.

Manuel Rodríguez Mantero.

Antonio García Ramírez.

Antonio García Ramírez (in the center) sent this photograph to his family from the Russian front.

Juan Antonio Luque Romero.

Pedro Donaire Leal.

Pedro Donaire Leal (a postwar picture).

José Luis López Moreno, Eugenio Pozo de la Cueva, and Manuel García Ramírez in María Luisa Park (Seville), during the Republic.

José, Carmen, and Antonio León García, one year before the assassination of their father, Joaquín León Trejo.

Concepción García Baquero.

Suceso Rodríguez Luque.

Carmen Muñoz Caraballo.

Elías, Rosario, and Sara Tebas Rodríguez, children of Manuel Tebas Escobar.

Otilia Escobar Muñoz, with black market baskets.

School photograph from the 1940s with orphans of men who were assassinated:

Sara Tebas Rodríguez (top row, to the left),
Dalia Monge Luque (next row),
Otilia Escobar Muñoz (next row, toward the right)

Manuel García Ramírez with photograph of his brothers Lutgardo and Antonio.

Leftists from Castilleja on the Málaga front with the Falangist militia: Standing, Celedonio Escobar Reinoso, Modesto Escobar Moreno, Antonio García Ramírez, Antonio Monge Pérez.

Evaristo García Ramírez, Antonio León García, and Narciso Luque Romero, family members of victims of the repression during the Second Sessions on Historical Memory of Castilleja del Campo, in 2005.

Alejandro León Saenz, son of Colonel Francisco León Trejo, and José León García, son of the schoolteacher Joaquín León Trejo. These two cousins were reunited thanks to the author's research.

Feliciano Monge Pérez, next to the monument to the victims of the 1936 repression, erected in 2005.

Letter from José María Ramírez Mauricio to his grandmother before the 1936 elections. Translation, on page 23–24.

Letter from Irene Ramírez Rodríguez to her father, José Ramírez Rufino, in the Sanlúcar la Mayor prison

My dear father you do not know how sorry we were when they took all of you away but then we were glad that you were in Sanlucar papa pepa has written to me and says that you are well and at peace there papa write me four words if you want me to send money or clean clothes there and I am going to send a bundle with Manolito write regarding what I said about the clothes and money for me or curro and me to go there Regards from all and receive a hug and a kiss from your daughter Irene Ramirez

Letter written from the Sanlúcar la Mayor prison by the Republican mayor José Ramírez Rufino

Dear children I have received the clothes from Braulio and I know you are all well telling you that we are all displeased they are the circumstances of life. There is no reason to be concerned because soon within a few days we will all be together do not send me anything like I said in the last letter. And with nothing more for today Regards to all and kisses for the children Your Father who loves you Jose Ramirez

Document from the Civil Guard in 1939, with the causes for the application of the war decree. Translation on page 245.

the anarchist Lucrecio Paz Delgado "El Cuartano." Like all the fugitives, he depended on the generosity, courage, and honesty of those who brought him food. His undoing was having trusted the wrong person. According to Feliciano Monge Pérez, *there was a man in Carrión named José María Mendoza, a goat herder, and he was told by corporal Martínez, he says, "You. Gain his trust out there. Take him food and so on, and the day we go out there, we make an arrangement and at the time more or less that you take him his food . . ." And that is how that bandit turned him in.*

Lucrecio Paz Delgado was captured and tortured by three Falangists from Castilleja, according to Antonio Monge Pérez. Celedonio Escobar Reinoso said there were only two who took part. During the first interviews, no one would name them. Sixteen years later, Feliciano Monge Pérez said they were Francisco Luque Cuevas "The Ill Wind" and Antonio Rodríguez Mantero "Antoñín," whose brother Manuel had been shot during the confrontation with Communists. Narciso Luque Romero named the same Falangists and added Casildo Escobar Reinoso, who was with Manuel Rodríguez Mantero the day he was shot. What can be said is that "El Cuartano" was captured and tortured by the Falangists Francisco Luque Cuevas and Antonio Rodríguez Mantero, and that another Falangist from Castilleja may have been involved. In 2008, after reading the Spanish edition of this book, Feliciano told me that it was not Casildo. I heard three versions of the capture and torture of "El Cuartano" during the first interviews. They contradict each other regarding where he was captured, where he was tortured, where he was taken, and how long he suffered from his wounds before being shot. But they all agree about the brutal nature of the torture.

According to Antonio Monge Pérez, *three from here brought him in on the back of a horse. And on the road there, somewhere between the Chichina estate and here, they cut off his parts. And his nephew who is still alive told me. His name is Elio, and he went to see him in Carrión, because he was in the jail there. That is where they took him. They came through here, carrying him behind on a horse. And then . . . his name is Elio, Elio Paz* [Nieves]. *He went to the Carrión jail with his mother. He says, "Look, nephew, they have cut off my parts."* In Celedonio Escobar Reinoso's account, *he was at an estate there called El Campanario. They caught him and brought him in and they cut off his parts there in Carrión*. And in Manuel Ramírez Mauricio's version, *one from here who was in a drainage ditch when they got him, well, when they caught him, they cut off his balls. And on the back of a horse they brought him here to town, to the jail. And from there they took him out and killed him*. I believe this last testimony confuses his capture with the incident in which "El Cuartano" hid in a drainage ditch to protect himself from the fire set by local Falangists who were looking for him. According to Celedonio Escobar, "El Cuartano" was a day or two bleeding from his wound when they shot him. Antonio Monge said, *They had him there for three days with his parts cut off. And after the third day, they took him out and shot him.*

Lucrecio Paz Delgado was shot the same night Manuel Tebas Escobar was taken from the Castilleja town hall, September 14, 1936, and they died together on the "side road off the Umbrete highway."[9] Lucrecio was either incarcerated in the Castilleja town hall with Manuel that night or he was in the Carrión de los Céspedes jail, in which case the truck that took them to the Umbrete highway had picked Lucrecio up in Carrión before passing through Castilleja. Two others from the town also died that night.

José Fernández Luque

José Fernández Luque had two nicknames: "El Perlo" (The Pearl) and "Pepe el de Simplicia" (Pepe, son of Simplicia). He does not seem to have stood out much during the Republic. He is mentioned in only one document in the municipal archive. On May 15, 1936, the mayor and councilmen approved paying him and another man, Francisco Rufino Pérez, ten pesetas to investigate the estates of the countess and the marchioness for the purpose of applying to them the Law of Obligatory Cultivation.[10] He was a tall, good-natured man, but timid, according to Narciso Luque Romero. *Here there was a poor man they used to call "El Perlo." Poor thing. He was a big man, but that does not mean anything. He was a kindhearted sort like . . . but he lacked spirit, the poor thing, he did not have the courage to endure that. Because each person is the way he is, of course. And he never thought they were going to kill him. He did not go into hiding.*

His confidence they would not kill him may have been due in part to his not having stood out as much as the town's other leftists. He may also have put too much trust in his Falangist cousins, the Luque Cuevas brothers: Francisco "The Ill Wind [*El Solano*]," Antonio "The Chatterbox," Manuel "The Little Ill Wind," and José. But these brothers did not care what happened to their cousin. According to Sara Tebas Rodríguez, *they told Pepe de Simplicia's mother . . . Simplicia [Luque Ramírez] was El Solano's aunt . . . and Simplicia went to her nephew El Solano. And she said to El Solano, "Child, your cousin for God's sake, do not let anything happen to your cousin, child." He said, "Go to bed and rest easy, aunt, nothing is going to happen to my cousin. Rest easy." When she got up the next morning, they had already taken her son away.*

Feliciano Monge Pérez's testimony is a variation on Sara's story. In his version it was not El Perlo's mother who begged El Solano to save her son, but El Solano's own father who begged for the life of his nephew. *You see, El Solano was the son of "Lutgardo, son of Jacoba," who was father to El Solano and that whole herd of cattle. But it turns out they arrested a nephew of his whom they used to call "Pepe el de Simplicia," and Simplicia was the sister of "Lutgardo, son of Jacoba," father to all those criminals. And they locked the nephew up in jail to kill him. One of the best men there was in Castilleja, so kind, a man who never harmed anyone, a marvel of a man, that one.*

And "Lutgardo, son of Jacoba" finds out, while he was sick in bed, and he finds out because someone must have told him, "Look, your nephew, they have locked him up." And he went and called his son Francisco, that murderous criminal, and he said to him, "Francisco, they have told me that the nephew is locked up. Can you avoid something happening to him?" And he told him, "Papa, do not worry because nothing is going to happen to him." Well. That same night he went and killed him. That same night he went and killed him. And when the father found out about that . . . see if he was evil, see if he was evil . . . it cost his father's life as well. Because he died right after it happened.

In light of the testimonies to the inoffensive, good-natured, and timid character of "El Perlo," together with his lack of political activity, the motive for killing him expressed in the 1939 document called "Relation of individuals of Castilleja del Campo to whom were applied the War Decree . . ." is rather astonishing. The motive that appears next to José Fernández Luque's name is "Dangerous extremist, and propagandist."[11]

José Pérez Rodríguez

Nicknamed "Sangalato," José Pérez was the exact opposite of his namesake José Fernández Luque, starting with his size. According to Narcisco Luque Romero, *He was a small man. But wiry too. All gristle.* He was also a man of action who distinguished himself when the Río Tinto miners invaded the town. That day he had interceded to prevent the miners on the town hall porch from shooting at the marchioness's house across the square. In the 1939 document "Relation of individuals of Castilleja del Campo to whom were applied the War Decree . . . ," the motive next to his name is "Coadjutor of the disarming of the population by R[*ío*]. T[*into*]. miners."[12]

He was married to "Carmelita," sister of the Monge Pérez brothers, Leovigildo and Antonio, who were on the list of those to be killed along with their father Leovigildo, all saved by the intervention of Juana Mantero Marmor, mother of the young Falangist Manuel Rodríguez Mantero. According to Feliciano Monge Pérez, she had told the authorities, *"Leovigildo and his two sons erase them and take them off of the list and leave the brother-in-law," and they killed my brother-in-law there in the town.* José Pérez Rodríguez was the only man from Castilleja assassinated in his home town. It was by his own choice.

While he was incarcerated, José Pérez devised a plan to confront the authorities and townspeople of Castilleja with the reality of the repression. According to Antonio Monge Pérez, *On one occasion they were going to take away in a truck from the jail here a brother-in-law of mine who was married to my sister. Well, when he was there in the jail locked up with the others, he told my sister, "Rest easy, they are not going to kill me outside of Castilleja. When I see them taking us out to kill us," since he knew, "they are going to have to kill me here. I am not going anywhere. No."* His plan worked to perfection.

The night of September 14, 1936
The assassination of José Pérez Rodríguez

It was getting dark when the truck arrived to take Manuel Tebas Escobar, José Fernández Luque, and José Pérez Rodríguez away. Lucrecio Paz Delgado may have also been taken from the town hall that night or he was already in the truck, having been picked up at the Carrión jail before it arrived in Castilleja. Celedonio Escobar Reinoso thought there were three men in this second group of victims, but he did not seem to be entirely certain: *The first bunch had already been killed. Then they killed them in batches. They killed three. Three? Yes. I think it was three who were taken. Yes. In the last bunch there were three.*

Celedonio immediately went on to describe the trick José Pérez used to distract the Falangists who were guarding them: *One was the father of a guy here named* [Juan] *Pérez* [Luque]. *They took him out and the man went and said, when they were taking him to the truck, he said, "Hey, I forgot my frock." And he turned back to get his frock and when he was turning to go back for his frock he took off running up that street.* Narciso Luque Romero also spoke of this subterfuge. Then Celedonio and Narciso described the outcome of the attempted escape. Their descriptions coincide almost completely with that of Antonio Monge Pérez.

Although Antonio omitted the trick of turning as if to go back for an article of clothing, he included so many details in his narrative that it provides a visual image of the scene: *He was a very wiry person, and then when they went to take them from the town hall, and there was a line of Falangists on one side and another line on the other and the truck at the edge of the porch. Well, from there they passed them to the truck. And then he, as he was leaving, gave one of them a shove and pushed him on his back and took off running up the street and they opened fire on him. And they did not hit him until he got to the facades of Aniceto's house and the carpenter's house . . . they were all full of bullet holes, like that . . . and then at the edge of Castilleja as you go to Carrión, in that little turn in the street there they caught him and, with his rifle butt, one of the Falangists from Carrión* [Antonio Cuevas] *smashed his head.* Knowing the town hall porch, the town's streets, and knowing where Aniceto Luque Luque and the carpenter lived at the time of the interview and the shortest route from these houses to the edge of town, it is possible to trace the course of José Pérez's flight.

The town hall porch is high and wide but it does not project out very far from the door of the town hall to the street, so only a few Falangists could form the gauntlet through which the prisoners had to pass. As he walked this gauntlet, José Pérez made a half turn to the right and threw himself at one of the Falangists, knocking him on his back. Then he leaped through this hole in the line of Falangists, ran at top speed to a stairway that descends from the side of the porch to the corner of the Plaza Calvo Sotelo, now Plaza Antonio Machado, and General Sanjurjo Street, now Miguel Hernández Street. Turning right, he ran up the latter street, a fairly long climb, to where this street ends at a right angle to Pedro Parias Street, now Virgen del Buen Suceso Street. It was there that José Pérez took a bullet in one of his legs. He then turned right toward the church and, limping, crossed the Church Plaza, now Plaza Óscar Romero, and turned left up General Mola Street, now Vicente Aleixandre Street, which comes out onto Count of the Atalayas Street, now Consitution Street, the road that connects Castilleja with Carrión de los Céspedes. That is where, according to Antonio Monge Pérez, he fell and was caught by Antonio Cuevas, the Falangist who crushed his head with a rifle butt.

The version of the end of José Pérez's flight provided by Narciso Luque Romero was a little different. He said that when José Pércz got to the edge of town, the same site indicated by Antonio Monge, he hid in a ditch and it took the Falangists a while to find him. Narciso emphasized how small José Pérez was and the fact that, by the time they were looking for him, it was already dark. Marina Luque Reinoso noted that at that time there were bramble bushes where José Pérez had hidden. Manuel Ramírez Mauricio told me that the Falangist from Carrión who found José Pérez and finished him off with a blow from his rifle butt was the victim's first cousin, but Manuel was mistaken. The victim and his executioner, Antonio Cuevas, shared the same nickname, "Sangalato," but not because they were related by blood. José Pérez Rodríguez got his nickname from his godfather, who was also the father of the Falangist from Carrión who killed him.The actions that night of the Falangist "Sangalato" from Carrión immediately earned him the opprobrium not only of leftists but of right-wingers as well. According to Marina Luque Reinoso, *Sangalato, who is still alive in Carrión, cannot go into any casino because everybody avoids him. As soon as he shows up, the people leave and he is left there alone. That was during the war, right then in the war, and during all of Franco's life.*

The gunfire in Castilleja's streets when José Pérez attempted to escape was a wake-up call to the town's conscience, giving more influence to right-wingers who opposed the repression. And there were many: Marina Luque Reinoso's father, José Luque López; Conrado Rufino Romero's father, Francisco Rufino Pérez; the town's doctor, Don Juan Luis Vergne Herrero; the mayor who resigned so as not to have to sign death sentences, Antonio Rodríguez Fernández "Antoñito el de Aurora." And doubtless several others. Perhaps they gained more influence after September 14, because it is one thing to watch trucks take men from the town and learn later that they had been shot, and it is quite another thing to hear gunshots by night in the streets of a small town and wake up the following day to see bullet holes in the facades of houses, a trail of blood left by one of the town's residents, and the pool of blood in a ditch where someone had finished off the victim with blows from his rifle butt.

The Falangist Antonio Cuevas "Sangalato" had turned an abstract process that took place elsewhere into a concrete and present horror. This would explain why the Falangist "Sangalato" had instantly earned the opprobrium of everyone, those on the Left because they regarded him as a murderous criminal and those on the Right because he had exposed them, complicating their collaboration in the repression. Those who saw the military coup as carte blanche to eliminate political or personal enemies continued their activities but, after September 14, they had to act with greater dissimulation.

The assassinations of José Fernández Luque, Manuel Tebas Escobar, and Lucrecio Paz Delgado

José Fernández Luque and Manuel Tebas Escobar had to witness José Pérez Rodríguez's suicidal "escape attempt." Lucrecio Paz Delgado may have seen it as well but, if not, he heard the gunshots from inside the truck. Perhaps all three knew the result of this manhunt before the truck took them off to their deaths. For José Fernández Luque, this additional shock was too much. When Narciso Luque Romero described the timidity of this tall man, saying that *he was a kindhearted sort but he lacked spirit, the poor thing, he did not have the courage to endure that*, it was the prelude to his story of how José Fernández died:

That is what I was getting to. When they came to take him away to kill him, of course, they loaded them into the truck, and when the truck was taking them away, since he knew where he was going, he had a heart attack or something, I do not know, and they did not have to kill him. He had already died. Like all of them, he was a very good man. All of them were like that.

Unlike the first group of prisoners taken away in early August, these men knew what awaited them. They were not going to another jail where they could hope to be freed some time. They were going directly to the firing squad. In this case, they were shot against the cemetery wall in Umbrete. At least Manuel Tebas Escobar was shot there. José Fernández Luque was already dead and Lucrecio Paz Delgado only needed the coup de grâce after having spent several days bleeding from the wounds of his mutilation.

Some observations

With the four victims of September 14, the number of men taken from Castilleja to be killed had grown to thirteen. The other nine were Antonio Cruz Cruz, killed the end of July, Alfredo Reinoso Monge and Cándido Nieves Perea, killed August 10, and the six men killed August 27: Manuel Escobar Moreno, Lutgardo García Ramírez, Enrique Monge Escobar, Manuel Monge Romero, José María Ramírez Mauricio, and Mayor José Ramírez Rufino. There are four other men who were shot, three of them natives of Castilleja, José Luis López Moreno, Braulio Ramírez García, and Manuel Ramírez Rufino, and one from Seville but residing in Castilleja, the schoolteacher Joaquín León Trejo. These four men were not in the town when the war began.

Although there is clear evidence of the influence of the Castilleja authorities in two of the killings yet to be described, no one else was taken from the town to be shot. Celedonio Escobar Reinoso spoke of the situation in Castilleja after September 14: *Afterwards fourteen or fifteen were incarcerated to kill them but by then hard bargaining began among the town's families. The one who had a brother or cousin and says, "What the hell! Why kill him?" Then there were influences to not kill them. Then the others began to take charge and they were all set free.* José Pérez Rodríguez's decision to die in Castilleja's streets had no doubt saved the lives of some of these fourteen or fifteen prisoners.

Notes

1 Minutes, 5 September 1936, Castilleja del Campo Municipal Archive.
2 Minutes, 12 September 1936, Castilleja del Campo Municipal Archive.
3 Various documents 1920–1940, Castilleja del Campo Municipal Archive.
4 José Manuel Martínez Bande, *La campaña de Andalucía*, 137.
5 Francisco Espinosa Maestre, *La Guerra Civil en Huelva*, 194.
6 Ibid., 265.

7 Ibid., 436.

8 Information provided by the historian José María García Márquez in June, 2007.

9 Civil Death Registry, Office of the Justice of the Peace, Castilleja del Campo.

10 Minutes, 15 May 1936, Castilleja del Campo Municipal Archive.

11 Dossier 24, Office of the Justice of the Peace, Castilleja del Campo.

12 Ibid.

Seven

Other Castilleja del Campo Victims of the Repression

Men who were not in town during the repression

Between the second half of August and December 28, 1936, four other men, natives or residents of Castilleja del Campo, were shot. Another was arrested and tortured, but survived. Two others were tried before military tribunals and given long prison sentences. Another made a daring escape to the Republican zone after learning that his name was on the list of those to be shot in the town where he was living. He had to leave his wife and two small children behind and would not see them again for many years.

Francisco Monge Romero

Francisco Monge Romero was born in Castilleja on June 5, 1909. His brother Manuel was shot on August 27, 1936, and his brother-in-law, Antonio Cruz Cruz "Adelino," was shot in late July. Soon after the war began, Francisco was arrested in Espartinas, where he was working as a chauffer. On September 30, 1937, he was condemned before a war tribunal for the crime of inciting military rebellion and sentenced to eight years and one day of imprisonment. He served his sentence in Seville, first at the Ranilla Prison, from which he was transferred on April 1, 1938, to the Provincial Prison. Then, on a date which is illegible in the document in his file, his sentence was commuted to six years and one day. On September 29, 1940, he was granted "conditional freedom," a form of probation. His sentence was liquidated on September 16, 1944.[1] I have no further information about his life before or after his imprisonment.

Pedro Donaire Leal

I have a great deal of information about this man, who was born in Castilleja del Campo in 1905. Two of those I interviewed in the winter of 1989/90, Aniceto Luque Luque and Manuel Ramírez Mauricio, mentioned him. In 2005 I met his children Matilde and Eugenio at a conference on Historical Memory. Matilde read a testimony to their uncle, Eugenio Pozo de la Cueva, and Eugenio read a testimony to their father, Pedro Donaire Leal. They told me their father had written a memoir but that he had not wanted people outside the family to read it because it contained personal information. Matilde had written the draft of a book on her parents' lives based on her father's memoir. The following account of Pedro Donaire during the repression is a summary of part of Matilde's manuscript.

Pedro Donaire Leal was married to Rosario Pozo de la Cueva, also from Castilleja del Campo. When the war began, they were working as school-teachers in Villanueva del Río, to the northeast of Seville. On August 9, 1936, Pedro and Rosario were celebrating their fifth wedding anniversary. Some of the town's Falangists interrupted the celebration to warn Pedro that his name was on the list of those to be shot and that he should flee immediately. Pedro spent three nights hiding in the mountains near Villanueva, worried about the fate of his wife and two children, whom he had left behind in the town. Meanwhile, Rosario went to Seville and met with Governor Pedro Parias. Seeing that she could expect no help from this "friend" of the family, she sent a message to her fugitive husband urging him to save himself by escaping to the Republican zone.

Pedro Donaire Leal walked for five days, suffering hunger and exhaustion, helped at times by peasants, and with the constant fear of the Falangists and civil guards who patrolled the area. On August 17, he encountered a military column carrying the Republican flag and told the commander he wanted to fight for the Republic. Having served during the monarchy in the infantry, where he had attained the rank of second lieutenant, Pedro Donaire was given command of a company in a new battalion being organized on the Córdoba front. In September he was promoted to captain and in late October he was assigned to Madrid. In November he participated in the defense of the Spanish capital. During this entire time, he had no news of his wife and children, nor they of him.[2]

Eugenio Pozo de la Cueva

Eugenio Pozo de la Cueva was born in Castilleja del Campo in 1910. He was Pedro Donaire Leal's brother-in-law. When the war began, he had been in Seville nine years, and was employed by the Public Works Department. He lived in a boarding house with two friends from Castilleja, Braulio and Bernardino Ramírez García, who were medical students. On the night of July 27, a Falangist patrol came to the boarding house and asked for Eugenio. Threatening him with pistols, they took him by car to the Falangist headquarters.

The next day he was taken to a meeting with the civil governor Pedro Parias. After this interview, Eugenio learned why Pedro Parias had been interested in his case. Back in the Falangist headquarters, he was subjected to repeated beatings to get him to reveal the whereabouts of Castilleja's schoolteacher, Joaquín León Trejo. Pedro Parias's interest in Castilleja's schoolteacher suggests that someone from Castilleja had informed the governor and former administrator of the countess that Joaquín had gone to Seville to resist the coup. Eugenio Pozo's ordeal lasted two days, July 28 and 29. His torturers may have realized that Eugenio did not know where the schoolteacher was hiding, which was the case, or during that time Joaquín León Trejo may have been arrested. In any event, after two days of torture at the Falangist headquarters, Eugenio was taken to the Jáuregui Cinema, one of Seville's many improvised detention centers, and from there to the Terceros Barracks.

Eugenio spent several months at these barracks, still suffering the effects of the beatings at the Falangist headquarters: swelling of his head, face, and hands, and hematomas over his entire body. As in all detention centers at the time, prisoners were not fed. They depended on the food their families could bring them. His suffering was psychological as well as physical. Every day after midnight, he saw companions taken away to be shot. One of these was José León Trejo, brother of Castilleja's schoolteacher Joaquín. José was shot on October 17.

During his imprisonment at the Terceros Barracks, Eugenio Pozo was obliged to sign a document redacted by the Chief Engineer of Public Works on orders from Governor Pedro Parias. The document stated that he was on a list of individuals who "belonged to the leadership of organizations opposed to the National Army, or have had close relations with the same," and "are immediately relieved of their posts, employment, or jobs they held in this Organization." Several months later, Eugenio was transferred to the cellars of the Plaza de España where he found Braulio and Bernardino Ramírez García, the two medical students from Castilleja del Campo who had been living in the same boarding house as he. From there, Eugenio was taken to the Ranilla Prison. He was released in January 1937 for lack of any accusation or charge against him and because he had not been tried before any tribunal. This information is based on the testimony of Eugenio's niece Matilde.[3]

Joaquín León Trejo

Castilleja's schoolteacher, Joaquín León Trejo, had gone to Seville during the week before the military coup after consulting by telephone with an older brother, Lieutenant Colonel Francisco León Trejo, then military commander of the Cuatro Vientos airdrome near Madrid. In the following days, Joaquín participated in the defense of the working-class neighborhood near the Plaza de San Marco. Afterwards, he went into hiding at the house of some friends, an older couple who had a toyshop on Puente y Pellón Street.

The friends with whom Joaquín had taken refuge warned him not to walk about much because there were pairs of armed Falangist youths patrolling the streets in search of people to arrest. Succumbing to his curiosity about what was happening in the city, Joaquín took a walk to a cafe named Saint Peter's Keys, on the corner of Regina Street near Saint Peter's Church. He was seated at a table near a window that looked out on the street, drinking a cup of coffee, when two Falangist youths got off a streetcar across from the cafe. By chance, one of them had been a student of his and recognized him. He told his companion, *"Hey, we have to arrest that gentleman. He is very Republican. That is Joaquín León Trejo."* They took him to the Jáuregui Cinema.

About the same time, José María Varela Rendueles, the last Republican governor of Seville, spent three days at this improvised detention center. He survived and left a description of it in his memoir, published after Franco's death. The theater's seats had been removed to make room for detainees. The heat and lack of ventilation were oppressive. So was the stench of sweat and urine. From dawn until dusk, prisoners stood in line for two toilets while guards took charge of the distribution of baskets of food brought by family members. The incessant din of the guards calling out hundreds of names drowned out conversation and thought. At night, there was complete silence. The prisoners lay packed on the cement floor. In the middle of that floor stood life size cutouts of Stan Laurel and Oliver Hardy, leftovers from when the theater was a place for laughter. Guards had put them there as a cruel joke. Between one and three in the morning, trucks would arrive to take another fifteen or twenty men to be shot. One of the Falangist gunmen read the names of the doomed with excruciating and sadistic slowness, while the specters of Laurel and Hardy looked on.[4]

This was the same improvised detention center where Eugenio Pozo de la Cueva had spent a few days. Joaquín León Trejo does not seem to have been at the Jáuregui Cinema at the same time. Matilde Donaire Pozo's testimony says nothing about their seeing each other there. Her uncle Eugenio would certainly have mentioned it to her, since his torture was motivated by the search for Joaquín's hiding place. After a few days at the Jáuregui Cinema, Joaquín was taken to the Carmen Barracks on Baños Street.

When Joaquín was arrested, his wife and his sons José and Antonio went to Seville, where they stayed at the house of their uncle José León Trejo, who was also under arrest. Uncle José was being held in the Terceros Barracks at the same time as Eugenio Pozo de la Cueva. José León García, Joaquín's son, and his cousin Joaquín León Fernández, one of José León Trejo's nine children, took turns carrying the basket with food and clean clothes to the two brothers under arrest. The daily ritual of taking a basket to the prisoners was a way for their families to know they were still alive. When the sentinels did not accept the basket it meant the prisoner had been shot. It was Joaquín León Trejo's nephew, Joaquín León Fernández, who delivered the basket to his uncle in the Carmen Barracks on August 23, the day the sentinels announced that Castilleja's schoolteacher was no longer there. Joaquín León Fernández was also the one who delivered the basket to the Terceros Barracks on October 18, the day after his own father, José León Trejo, was shot. This information is based on the testimonies of Joaquín León Trejo's sons, José and Antonio León García.

Manuel Ramírez Rufino

A builder by trade, Manuel was the brother of Castilleja's Republican mayor, José Ramírez Rufino. When the war began, Manuel was 58 years old and living in Aznalcóllar, where he had recently married a woman from there. He was shot during the repression that followed this mining town's occupation on August 17, 1936. I have heard the rumor that he was shot by Francisco Luque Cuevas "The Ill Wind," one of the Falangists from Castilleja who participated in the occupation and sacking of Aznalcóllar.

José Luis López Moreno

When I recorded the first interviews, in 1989/90, only one person mentioned José Luis López Moreno, and only in passing. Marina Luque Reinoso was talking about the *town's sons* who were living in Seville and were shot, primarily the medical student Braulio Ramírez García, but she added, *and another lady from here who was named Orosia whose son they also killed and whose name was José Luis. They killed him too, and he too was a son of Castilleja*. In the year 2000, I found a document in the municipal archive with his full name and his profession. He was a mechanic.[5]

I visited Manuel García Ramírez, one of the oldest of those I interviewed, and also one of those with the sharpest memory. Inspired by my research, he had been drawing up his own list of the men from Castilleja killed in the repression. When I asked him about José Luis, Manuel was devastated, as if he had been disloyal to a companion, and said, *Ay, José Luis, how could I have forgotten him. He was a close friend of mine*. Manuel rummaged through a drawer full of old photographs until he found one from 1932 when he was doing his military service in Seville. Manuel, in uniform, is strolling in María Luisa Park with José Luis López Moreno and Eugenio Pozo de la Cueva. Manuel also remembered that José Luis was shot the same day José Antonio Primo de Rivera, founder of the Falange, had been shot in the Republican zone, November 20, 1936.

Curiously, among the files from the Seville Provincial Prison, there is one for Orosia López Moreno, José Luis's mother. On December 29, 1936, Orosia was turned over to the prison by "the forces of public order." On March 15, 1937, she was condemned to twenty-four months of governmental detention. She was released from prison on May 11, 1938. In her file, there is no explanation of the reason for her arrest. The most logical motive would be that, on finding out her son José Luis had been shot, she had gone to Seville and caused a commotion over the loss of the son she had raised, undoubtedly with great sacrifice, and who probably helped her get by with a portion of his salary as a mechanic. According to her file, Orosia was fifty-five years old in 1936, worked as a servant, was single and the mother of one child.[6] Apparently, in the opinion of the military authorities, this single mother of advanced age, and no doubt very poor, whose only child had just been shot, was regarded as such a grave threat to the new regime that she should be locked up for twenty-four months, a sentence eventually reduced to sixteen months.

Braulio and Bernardino Ramírez García

These were the two brothers from Castilleja who were studying medicine. I have more information about Braulio than about Bernardino. Braulio, three years older than his brother, had just completed his studies, receiving his medical degree in May 1936. Shortly after the military coup, the two brothers were arrested in the boarding house where they lived in Seville, the same boarding house where their friend Eugenio Pozo de la Cueva lived. When speaking of her uncle Eugenio, Matilde Donaire Pozo also mentioned Braulio. He was from a humble family and studied medicine with scholarships he earned through his intelligence and hard work. While still a student, he made house calls to patients to give them injections. Eugenio Pozo de la Cueva often accompanied him and told his niece that when the patient was poor, Braulio did not charge them.[7]

Three of those I interviewed spoke of the hatred Castilleja's priest Felipe Rodríguez Sánchez had toward the Ramírez García brothers. One was Isidora Mistral, a right-winger who, when speaking of Don Felipe, said, *And there were some students here, medical students, wonderful young men. And he had a deep-seated hatred for them.* She did not specify the reason for this hatred. An incident described by Feliciano Monge Pérez suggests that the anticlerical ideology of the Ramírez García brothers played an important role. *Braulio got his medical degree at that time when things were coming to a head, and his brother was named Bernardino, who also was studying to be a doctor but he could not make it. Events overtook him, and he never got beyond his internship.*

Alright, well, one day celebrating the Corpus out came, as the saying goes, the lord under his baldachin, Don Felipe, and Braulio, who was already a doctor, was in the doorway of my uncle Francisco's casino on the square. And when the lord under his baldachin passed by, Don Felipe said to Braulio, "Braulio, come on, take up one of the poles." And Braulio . . . Braulio was a Communist, and he said that he was not going to do it, he says, "I do not hold baldachin poles." He says, "Go on now, take the pole." "No, I will not hold the pole." And at that moment he says, "Well, one day you will remember." He was saying it for him. And that is what happened.

When the time came he went and had him arrested. Don Antonio Cortés, Don Luis Recasén, and another one of the important doctors there in Seville came to plead that he be pardoned. They were from the Macarena Hospital, the only one there was in Seville, and that is where that man Braulio studied, and they were on his side. And they came all the way to Castilleja so Don Felipe would pardon him and he said to them, he says, "If only He who is on high had come instead of all of you. There is no one who can save him now."

Manuel García Ramírez, these two men's cousin, also offered evidence implicating Castilleja's priest in Braulio's death. Manuel visited Braulio while he was under arrest and Braulio told him what the police said when they came to his boarding house. *My cousin Braulio had already completed his studies in May and they assigned him to a town . . . because he did not want to leave Castilleja nor did the doctor who was working here want him to go but he went to substitute for a friend of his who had gone on vacation. And with his suitcases packed, the war broke out. Well, Castilleja's priest denounced him in a letter. That is what the policeman told him, the same day he told my cousin . . . with the seal of the Castilleja parish, denouncing him as a Communist. And that was that. I went to see him in the cellars of the Plaza de España in Seville. That is where they had him. And he was killed on the Day of the Holy Innocents.*

The date of Braulio's death given by Manuel García Ramírez, the Day of the Holy Innocents, was confirmed in Matilde Donaire Pozo's testimony. Her uncle was incarcerated with Bernardino and Braulio in the cellar of the Plaza de España when Braulio was taken away to be shot: "On December 28, 1936, at about three in the afternoon, Eugenio, Braulio, and Bernardino were playing dominos when a truck arrived for one of the so frequent roundups of prisoners. Braulio was on the fateful list."[8] His brother Bernardino was imprisoned for a while longer. According to his prison file, he was condemned in January 1937 to twenty-four months of governmental detention and was transferred from the Plaza de España to the Seville Provincial Prison on January 15. In July 1937, he was transferred to a labor battalion in Alcalá de Guadaira. His sentence was completed on November 21, 1938.[9]

Braulio Ramírez García was the last native or resident of Castilleja del Campo shot in the repression, as far as I know. With his death, the number of mortal victims rises to seventeen. For a list of the men from Castilleja who were shot, with relevant data for each victim, and an analysis of that data, see Appendix B. For sources of information on the victims, see Appendix C.

Notes

1 Francisco Monge Romero's file from the Seville Provincial Prison, Archive of the Second Territorial Military Tribunal.
2 Matilde Donaire Pozo, "Largo camino hacia la paz" (unpublished work, photo-copy courtesy of the author).
3 Matilde Donaire Pozo, "Eugenio Pozo de la Cueva, mi tío" (testimony, Second Sessions on Historical Memory, Castilleja del Campo, 4 June 2005).
4 José María Varela Rendueles, *Mi rebelión en Sevilla*, 155–9.
5 Recruitment and Military Service Records, Castilleja del Campo Municipal Archive.
6 Orosia López Moreno's file from the Seville Provincial Prison, Archive of the Second Territorial Military Tribunal.
7 Matilde Donaire Pozo, "Eugenio Pozo de la Cueva, mi tío."
8 Ibid.
9 Bernardino Ramírez García's file from the Seville Provincial Prison, Archive of the Second Territorial Military Tribunal.

Part Three

War

Eight

Men of Castilleja del Campo Go to War

Mobilization

Eighty men from Castilleja del Campo were mobilized into the forces of the insurgent generals, either in a Falangist militia unit, the Spanish legion, or the army. For a list of the names of these men and the source of this information, see Appendix D. The principal burden fell on those who were between seventeen and twenty-six years of age in 1936. There were sixty-four men in that age range who went to war, 90 percent of the seventy-one men in that age range living in the town.[1] The ten men I interviewed in the winter of 1989/90 were all in that age range. For a list of these ten ex-combatants and comments on their data, see Appendix E.

"Volunteers" in the Falangist "centuria" and enlistment in the Spanish legion

Like their Italian counterparts, Spanish Fascists drew inspiration from the Roman Empire. The name *Falange* is Spanish for phalanx, the Roman infantry formation. Falangists organized their militias in units of one hundred men and named them "centurias" after the Roman military unit. In September and October 1936, there was pressure to volunteer in a centuria being organized in Carrión de los Céspedes and Castilleja del Campo, according to Aniceto Luque Luque. *Then the organizations, Falange and so on, began, "Alright, you have to sign up here." I am as right-wing as you please, but I am not signing up with any organization. I am not going anywhere as a volunteer. Now, when the army mobilizes me, I have no choice but to go.* Later Aniceto would be drafted into the army. *They were respecting me because I was the son of a widow. And later, well, it was all a lie. The time came and they mobilized me in the army like anyone else.*

Right-wingers like Aniceto Luque could resist the pressure to volunteer for the centuria. It was not so easy for leftists. José Escobar Moreno and Celedonio Escobar Reinoso, the brothers-in-law who hid at night in the countryside in August and September, were saved when they enlisted, the former in the legion and the latter in the centuria. The story of how these two men went to war is interwoven with that of two other fugitives, the brothers Leovigildo and Antonio Monge Pérez, who also escaped the repression by going to war. There are two versions, one provided by Leovigildo and Antonio's brother Feliciano and the other by Celedonio Escobar himself. They present typical examples of the way many leftists were saved from being shot and provide a glimpse of how different influences inside and outside the town interacted in their destinies.

Feliciano tells how Leovigildo Monge Pérez and José Escobar Moreno "El Regular" were saved by the influence the Falangist Casildo Escobar Reinoso, the countess's armed guard, had with Pedro Parias, formerly the countess's administrator. *They wanted to kill my brother Leovigildo any way they could. And then they got him and denounced him along with another from the town [Celedonio] who was Casildo's brother. And it had a lot to do with Don Pedro Parias, because Don Pedro Parias later was also the civil governor in Seville. And he [Pedro Parias] said to him, he says, "Look here, Casildo, your brother-in-law José [Escobar Moreno] and Leovigildo, you have to get them out of the town, because the denunciations are falling here like rain, and I cannot hold out any longer."*

And then the two of them went and reported in Seville in the legion, which was like their life jacket, and there was a captain there who was the one who took down their affiliation and so on. And, naturally, [José Escobar Moreno] "El Regular" was a very tall and strong man but my brother [Leovigildo] was an average man. And when they got there the captain who was there says to them, "Who has sent you here?" They tell him, "Well, the mayor of the town [José Cuevas Reinoso]." He says, "Well, this man stays here," for El Regular. Because he was a tall man for the legion. He says, "But this one has to go home." And when my brother got back and reported, well, they immediately took him away in the army, in shock troops, and he was on all the fronts in Spain, and on the worst ones, that is where they went.

Celedonio Escobar Reinoso's version is centered on how he and Antonio Monge Pérez enlisted in the centuria, but he also mentions the story of José Escobar Moreno and Leovigildo Monge Pérez. *My brother [Casildo] was the armed guard on the countess's estate here. And he went and saved me because the first civil governor in Seville after the Movement was Don Pedro Parias, and he was the administrator of that estate here. He had close ties to this town. He used to say he loved this town as if it were his mother. But then he did not respect it because of the influences, because there was a case here, when he [Castilleja's priest Don Felipe] saw he could not eliminate me, because I had already had a lot of run-ins with that priest during the Republic, and when he saw he could not get rid of me because of my brother's influence, he went and he said to him* [to Pedro Parias] . . . *well they had already killed ten or twelve . . . he says, "This one, we have to get rid of him because they have already gotten rid of others and there is no one who can get rid of him." Then the governor called my brother* [Casildo] *and he went and he* [Pedro Parias] *told him that one of Antonio's brothers, Leovigildo, the oldest, and a brother-in-law of mine* [José Escobar Moreno], *they put them in the legion to not kill them. But the priest's influence in Leovigildo's case . . . you understand that in those times the legion was where they put all the ones they were going to kill . . . because of the influence of that man* [Don Felipe], *it turned out that Leovigildo, Antonio's brother, did not go into the legion.*

As to me, well, my brother told him [Pedro Parias], *"Well look, he* [Celedonio] *is a kid who is not twenty years old yet." He says, "Alright, well, if he is not twenty, let him go into Falange because I cannot resist any longer. The influences to kill him are too great." And then my brother came back from Seville, and he said, "Look, go with the Falange. If not," he says, "I cannot help you, eh? If you do not go, I cannot do anything. The governor told me, 'I cannot help him because the charges against him are too much.'"* [Antonio] *Monge and others joined the Falange and . . . some twenty of us went from this town. We had to go into Franco's forces. They signed us up so as not to kill us.*

Celedonio's version contradicts that of Feliciano Monge Pérez as to why José Escobar Moreno "El Regular" joined the legion but not Leovigildo Monge Pérez. According to Celedonio, it was not because Leovigildo was too small for the legion, but because Don Felipe took an interest in helping Leovigildo avoid ending up in the legion where *in those times the legion was where they put all the ones they were going to kill*. It seems that Don Felipe interceded on behalf of Leovigildo because he was the son of the leftist who had tried to save Don Felipe's nephew, the young Falangist Manuel Rodríguez Mantero, killed by Communists in May 1936.

Feliciano and Celedonio's testimonies present a glimpse of the situation in Castilleja in the fall of 1936. One sector of the town had absolute power over the destinies of young leftists, whether they would be shot or sent off to war and, if the latter, even determining in what units they would serve. But those who wielded this power were divided among themselves because of personal or family ties. Some, for example, wanted to eliminate José Escobar Moreno and Leovigildo Monge Pérez, but the Falangist Casildo Escobar Reinoso opposed the elimination of the former because he was his brother-in-law, and the parish priest Don Felipe opposed the elimination of the latter because he was the son of the man who had tried to save Don Felipe's nephew. On the other hand, Don Felipe wanted Celedonio Escobar Reinoso eliminated because of the run-ins they had had during the Republic, but Casildo was opposed because Celedonio was his brother.

Meanwhile, the civil governor Pedro Parias and the Falangist mayor José Cuevas Reinoso used their power as they saw fit on a case by case basis, although always within the limitations imposed by the pressures from one side or another.

Another young man from Castilleja, Conrado Rufino Romero, a right-winger, also joined the centuria. He did so enthusiastically. *I used to read the newspapers, and the war was . . . that was a delight. There was a journalist they used to call "Tebib Arrumi"* [Víctor Ruiz de Albéniz]. *I used to read the newspapers and, according to "Tebib Arrumi," well that was like one of these walks you take for an excursion the way they were receiving us in the towns. Later I realized it was not like that.* Conrado was with the centuria only a few months when his father demanded his discharge because Conrado had not yet turned eighteen.

Training in the Falangist centuria

The disappointment Conrado was to experience during the war began when he saw how poorly he had been prepared for life at the front. *Well, they called us from here and they took us . . . I do not remember how many of us went but there were quite a few of us. They took us to Carrión. We caught a train to Seville to where the Falangist headquarters was. There they equipped us with a coverall, one of those uniforms, and some leather belts, and a rifle. And they boarded us on a train to the Málaga front. Without experience. I mean, we did not even know what a rifle was. There I was months. With people from here, from Castilleja and from Carrión. And then when my father demanded my discharge, I came back. And as soon as I turned eighteen they called me again, and they put me in a different unit.*

The lack of training in the centuria is corroborated by Celedonio Escobar Reinoso. *In October they took twenty of us from here. They did not even give us arms. We were mobilized and there was not even any training. They took us to the Málaga front, twenty from here and from Carrión some sixty or eighty. A little over a hundred of us went. And we did not even carry arms. We boarded a train and when we arrived there, we relieved the ones who were there, and they gave us their arms and went home.* Antonio Monge Pérez also went to the Málaga front with the centuria and lamented the lack of training: *Those of us from here, those who went from here, we went to Seville in the first Falangist Battalion. Did I say those of us who went? No! Those of us they took because we did not want to go, as is only natural. For training, nothing. They trained us here. We fired off a few shots. Very few. And then, about the discipline for war, nothing. Nothing except how to handle a rifle and two days later they took us to the front, and that was that. Nothing. That is how it was.*

The Falangist centuria arrives at the front

The lack of training cost Antonio Monge Pérez a humiliating punishment. *Having just arrived at the front in the town of Almargen, since I knew nothing about the military, well we were there in a room, and I was sitting at a table with a brazier under it, and I was like this* (he crosses his arms on the table and rests his head on them), *and there was one of them sleeping there in a side room, one of those who rounded up people to bring here and kill them, whose name was Benjamín Caraballo* [Corchero]. *He had already served and he knew the responsibility there was for taking a sentinel's weapon, and I, since I had not served, I did not know. I had the rifle in a corner of the room. In the barracks. And the barracks' doors were locked, eh? It was in the town, which had already been taken, and the guards were all around the town. In short, there was no danger.*

And I was like I told you, and he had been lying down, and he was the corporal, and he passed behind me in his socks, like he was going out to urinate, and when he passed behind me he took the rifle and put it under his mattress. And then in the morning he says, "Hey, and the rifle?" I say, "How should I know? I had the rifle here and someone carried it off." "Because you were asleep." I say, "I was not asleep. What happened is that someone came by and, with stealth, took it away from behind me." He says, "What shit!" He reported it, and the one who was in charge there ordered them to shave my head, and they shaved my head. As a punishment. So. Well. That was that. But since we knew nothing about the military . . . but from then on, when resting like I said, you put the rifle between your legs. That is the way. You grasp it between your legs and then nobody can make off with it. The punishment inflicted on Antonio Monge Pérez in Almargen was the same one his mother Felisa Pérez Vera had suffered in Castilleja. The application of a punishment normally used on women would be especially humiliating for the implication of "effeminacy" that it carried.[2]

When Antonio Monge Pérez arrived in Almargen, he saw the other side of the repression: *Well, here* [in Castilleja] *leftists were killed and, of course, a thing happened that is interesting to know. We were at the Málaga front, like I already told you. It was the first front that we saw. Conrado* [Rufino Romero] *was there and Celedonio* [Escobar Reinoso], *because we went with the First Battalion from here in Seville. Then, we got to a town named Almargen and there the leftist people had killed rich people, you know? Many people . . . even if you do not . . . there are always people predisposed, and ready to kill people too. On that side they killed as well, people who were right-wingers. We saw it ourselves. That was how it was. Although it was not many but they were the elite people and all. But it was not the barbarity we had here, but, I mean, they killed too.*

Some of those who went to Almargen with the First Falangist Battalion saw the repression inflicted on right-wingers as a pretext for abusing the civilian population, according to Antonio. *There are many persons who have little conscience and abuse poor people like I saw some who were in the Falange. When we got there to relieve the other troops, since they found out there in the town that those people had killed people there, well, they used to say to many of the poor people's women, "Listen, wash my clothes!" And, "Well I . . . the truth is I do not have soap because it has been a long time since I have earned any money." "Well that is not my problem. You look for it somewhere, and tonight I want these clothes clean." And they used to abuse people like that. The poor women had to find soap, we do not know how, and wash the clothes of the Falangists because they were very frightened of them because they were the ones who killed people, those in the Falange. It was not the troops. Generally it was the Falangists who killed people more than any of the others.*

And then, poor things, they were terrified. Well, the women washed for them and did everything they wanted because, naturally, they knew they could shave their heads if they were not shorn already. Because they used to shave the heads of many women and give them a purgative of castor oil. Ay, what a catastrophe! Ho! Ho! Ho! Imagine! Oy! Oy! Oy! Castor oil! Have you ever tried it some time? I have. When I was a boy. As a child, I did. My parents gave me a few spoonfuls, and that has an effect that is all out of proportion. It was used back then to clean out the stomach. And then it was given to many people, bread soaked in it. You would have to have seen what that does. Well, all the bad things that could be thought up, they would do.

On October 31, 1936, the Castilleja administrative commission made a donation to the centuria, agreeing that "Don Casildo Escobar Reinoso be paid the sum of twenty-five pesetas as a donation that this Municipal Government makes to him so that as Militia Chief of Spanish Falange of this town he distribute them as he sees fit among the elements of said organization presently stationed in Almargen."[3]

Mobilization in the army

Manuel García Ramírez, whose brother Lutgardo was assassinated on August 27, was in the 1932 call-up. He was going to be forced to join the legion but he was saved from that fate because he was ill. *I was already through with the military. I had served when I was twenty. I was already discharged. And a short while later the war broke out and they mobilized me again. And they were going to send me to the legion, along with three or four others from the town. But I developed a pain, probably because of what we were going through, and the doctor told me I was in no shape to go. And then in the meantime they mobilized my call-up and I went into the army. I do not remember the date. And I was in*

Seville in the barracks where I served before and I was there a short while and they took me to Cerro Muriano, Córdoba. In the cavalry.

Miguel Rodríguez Caraballo, a right-winger, was also remobilized. First he reported in Seville with the Falangist José María Fernández Rodríguez "El Niño Guapo" on July 18, when Queipo de Llano had just taken over downtown Seville. *I was already discharged and they called me in 1936. On July 18 they called the two of us here, El Niño Guapo and me, because then things were not at all clear and they called the ones whose ideals they could be sure of, no? And the two of us went to Seville and we reported to the governor who was a gentleman who was in charge of the palace estate. He was the administrator, Pedro Parias. And I had a great friendship with him because I was practically brought up on that estate. And we went to the provincial government and it was all full of bullet holes everywhere and he told us to go home because he said things were not at all clear. And he says, "I will call you when things are more settled." Well they called me again and in the barracks the colonel there, he says, "You, how is it you have reported here?" I say, "Well, look, do me the favor, because I am a great friend of the governor, ask the governor." He says, "Ah, well then, that is it." He was an intimate friend of the governor, that colonel of the Quartermaster Corps.*

Another right-winger, Leopoldo Moreno, was already serving in the army in Seville when the war began: *The twenty-ninth of January 1936 I entered the service at four o'clock in the afternoon. And on July eighteenth at two o'clock in the afternoon the Movement began already in Seville. I was serving in the Quartermaster Corps. And well, we saw the shootings there and all the things that were going on. The people in the street. The Movement. The whole army in the street. And there were three or four days of shootings. Until at least the twenty-second. Then they took San Julián, a neighborhood there that had the most thugs.*

Leopoldo served in Seville in the Quartermaster Corps during the entire war, a job that made him a privileged witness to the repression against the military men who had remained loyal to the Republic in the first months of the war: *General Campins did not surrender. In Granada the troops did not surrender. And there was another general as well, the general who was in charge in Seville, Don José Fernández de Villa-Abrille. Queipo de Llano told him to join the Movement and he did not join the Movement. And they arrested him. They arrested him and they were holding him in a chalet that was named Ave María, with an infantry guard that was there. And then I used to take them bread every day from the Quartermaster Corps. Later they put him on trial. I do not know if they dismissed him from the army . . . they did not shoot him.*

They shot Campins, the captain general there in Granada. I saw him at eleven o'clock in the morning there in La Macarena. They stopped all the troops. I was going to the military hospital with bread for the wounded and the troops who were there in the military hospital. And they wanted everybody to stop, and I stopped. I saw when a priest confessed him, and he asked, "Can I smoke a cigarette?" And he lit a cigarette, and right then the troops . . . a captain of the Civil Guard who was in charge of the troops ordered them to fire. Well, they put him on one of those litters and they carried him to the cemetery. General Campins who was in charge in Granada.[4]

The others I interviewed who were mobilized into the army were Aurelio Monge Romero, who was in the 1939 call-up, Antonio Delgado Luque, of the 1940 call-up, and Aniceto Luque Luque, 1936 call-up. Aurelio Monge was mobilized into the army toward the end of 1936. *They mobilized my call-up and I went. I was in Algeciras. From Algeciras I went to Tarifa. From Tarifa to Ronda. From Ronda they sent me here to La Palma del Condado. We had completed basic training and we were here two months, near La Palma del Condado toward the mountains. Then there were fugitives who had escaped to the mountains. We went to an estate there they called La Zorrera to stand guard. An outpost there. I stood very few guards because they assigned me to a burro, because I had to come down from the mountains every day to get food in La Palma. To the town. There were ten or twelve men there standing guard. And I used to take them food every day and come back before nightfall. And then when we left there, well we went to the Córdoba front. To Villafranca on the Pozoblanco front.* Antonio Delgado remained in Castilleja for over a year before being mobilized. His unit was assigned to the rearguard: *I entered the army in October 1938 in Villa del Río, Córdoba, because we belonged to . . . we were all young, all sons of widows, just turned eighteen and we were never in combat, but instead maintaining order in places that had already been taken.*

From military improvisation to modern warfare
The failure of the coup

The first heavy combat experienced by men from Castilleja del Campo was during the taking of Málaga in February 1937, an action in which the Falangist militia from Carrión de los Céspedes and Castilleja participated. By then the nature of the war had changed. The July 18 rebellion was planned as a violent takeover that would last a few weeks at most, but it was soon clear that the military uprising had failed in slightly over half the country. What was to be a swift coup had turned into a war for which neither of the two sides was prepared.

The great advantage of the insurgent generals was the Army of Africa, the only force with the personnel, training, materiel, and experience to enter into action immediately, but this army was trapped in Morocco. For its part, the Republican government had lost control even of the territory where the coup had failed. The need to distribute arms to the workers' organizations in order to contain the coup meant that power in the Republican zone was in the hands of militiamen who not only disobeyed the orders of the government but often those of their own party or union. The coup had unleashed the very revolution it had claimed to prevent.

Neither side had the means to enter combat without foreign support. The insurgent generals needed arms for their forces in Spain and a way to transport the Army of Africa across the Strait of Gibraltar. The Republic needed arms of all kinds, as well as the training and organization of the workers turned militiamen, not only to defend itself from the enemy but to recover control of its own territory. In less than four months, an improvised and spontaneous conflict would turn into a modern war in which various foreign powers and forces would intervene, Germany and Italy on the side of the insurgents, and the Soviet Union and the International Brigades on the side of the Republic.

Objective Madrid

Until the end of November 1936, a short war still seemed possible if Madrid could be taken by the insurgent generals. But the troops and Falangist and Carlist volunteers sent by General Mola from the north were stopped in the Guadarrama Mountains by militias from Madrid and military units loyal to the Republic. Meanwhile, the Army of Africa was arriving in Seville, slowly at first, but later more quickly, due in large part to the transport planes provided by Germany and Italy. Once control of most of Andalusia had been assured, these forces began the long march toward Madrid, arriving within seventy-four kilometers of the capital by the end of September. In one of the most controversial decisions of the war, Franco decided to postpone the attack on Madrid and rescue Colonel José Moscardó, besieged in the Alcázar fortress in Toledo. Whether this decision cost Franco the taking of Madrid is a question that may never be answered, but it is clear that the Republic gained a month and a half to organize the defense of the capital and receive foreign aid.

Madrid prepares to defend itself and receives Soviet aid

With the Army of Africa's detour to Toledo, the Republican government was able to take advantage of the entire month of October to prepare the defense of Madrid. It could count on professional officers loyal to the Republic who organized, trained, and led "mixed brigades" composed of militiamen, soldiers already serving in the zone, and new recruits. One of the officers who provided these services was Captain Pedro Donaire Leal, a native of Castilleja del Campo, who was sent to the capital at the end of the month. During the battle of Madrid, the defenders would also receive foreign support, which would be as important morally as it was militarily.

The attitude of the Kremlin during the first months of the Spanish civil war was extremely cautious. Until October, the USSR sent only food and medicine to the Republic, but in mid-September Stalin seemed to realize that Soviet passivity with regard to the Republic would be perceived by the international Communist movement as betrayal of the revolution. For its part, the Comintern also began to act during the month of September, establishing an organization in Paris dedicated to the recruitment of anti-fascist volunteers from all over the world, the International Brigades. These seeds planted in September by the USSR and the Comintern would bear fruit during the following month. On October 4, the first Soviet armaments arrived in Cartagena. On October 12, some five hundred volunteers recruited by the International Brigades disembarked in Alicante. It is important to bear in mind that aid from the Soviet Union and the Comintern began after more than a month and a half of massive German and Italian military aid to the insurgents. Without the spirit of resistance of the Madrid populace, it is doubtful this belated aid would have saved the capital.

The battle of Madrid

The attack began on Sunday morning, November 8. Successive waves of legionnaires and Moroccan mercenaries charged the main bridges over the Manzanares River only to fall back or die under the machine gun fire of the defenders. Hundreds of militiamen died at the barricades and parapets but others, unarmed, emerged from their hiding places to take up the machine guns of their fallen comrades. Meanwhile, telegrams were arriving at the Nationalist general staff headquarters congratulating Franco for his victorious entry into Madrid.

That afternoon, the Eleventh International Brigade arrived in the capital from Albacete and was received with great enthusiasm by the populace which, for the first time, felt it had the backing of the international Left. But the support brought by the brigade was more moral then material. The main credit for the defense of Madrid belongs to the Republican officers who, in the postwar, would minimize their contribution, for obvious reasons. The desire of many Republican officers to maintain silence about their actions in the defense of Madrid was born during the battle itself, as was the case for the Castilleja native Captain Pedro Donaire Leal. It was important that his heroism remain anonymous to avoid reprisals against his wife Rosario and his two small children, Matilde and Eugenio, in the Nationalist zone. Another such case was that of Colonel Francisco León Trejo, commander of the Cuatro Vientos airdrome, whose brothers José, Manuel, and Joaquín, Castilleja's schoolteacher, were in Seville.

The failure to take Madrid on November 8 showed that the Army of Africa was not invincible when the opposing forces and their materiel were comparable to their own. The capital's defenders had considerable resources at their disposal. The German and Italian tanks of the attackers were resisted by the Russian tanks of the defenders. In the second week of November, the aerial support provided the insurgents by the German Condor Legion confronted "Mosca" and "Chato" fighters from the Soviet Union. As far as personnel were concerned, the officers in the capital commanded a large fighting force. Among these officers was the Castilleja native Pedro Donaire Leal. When the battle began, he was with the men under his command in the Moncloa zone and the Paseo del Pintor Rosales, facing the enemy charges from the Casa de Campo. Later he received orders to take his troops to the Bridge of the Franceses, also facing the Casa de Campo. There they resisted for two or three days under continuous fire until being relieved.[5] The battle of Madrid lasted until November 23, when Franco's General Staff decided to suspend the frontal attack on the capital.

The battle of Madrid as watershed

Before the battle of Madrid, the civil war resembled the Spanish colonial campaigns of the Moroccan War. Columns of Nationalist forces advanced rapidly, taking poorly armed or completely defenseless towns and cities and leaving behind civilian populations terrorized by the repression. After November 1936, the type of combat changed. Troops dug trenches along a front that was more than two thousand kilometers long. Territorial conquest would require battles with enormous losses in personnel and materiel. The conflict would resemble the First World War, at least for the soldiers defending the trenches or taking part in the battles. For the inhabitants of cities in the Republican zone, the war would be a new experience in the history of warfare. There the German officers of the Condor Legion would experiment with massive aerial bombardments and its psychological effect on the morale of civilian populations. The terror inflicted from the skies over Madrid, Barcelona, Valencia, and Guernica was a foretaste of the aerial attacks on London, Hamburg, Coventry, and Dresden during the Second World War.

Another change in the war during the battle of Madrid was the internationalization of the conflict. From then on, large numbers of personnel and quantities of war materiel would arrive in Spain from Germany, Italy, and the Soviet Union, along with the volunteers of the International Brigades. Given the early help provided the insurgents by Germany and Italy, and the passivity of the European democracies, Soviet aid was crucial to the Republic. This aid increased the prestige, influence, and size of the Spanish Communist Party. Many of the new members were not Marxists but members of the middle class who saw the discipline of the party as protection against the spontaneous repression carried out by uncontrollable elements.

Many military men joined the Communist Party because they saw it as the only political force that could organize an army capable of defeating the enemy. The military coup had been justified as a means to avoid a Communist revolution led from Moscow but, in fact, it gave the Spanish Communists who took their orders from the Kremlin an influence they never would have attained without the war. This influence would be felt in the repression carried out in the Republican zone. After the period of the spontaneous killings, many of the victims were not right-wingers but leftists who did not agree with the orthodox Communists who adhered to the Soviet line.

International intervention prolonged the Spanish civil war and made it as deadly as possible. It was a critical moment in arms development. For over two years, the most advanced machines of destruction in the history of warfare were arriving in Spain, which, in July 1936, had been a technologically backward nation. The countries that sent weapons, men, and technical assistance to each side did not want the war in Spain to provoke a general European War. Starting in 1937, Germany and Italy would provide Franco the help he needed to avoid a Republican victory, and the Soviet Union would send the Republic enough aid to counteract what the Nationalists were receiving from the Nazi and Fascist powers. The assistance to both sides would increase throughout the conflict, but at no time would it be sufficient to assure either side a swift victory.

The prolongation of the war benefited Franco who, in early 1937, told the Chief of Staff of the Italian troops in Spain, Colonel Faldella, "In a civil war, a systematic occupation of territory, accompanied by the necessary 'cleansing,' is preferable to a rapid defeat of the enemy armies that would leave the country infected with adversaries."[6] Franco may have already arrived at this conclusion in late September 1936, when he decided to take the detour to Toledo, jeopardizing the taking of Madrid. The liberation of the Alcázar fortress in Toledo may well have been motivated by Franco's desire to prolong the war. He later told the right-wing journalist Manuel

Aznar, grandfather of a future head of the Spanish government, "Upon entering the Alcázar I had the conviction that I had won the war. From then on it was only a matter of time. I was no longer interested in a sudden victory, but rather in a total victory brought about by the wasting away of the enemy."[7]

And that is what happened. After the battle of Madrid, and for the next twenty-eight months, Spain would suffer a combination of the horror of trench warfare and battles of attrition reminiscent of the First World War and the terror of aerial bombardments and mechanized warfare that prefigured the Second World War. This was the hecatomb stored in the collective memory of a generation of men from Castilleja del Campo and reflected in the testimonies of the ten men of the town I interviewed in the winter of 1989/90.

Notes

1 Census of 1935, Castilleja del Campo Municipal Archive.
2 Francisco Espinosa Maestre, *La Guerra Civil en Huelva*, 436n2.
3 Minutes, 31 October 1936, Castilleja del Campo Municipal Archive.
4 General Miguel Campins Aura was shot on August 16, 1936. General José Fernández de Villa-Abrille was still under arrest in the Ave María chalet during the postwar.
5 Matilde Donaire Pozo, "Largo camino hacia la paz," 11–12.
6 Francisco Espinosa Maestre, *La columna de la muerte*, 140.
7 Ibid., 475n362.

Nine

Men of Castilleja del Campo in the War

Men from Castilleja in offensive operations

The men in the Falangist centuria saw their first heavy combat in February 1937, during the offensive to take Málaga. It was successful because the Mediterranean port's defenders lacked experienced commanders, but geography favored the defense of the region and there was strong resistance.[1] This is reflected in Manuel Ramírez Mauricio's testimony: *Well, the first experience we had there was when we took Málaga. We entered through a series of ravines where there were tall rocks, and there were machine guns on both sides, manned by them. And we took a road to the right where the whole front was and there we made a stand. Some got behind the rocks, and the rest of us piled up two or three of the dead and that is how we protected ourselves. And the Reds put up a strong resistance. There were a lot of personnel there. That is why a lot of personnel died there. I mean when a bullet came, well it took out one or two people. And there were machine guns, there were cannons, there were tanks, there were . . . I mean, there was everything.*

Another of Manuel Ramírez's testimonies reflects the internationalization of the war. The first massive participation of Italian troops occurred during the Málaga offensive.[2] Manuel also describes the danger of friendly fire in mechanized warfare. *We were together with some Italians there on a ridge they call El Cerro de la Perdiz, next to Nerja in this direction. Well, almost all of them died there. Because there was an aerial bombardment, you know? Because they did not know if those forces were with us or with them, eh? Our own planes from this side dropped bombs there and since it was all full of Italian positions, you know?, in a line that was seven or eight kilometers long, or ten, whole battalions there, well, they pulverized them all.* After the taking of Málaga, the centuria from Carrión and Castilleja was sent to several fronts, but almost always in Andalusia.

Conrado Rufino Romero, in a different Falangist unit, described combat in the province of Córdoba, combat made more difficult by the heat. *I remember an offensive, an operation they carried out from Valsequillo, Los Blázquez, from Fuente Obejuna in that direction almost to Pozoblanco. I do not remember how many days that offensive lasted but they were terrible days because it was hot and there was no water. If we arrived some place that had a little brook, or there was a well, then since there were so many people, they muddied the water, and they ruined it, and it was a real hardship. Once they brought us some metal tanks in some trucks. With water. They lined us up and there were so many people that they broke ranks and split open the tanks with machetes and most of the water went to waste. I mean, it was a calamity everywhere you turned.*

During this offensive, tactics to be used in the Second World War were employed. *Of course, there was one thing to consider. Here when you had to charge the heights . . . they used to say "the heights" for a hillside, a town, because the towns were generally on a hilltop, and they would say, well, "That town up there you have to take it." First off, the artillery would start in. And then the aviation. When we got there, it was all pulverized. There were some that resisted, but others were pulverized. Sometimes there was no longer anyone there. The town was half-destroyed. Other times, well, when we were advancing, well, when their troops regrouped, they stood their ground. They stopped us and, after days of fighting, we would advance again.*

Those who were mobilized in the army participated in offensive operations in various parts of Spain. Aurelio Monge Romero began his military service transporting supplies to a unit in the mountains to the north of La Palma del Condado, Huelva, a unit that was on the lookout for fugitives. Then he was sent to the Córdoba front and from there to Estremadura. His experience there shows that even abandoned towns could be dangerous. *I have known more fear than God. And caught in the middle of open ground. That was in Zorita, a town in the province of Cáceres. Near the city of Cáceres. And the people could not stay in the town. They came out to the countryside because of the aviation. Whole families were sleeping in meadows under the cork oaks and the holly trees. That is where the people were living there. All the people and their things there. And the troops there too. And the town empty.*

And every day a labyrinth. Fuck if it was not a labyrinth. Because one night we had to enter the town with the help of the aviation. The aviation covering us. And we got all muddled up because the sentinels made a mistake and they killed one of our mules with the machine guns until the liaison came and said that those were our troops. There were times that you did not know who was who because they were dressed the same as we were too. The only thing was that they did not have a little ball and tassel hanging from their caps and we did. But often you took your cap off because you did not know where you were. Everybody all muddled together.

Celedonio Escobar was in combat in the Pyrenees at the end of the war. *Later I froze my foot in the last offensive they had right near the border with France. It was the last time we got to the front and there was a snow storm. And we had to get up to where we had to make camp. And we had to get to the top. After the snow storm there was an ice storm too. You know when the snow freezes, when you can no longer walk on top of it. Along a trail that was full of people who were falling, who were breaking . . . there were one hundred and forty of us I remember in the company and eighteen of us got to the top. The others fell because of the ice. They slipped and fell and that is where they stayed. It was a disaster because of the frozen snow.*

We got to the top. Of course, there we were but it turned out that the next day we were going to attack. There were more than two hundred batteries and I have no idea how many of us creatures there were there. We were all concentrated there for the offensive. But there was no way. We dug the snow with ice axes. We were carrying ice axes to make trenches. And there were not even fires or anything. They did not want us to make fires because they were firing artillery at us. And the next day, I remember, or three days later, the command came, "You have to comb the terrain meter by meter." And when we advanced, with four artillery shells it was all blown apart. The trenches were all full of people blown apart. I was three months in the hospital, because of frostbite, you know? They say that . . . with alcohol is the only cure they have, alcohol. Scrubbing and scrubbing to get the blood moving, you know? It hurts like you cannot imagine.

On the stabilized fronts

The majority of soldiers spent the war on fronts that barely moved. From 1937 until almost the end of the war, Conrado Rufino Romero was on the same front: *There on the Córdoba front. Some positions they had there. They called one of them Chamorra. And the other they called Los Chivatines. Very sad memories because there was nothing there but gunfire, and rain and lice and mud puddles. Very sad memories of those positions. Because then I was of an age that, well, the war robbed that age from me. Those three years, from seventeen to twenty, the war robbed those years from me. And when I see the young men here at that age enjoying life and having fun, it is not that I become envious but, I say, I lost all that. The war robbed me of all that. Bad, bad, bad experiences. Not because of the fear of the bombs and the artillery. It was more the fear of the puddles, the trenches, the abject misery. Of having to go two months without even changing your clothes. It was the lice. The lice were . . . they were there at morning roll call . . . your whole body covered in lice. And what can you do if you cannot even light a fire to dry your clothes?*

Aurelio Monge Romero summarized his military career, enumerating the fronts on which he had served. He included an incident on the Córdoba front in which nature itself was the danger and then, in his description of the Madrid front, the danger was the proximity of the enemy: *Then when we left* [La Palma del Condado], *well, we went to the Córdoba front. Once, in the summer, a brush fire started. A whole lot of uncut forage that was there nearby. And*

*with our machetes . . . in some places there had been fences with tall stakes for the
cattle and all, and we had to shinny up the stakes and hang on with our machetes
until the fire passed under us. Because we were loaded down with hand grenades.
And then they sorted out the battalions and we were assigned to the Madrid front,
my battalion was, and there is where I finished out the war. In Madrid. Those on
this side here, the Nationalists here, the others, the Reds, there only one hundred and
fifty meters away. And keeping an eye out by means of some mirrors they had set up
there. Well, we had to watch through the mirrors because we could not look through
the peepholes because the moment you looked through, poom.*

Like Conrado, Aurelio Monge complained less about the danger than
about the living conditions, the bad weather, the vermin, the substandard
clothing, inadequate food, and lack of water. *And always a good deal of thirst.
We used to have to go to the wells with those scoops from the machine guns, those
pumps to cool the barrels, and we used to get water from the well with the scoop,
pushing the cicadas to the side. Enormous cicadas that would fall into the wells. And
we used to bury the water in the ground there so it would stay cool. And in some positions, at night they used to come with tank trucks to bring us water because there was
no water or anything there. The clothes were awful. And shoes that were inadequate.
Half the time rope-soled sandals. The soldiers' clothes were terrible. And the food. I
have gone sometimes more than a week without hot food. Cans of sardines and cans
of peas, cold rations. I have eaten hardtack without salt and I had to use a machete
to break it, hardtack that was two inches thick. And it did not taste like anything.
Awful. And enough lice to stop a train.*

The same complaints about the inadequate clothing and food appear in
many testimonies, like this one from Manuel Ramírez Mauricio. *In winter,
the same clothes as always. Coveralls or some pants or slippers. Other times some
rope-soled sandals. And other times some shoes, depending upon what they could give
us or what we could find. And at night to stand guard, a shawl to wrap yourself
up in, you know?, like a cape. A woolen blanket-cape, you know? To withstand the
snow or rain that was coming in. It was not sufficient because you had to wear it all
night. The first to stand guard would wear it, and from the first guard it would
pass to the second guard, and from the second to the third, until morning came. You
know how that cape was when the second guard and the third took it? Soaking wet
was how it was. You were all warm when you left the shanty, you know? "Get up
and get out there. Here, put this on and get going." And the other would go back to
crawl into the shanties to sleep.*

*The food, sometimes not too bad, and other times terrible, with a lot of flies in the
pot. Because the kitchen used to attract all the flies, you know? And even though you
would go like this* (sweeping with his hand), *to and fro, it was no good. The pots
always had flies stuck in them because there were always flies around and they would
take them out so we would not see them. But those of us who were helping in the*

kitchen, peeling potatoes, or chopping up this or that or whatever, the meat, or what there was to throw into the food, we would see them. To make coffee, we put a sack of grounds with a little bit of sugar in a tub, and with a little coffee, you know? And they would put it in there and stir it up with a ladle and serve it and that was that. And from there they would ladle it out and throw it in the bowls we used to have for drinking and for eating.

We used to eat . . . when there was almost nothing, when we were going hungry . . . the bread we had thrown out the day before, because we did not feel like eating it . . . we had thrown it out for the dogs, because there were always a lot of dogs . . . and the rats had grabbed it and carried it off to the old shanties. Rats. And they used to put it into the cracks between the stones, you know? For them to eat later. And we would tear down the shanties to get at the bread, and remove the sulfur color, you know? We would scrape it a little and hold it over the fire to toast it a little, and we would eat it.

The terrible conditions at the front led to diseases such as typhus, spread by lice. On a number of occasions, Aniceto Luque Luque suffered from what he called paratyphoid sweats. Antonio Monge Pérez also became sick. He attributed his illness to the poor quality of the rations and to the lack of variety in the soldiers' food, and he described a dangerous attempt to procure a healthier diet: *They put me on leave because we used to eat canned sardines and so I got a very bad infection. Because they gave us sardines for dinner and for supper and with coffee for breakfast. And so I came down with an infection. Another one from Castilleja and I caught it and it turned our blood to water. Of course. Canned sardines all day. You see, we used to have to open the can like this* (makes the gesture of holding the can at arm's length) *so that the smell of the sardines did not reach us because otherwise, we could not eat them. Imagine what it is to eat them for dinner and for supper there for a whole month.*

And then, I remember there were fava beans planted between the Reds and us, and we went out to see if we could pick some fava beans for the midday dinner at least, for a change of food. But, of course, the Reds were on a high ridge and they saw that we were going out there to pick fava beans and they started in with the machine guns. That was the end of that. And a lucky thing that we made it to a gully. And we had to stay there until nightfall because if you stuck out your head it was . . . poom, poom . . . and we had to keep on eating canned sardines. What a feast! The way things were. Yes.

During the interviews, the ex-combatants related experiences they had kept silent for many years. According to Aurelio Monge Romero, *one did not want to talk about the war because one had been through so much. So much misery and so much hunger and so many calamities and so much suffering . . . because I have spent many nights sleeping on the hard ground with only a little blanket or with a cape for a cover, with a cartridge belt on, and a gun for a pillow, and at midnight to hear, "Come on, get up now, the enemy is coming." Uff! And that was a shock.*

The fear of attacks was constant. Conrado Rufino Romero described a particularly bad night. *I have seen eight attacks against us in one night. Because they wanted to take the position where we were and they could not take it. They attacked eight times and each time they had to retreat. And it even became a big joke. We started in with music singing, "Another bull, another bull, bring out another bull." As if we were telling them to attack again. And they would attack with "the Republic!" Poom, poom, poom, poom. And of course, we drove them back again. Eight times in one night. And they used to attack primarily on rainy nights. I do not know why. On rainy nights it was almost certain they would attack, eh? I never found out why.*

Celedonio Escobar Reinoso was wounded during one attack. *They wounded me here* [in the leg]. *I had a very big piece of shrapnel lodged here. On the Zaragoza front in the province of Lérida. I remember when they got me. I was manning a machine gun because they were attacking. A lot of them. The corporal had thrown himself into the trench and he says to me, "Look out. They are practically on us. Get down here man." I grabbed the machine gun and started to fire. They operated on me in Zaragoza and took out a piece of shrapnel that I had lodged down here.*

These descriptions are of attacks carried out by shock troops. Artillery bombardments were worse. Antonio Monge Pérez described the impotence one felt and the temptation to take extreme measures to escape the danger of a certain death. *I remember once we had a huge shelling. And then they knocked out a position with sandbags and stones, a position that covered at least three hundred acres of terrain, and they pulverized the whole thing. And one of the men there right next to me shot himself in the hand. I say, "Kid, what is the matter with you?" He says, "Look, they shot me." "But, man, for God's sake, why have you done it like that? You have scorched your hand. Man, to shoot yourself, you stand like this, you pee in a handkerchief, and with the handkerchief wrapped around your hand you hold it at arm's length. But you go and shoot yourself like that and burn your hand and maybe . . ." It seems to me they told me later that they shot him for abandoning his post.*

But of course, I was there manning a machine gun, and sometimes I would raise my hand and stick it out like this because I say, "One of these shells is going to get me and I am a dead man." Because they were fifteen and a half caliber shells. The projectiles were this long and I say . . . and they were raining in . . . and I was manning a machine gun, but since the enemy was not coming, well there I was. I was not shooting at anyone. I would put my hand straight up and the explosion would move it. I would stick it out to see if I could get hit somewhere. I say, "Alright, let us see if with just a bullet wound, there may be something left of me." But no. The shots were coming from far off and they were coming every which way.

But the other poor guy who came up to relieve the one who shot himself, a shell got him and there was nothing left of him. His shoes, with his feet in them, torn right off. And his rifle was pulverized too. Imagine what it takes to pulverize a rifle. The poor thing. Since it was summer, there was a stain on the ground and stones there and there was not . . . I do not know if they could find four little pieces that remained of him. There was nothing left. Because they were projectiles that used to weigh at least fifty kilos. At least. We went through so many things. The things that happen in war. It is only logical.

Contact with the enemy

Fraternization with the enemy was common during the Spanish civil war. It served various purposes, such as the exchange of products that were lacking in one zone or the other. According to Aurelio Monge Romero, a leftist, *when there were new troops that relieved those on the other side or on this side, you had to be careful. But when we had been there long enough, we used to go out at night and they did not have tobacco and we did not have cigarette paper. And we would exchange cigarette paper and newspapers and things like that.*

Conrado Rufino Romero, a right-winger, spoke of the advantage of agreements with the enemy. *There were exchanges of tobacco from here for cigarette paper from there. And if there was a water trough between the two sides, there would also be agreements for them to go at a certain time and for us to go at a different time. I never went to exchange paper and tobacco, but there were some of those serving with me who went. I never went because one did not know how they were going to receive one. I mean, that was an adventure. And I did not smoke then. But yes, I know that people went out to exchange paper for tobacco. I also know that if there was a well that was between the two sides, then they would negotiate an agreement. And other times they made agreements not to shoot because it was Easter or something like that and we would go a few days without shooting. And other times we even used to go for walks there along the trenches and we did not shoot at them nor they at us. And then some troublemaker would fire two or three shots off in that direction and we were back to the same mess.*

For Manuel Ramírez Mauricio, the greatest impediment to contact with Republican soldiers was the officers. His testimony gives the impression that for leftists in Franco's forces, fraternization with soldiers from the other side alleviated the loneliness of serving in an army that was fighting for an ideology they did not share. *Contact? Yes, yes, yes. Talking to them, like Celedonio* [Escobar Reinoso] *and I used to take the forward positions so we could talk with them until the superiors found out and stopped us. In the trenches, where there was barbed wire toward our side, and more barbed wire toward their side, we used to open the barbed wire, you know? With the barbed wire raised up. And there we used to talk with them until a corporal or a sergeant came to relieve them or to relieve us, you know? And maybe the following week we were shooting at each other. The following week or the next morning.*

On another occasion, we used to go sometimes, in the town of Villa del Río . . . There was a river between us that carried very little water and there was a little mill to grind wheat for flour, and we used to cross there. They gave us paper, and we gave them tobacco. And we would come back when we had rolled a cigarette and talk. Like you and I right now. And there were some pools formed there that had water, so we used to wash our clothes, and they also used to go wash their clothes, you know? And later we would do our washing there together. But the officers did not want to see us together.

Many of the combatants in the civil war were fighting on the side that did not correspond to their ideals. They had more in common with enemy troops than with their own officers. I asked Manuel Ramírez whether, during such intimate contact with Republican soldiers, it had not occurred to him how easy it would be to desert. His response was the same one all the leftist ex-combatants I interviewed gave. *Yes, but the fear we had is that they would kill our family here. Because they used to kill them.* He then went on to describe an incident that underscores the absurdity of the war.

For Christmas we were in a position . . . The second Christmas. Thirty-seven. Well, we were talking there from one side to the other, they with us and we with them, to get together a few of us on Christmas Eve there on their side in a shanty to eat and drink. Drinks and sweets and things. Seven of us went. There were seven of us and we were there eating and drinking as much as we wanted. When the time came to return, before daybreak, well, "Hey, farewell then," or "Compatriot, this, that, and the other," or "To your health, comrade," and we came back. And on New Years Day, I did not go. Another five or six went. And they went and came back again the same as happened before. And they understood why we had to be there. Of course. They understood it just like we understood them. Because we were talking with them and, "Well, look, we are here with this side and we have to be here by force, with them, because otherwise, they will kill our people, the family from there that we left behind." And they say, "Well, it is the same for us." And the ones I met from the other side, they were further to the Right than me.

Permeable frontlines

The fear of reprisals against family members was greater for combatants

from small towns. The local authorities sent reports on the soldiers' political and religious background to the officers of their units, and the local
authorities received reports from the soldiers' officers on their behavior at
the front. In small towns like Castilleja del Campo, where everyone knew
each other, it would be easier to punish family members of soldiers who
deserted.

Nevertheless, the ex-combatants' testimonies indicate that desertion in
both directions was fairly frequent. Manuel Ramírez Mauricio: *I saw men
who crossed from that side to this side. One night in Cuevas del Becerro, in the second
town on the Málaga front, while I was standing guard. There were little cans
hanging from the barbed wire, you know? So that if we heard . . . if someone was
coming or something, we would hear those cans. There was a very thick mist that
night while I was standing guard there. And another guard further down and
another, all around the town, you know?*

*And those little cans clanged and I say, "Halt! Who goes there?" And he says,
"Spain." "The password!" I do not remember what password it was. A password.
"Alright then, forward!" And then he started to cross and I say, "No. Halt! Halt
right there!" And I called for the corporal of the guards, you know? And it was
passed down the line from position to position: "Corporal of the guards," "Corporal
of the guards," "Corporal of the guards," until it got to where the corporal of the
guards was. And the corporal of the guards, "What position?" And he took down
the number of the position. Then he came and he . . . eh?. . . and that one did not
go anywhere. He stayed there with us. Serving as a soldier like us. And nothing
happened to him for crossing over. He crossed over with his weapon, you know? He
crossed over with his rifle to this side and nothing happened to him for bringing his
weapon.*

Conrado Rufino Romero spoke of other cases that show the danger
confronted by those who crossed over as well as those who took them in.
*There were some who crossed from this side to that side. One of our soldiers crossed
over there. I mean, more than one crossed over. But one of them died. He did not die
because we killed him. The cavalry posted near him killed him. We fired off shots
but we did not hit him. Because we did not shoot for real, because he was a friend of
ours. And what happened is the boy, well, he was assigned to the front position that
morning and he took advantage of it to take off. He grabbed a machine gun he had
there and he left. And when our sergeant realized it, he began to say, "Fire, fire, so
and so is getting away!" And we shot because we had to shoot, but those to his left
killed him. He had all the bullet holes on his left side. We did not shoot at him. I
mean not to hit him. We did not shoot to hit him.*

*And I saw a lot of them cross over to this side. They had to come clapping their
hands without stopping. Because it could have been a trick. It could have been to get
close to us and throw, for example, a hand grenade. They came clapping their hands*

so we could see they had nothing in their hands. From here they would take them to some battalions that . . . they observed them there, for example, three or four months, and when they saw by their behavior that they had crossed over to this side because they held these ideals or something, they would take them to the front with us. And there were some there, serving with me, who had been with the Reds. Then Conrado related a truly surprising incident. *I was with three Germans who came as volunteers in the Falange. And after they were with us three or four months, they crossed to the other side. To the Republican zone. To the Reds. Three of them. They were Communists or something, of course. They were in the Falangist barracks there and they went out on an expedition to the front and they went over to the Reds.*

The motive for crossing over was not always political, according to Conrado. *There was another who also went over to the Reds because he did not want to marry the girl who was going to have his child. There in the province of Córdoba. We were on leave in a town and he met that girl and the girl got pregnant. And she reported it to the commander and the priest we had there and . . . the boy was from Utrera or Carmona, one of those towns. Well, he said to me, "I am not getting married, I am not getting married." Well, they had all the papers there in his town and all, for him to get married the next day. Well, that night he went over to the Reds. To get out of that obligation he went over to the Reds.*

Juan Antonio Luque Romero "Antonio Canitas"

Only two men from Castilleja del Campo served in the Republican army. One was Pedro Donaire Leal, who escaped to the Republican zone on August 17, 1936. With the rank of captain, he participated in the defense of Madrid. The other was Juan Antonio Luque Romero. He served in Franco's forces until the middle of 1937 when he crossed over to the Republican side. His brother Narciso told the story of the two combatants in the family, Juan Antonio and Manuel, and how the death of their mother changed Juan Antonio's destiny. *Antonio had leftist ideas and no one could move him from there. But beyond that he was like all the rest. A very good worker. And a very good companion to those who worked with him. He was in the 1932 call-up. He was thirteen or fourteen years older than me. And my brother Manuel, he was in the 1935 call-up, and the war caught him already serving. He was to be discharged in August, but then came July 18 and they did not discharge him. They kept him there serving in Peñarroya, one of the toughest fronts in Spain. He was in heavy artillery and he was there the whole war on that front. But Antonio had already done his service. He was already discharged but they called him up right away and they took him to the Guadalajara front.*

And my mother, the poor thing, well, since they took my two brothers off to war, and they killed my poor brother-in-law [Manuel Monge Romero, shot on August 27, 1936], *my mother, well she was distressed because she had a bad heart and all, and the sorrow and all, the calamities, well she started to die. We were always encouraging her, "They are coming back soon, the war is about to end." What she wanted was to see her sons. In short, the poor thing was getting worse, worse, worse, worse, and my sisters and my father* [Antonio Luque Tebas] *sent them telegrams, to each of my brothers so they would come. And they put on the telegram, "Mother's condition is serious." Then they showed the telegram to their captains and then Antonio . . . that front was quieter . . . they gave him leave as soon as the telegram arrived and he came in two or three days. In short, when he arrived, nothing, she had already been buried, of course. You had to see how the poor thing arrived, because he was dressed like a soldier at the front. He came by train and he came walking from Carrión to here at midday with the heat and those clothes on, covered in dirt and vermin, the lice. It filled you with pity the way he came.*

Then his ten days were up and they had not given my brother Manuel leave, mother or no mother. But Antonio, when his ten days were up, well, [my father says] *"Antonio, you have to go back." He says, "Well I am not going." Because that was how he was. He* [my father] *says, "Yes man, yes, because you know we are at war and they gave you ten days." He says, "Alright, I am not going. Until I see Manuel I am not going back because I . . ." The poor thing was seeing the panorama the way it was. ". . . the most likely thing is they kill him or me or the two of us because we are on the front lines and, in short, the war is at its height." It was 1937. He* [my father] *says, "But, man, think of what . . ." He says, "No way, I am not going back until I see him. So do not tell me again, because I am not going." And Manuel did not come until thirteen days had gone by and my mother already dead. So Antonio had one day with him, with Manuel, and then well, "I am going back now. Now that I have seen Manuel."*

He caught the train and he went back to Guadalajara. But he had to report to that captain of his and he reported, and he began to look him up and down and he says, "Now you come back?" He says, "Now I am back." "Well you are three days late." He says, "Yes, I know, but I am going to tell you something. I have another brother of mine in artillery in Peñarroya on the Córdoba front and since I know that if they do not kill him or they do not kill both of us . . . and I was not coming back without seeing him because he is my brother. You will forgive me but I was not coming without seeing him." "No, here there is no brother or mother or anything. Here there is the flag and your rifle." He says, "No sir, you are mistaken." And he says, "Your mother is the flag and your musket and your cartridge belt. That is your mother." He says, "No sir, you are mistaken. My mother is the one I left buried in Castilleja del Campo, province of Seville. That is my mother, but beyond that, for me there is no other mother." He says, "Get out of my sight before I . . ." "You do what you want but . . ." Like that. "Go on, go on, get out of here and get to the front trench

*before I put two bullets in you." He says, "That too? Well, go ahead and shoot me.
There is your pistol hanging there. Put those two bullets in me."*

*In short, there they had a big brawl. He says, "Alright. And another thing I am
going to tell you, my captain, the one who . . ." The poor thing could no longer control
himself . . . because he had a temper that . . . ". . . the one that ought to go there to
the forward trench is you, because you draw a salary that you have to defend. As for
me, at two cents, what do I have to defend? They pay me two cents every day. And
I have nothing to defend. If you want, put those two bullets in me. It is all the same
to me."*

*In short, he could no longer remain there seeing that guy every day . . . but knowing
that he had another brother he did not want to cross over to the other side because
maybe it could come to one of them killing the other, eh? And that would have been
too much. But he did not think twice about it. So he would not have to see that guy
again, he up and . . . twenty-three of them crossed over. And with him there were
twenty-four. They talked it over and one night, he says, "Alright, let us go." They
had already talked it over because they used to talk, the Reds and the Nationalists
used to talk. They were nearby and they told them when they could, "Look, well
tonight twenty-four or twenty-five of us are going to cross over. So now you know.
Do not shoot because it is us." And they crossed over and they were there until the
war ended.*

*They took him to Madrid and he was there until they entered Madrid, which
was the last place that fell. There is where they captured him. And Don Pedro
Donaire was there too. Don Pedro was a personage, a man of learning who knew a
lot, a smart man, and they put him in charge of a company, what he was in charge
of. And there Antonio and Don Pedro found out that the two of them had crossed
over.* After the war, Juan Antonio Luque Romero would pay dearly for his
decision to cross over to the other side, just as Captain Pedro Donaire Leal
would pay dearly for having served in the Republican army.

Soldiers in support units

Manuel García Ramírez

Of the ten ex-combatants interviewed, four of them served in support
units. The only leftist among these four was Manuel García Ramírez. He
had already done his military service during the Republic, but was remobilized. They took him to Cerro Muriano, Córdoba, in the cavalry. *I do not
know why . . . they probably sent bad reports on me since I was a leftist and they
never sent me to the front. I always had noncombat duties. Sometimes taking care
of the horses, other times in the kitchen. I did not go to the front ever. If I had gone
to the front, I would have crossed over to the other side, eh? Guaranteed. Without*

fear of what might happen. None at all. I never even took up a musket. Not once.
Manuel's testimony seems boastful since so many of the town's leftists
with opportunities to go over to the other side did not do so for fear of
reprisals against their families, but bragging would have been untypical
of this man who always measured his words. His declaration reflects his
family's situation.

Manuel's brother Lutgardo was shot on August 27, 1936. While
Lutgardo was in jail, his father Manuel García Romero "Manolito el
Cortaor" went to Seville to ask Pedro Parias to intervene and save Lutgardo's
life. The governor kicked him down the staircase, which so distressed
Manolito that he had a stroke upon returning from Seville. Another stroke,
on January 28, 1937, killed him. With one brother assassinated, a father
who died of sorrow at 59 years of age and three other brothers, Antonio,
Eliseo, and Félix, mobilized in Franco's forces, it is difficult to imagine what
else could have been done to this family.

While other leftists were mistreated in Franco's forces, the army was a
sanctuary for Manuel. *And later they assigned me to a kitchen for the officers. To
prepare meals for the officers. And with me they behaved marvelously. I tell it the
way it was. Marvelously. So much so that the captain, when I was discharged after
the war, said to me, "Manuel, if they make trouble for you in your town, all you
have to do is come here." To see him. In Seville. Seville was where he lived. I mean,
they behaved very well with me. When there was an offensive they would give me a
pass to come home. Because they did not need me those days. They would be eating
cold rations. "Well these days you go home."*

Leopoldo Rubio

Leopoldo Rubio was already serving in Seville when the war broke out. Life
in the army suited him and he continued serving after the war. *I was five
and a half years, always in Seville. In the Quartermaster Corps that supplied the
troops. There were days when the bakers would make fourteen thousand bread rations.
And when it was needed for the troops at the front, you know?, they would requisition the bakeries in Seville. The order would go out, "Alright, knead dough for bread
to send to the front." And there were days and nights when ten or eleven trucks would
go out loaded with bread for the fronts.*

He was able to spend a lot of time in Castilleja. *Almost every week I used
to come, but on the sly. Because they did not give me leave. There was a control there
in La Pañoleta. There where you enter Seville there was a military control and they
would ask to see your papers. But I used to give bread to a corporal there in the print
shop, you know? I used to give his mother one or two rolls of bread every day and he
would go and make me a pass and nothing to it. I used to take it to the civic guards . . .*

that is what they called them, the civic guards . . . and he says, "That is all. You may pass!" I used to come on the bus, the Damas Company bus.

Miguel Rodríguez Caraballo

Miguel Rodríguez Caraballo had already completed his military service during the Republic, but was remobilized. At first, things went well for him. He was serving in the Quartermaster Corps in Seville with Leopoldo Rubio: *I was six months in Seville. I used to come here* [to Castilleja] *every Sunday on leave and when I arrived there one night* [in Seville], *Leopoldo was waiting for me at the door of the barracks. And he says to me, "Look, they signed you up there." I was a little surprised because there I was a little . . . you know, in with the colonel, no? But the time came and I had no alternative but to go. In short, they put us on a train heading north, ten or twelve of us.*

And we went from there directly to Llerena, in the province of Badajoz. And there we all worked together to establish a supply depot in an old church that had been abandoned and we set up a warehouse. And from there we used to supply all the troops in that area there. Every day we would go out with a truck full of comestibles to Azuaga and to Granja de Torrehermosa. Every day we took a truck full of food to distribute to the depots right up by the front. After that, they dismantled that depot because it was too far from the front. And from there we went to Cabeza del Buey.

When we arrived in Cabeza del Buey the lieutenant there put us where another depot was to be built and the Red aviation came. Well, of course, the two of us arrived, the lieutenant and I in a car, and he got into the shelter when the aviation arrived. I mean, where the depot was going to be built, there was a shelter. And I did not know where to take cover. There was a doorway and I threw myself down there and there I was. The Reds were looking for the supply depot and when they located it they dropped a bomb and the cans of sardines flew, oh hoo, all the way to the mountains around there.

The same town was later attacked by Republican infantry and Miguel had to stay to destroy the depot if it was taken by the Republicans. *Once there in Cabeza del Buey we were surrounded. The lieutenant told the commander of engineers who came to get the soldiers out . . . "And this one here I want you to leave him with me to guard the depot." And then reinforcements arrived. Everything was prepared to make a run for it. And the lieutenant says to me, "You, do not dare to . . ." I tell him, "Me? The first one to take off running is going to be me." "You stay here to pour gasoline on the depot and burn it so the Reds do not find . . ." I do not know what happened because there was no one left in the town. And there in the city hall . . . it was open . . . I climbed to the top floor because there was a plain in front of the town and I saw the troops doing battle there.*

After another aerial attack, Miguel Rodríguez was transferred again.

Afterwards, the Reds also located the depot there in the train station and I was at a table by a window to make the vouchers and so on. And I went to eat and the aviation came and when I got back, a bomb had fallen right there in the window where I worked. The whole place was, I mean, it was the most horrible thing I have ever seen, the brains of one of the legionnaires whom we knew well were stuck on the wall. And the dead mules there. Oh hoo! So I told the lieutenant, I say, "Get me out of here, because I am going to die here." And he relieved me of duty in the depot. After that, the company was disbanded and they transferred me to Espiel.

Miguel was in Espiel when the war ended. He experienced hunger there and another fright, this time because of a threat from the officers: *There in Espiel we did not go through hell. Oh hoo! We almost died of hunger there. In the mountains. Near Córdoba. I was there for only a short time. And they put up a bakery. And there were two captains who were from up north, and they were not at all good. "Whoever is a baker take one step forward." And we all stepped forward. And, "Be careful because if you do not know how to bake, I am going to shoot every one of you." But there were a few there who were bakers, two of them from Escacena and another from near Granada and they say, "Do not worry, any of you." And the bread turned out better than a mother.*

Antonio Delgado Luque

Antonio Delgado Luque, of the 1940 call-up, was the youngest ex-combatant I interviewed. He was mobilized in 1938 and his unit, which consisted primarily of young men who were the sons of widows, was never in combat. Instead, they were maintaining order in the places already taken. He remembered his life in the army as a relatively pleasant experience, except for the homesickness. *We were in several different places during the war. We started out in Villa del Río. I was there quite a few months because the front line was a little further ahead. We were there until they sent us to the area around Badajoz. And from there we went to the province of Granada. Between the province of Granada and Almería. And later they took us to the area beyond Porcuna, Córdoba. A salient that remained there, and that is where we stayed. Always backing up the combat forces that were there ahead of us. And we were there for a long time. That is all I can say about the war because I was never in combat.*

I think life there, out of ignorance . . . now things are clearer . . . out of the ignorance of youth . . . we were playing and adapting, free of obligations or anything. Now, of course, those who were on the front lines had other concerns and all. They had to march up the roads covered by the aviation. But for us it was a lark. I had a relatively easy time in the war, you know? Except for being apart from what you are familiar with, because of our age, because we were young, it was a lark. And that is how the war was. Considering the strong attachment people from

Castilleja del Campo have for their town, it is significant that the only ex-combatant who mentioned missing home was a young man who had an easy time of it in the war. Those who saw combat gave it little thought because they had a much bigger problem to deal with, the struggle to survive.

The harassment of leftists in Franco's forces

It is impossible to know how many of the men from Castilleja in the war were leftists but, given the economic and ideological composition of the town, it was probably well over half of them. Eight had brothers who had been killed in the repression. For a list of them, see Appendix F. These eight men were risking their lives to defend their brothers' assassins. But all the leftists in Franco's forces were fighting against their own ideals. The bitterness of this conflictive situation was described by Antonio Monge Pérez. *I am going to tell you something in all frankness. I did not cross over to that side because I feared reprisals against my parents and I, of course, no one wants something to happen to their parents, as is only logical. If not, I would have gone to the other side and I would have gone to France so I would never again see the people here who were so evil, because the truth is we never suspected they were capable of killing people like that.*

The harassment these men had experienced in their home town followed them all the way to the front, especially those who were in the Falangist *centuria*. The officers in this unit had known them all their lives. Antonio Monge, for example, was set up by a Falangist corporal from Castilleja who took his rifle while he was on guard duty, costing him the humiliating punishment of having his head shaved. And Manuel Ramírez Mauricio related an experience he had with a sergeant in the centuria. *We who were on the Left had to keep our mouths shut and watch what we did. Because when they saw anything they did not like, they punished us well. One day, they gave one of them a pistol when he became a sergeant, so he would be in command. And he said to me, "Chico." I say, "What?" He says, "Let us go out to some olive trees on the edge of the town and try out this pistol." I, innocently, well we went there and when we were outside the town, since they used to do whatever they wanted to do, well he stopped and he says, "I am going to shoot." And he was shooting at an olive tree. And he says, "Go see if a lot of them have hit the tree." I say, "No. For that, you walk on ahead of me. You know more about it." And, "Why?" I say, "It is not going to turn out that you take another shot at me like you did at the olive tree, eh? And then you leave me here." Because that is what he wanted. That is what he wanted.*

Like another poor thing who was there and quarreled with a warrant officer and he says, "Hey, let us go out and pick some sweet potatoes." To eat, because there was a lot of hunger then. Then when they got out on the road to a gully that was a little lower, he shot him twice and left him there. And he sent three or four Falangists out there to dig a shallow grave and bury him. There were a lot of bad things there. A lot of bad things.

At least two leftists from Castilleja in the centuria transferred into the army to escape this harassment. One was Antonio García Ramírez. His brother Manuel showed me a photograph of him. *They took this brother away in the Falange when he had not even entered his call-up year. There was a competitive exam for sergeants and so he signed up and he went. To get out of the Falange he went into the army. He got to be a sergeant. There he is in the photograph with his stripe.* The other leftist from the town who signed up for the sergeants' exam was Celedonio Escobar Reinoso: *I went to the academy for sergeants to get out of the Falange, because there they were all criminals, assassins. They were always coming around . . . at any given time, the Falangist troops, and saying, "These are all Communists. You came here so they would not kill you."*

It was not that I was a Communist, only that I had a different ideology, you know? I never belonged to any political party. It was just that I was on the side of the oppressed classes because I was one of them. I was on the Málaga front. Then I was on the Córdoba front. Then I took courses to be an officer. And when I left the Falange, I up and requested that they post me to the north so I would not end up around here. I volunteered for the north. They sent me to Zaragoza in the Army of the North. I made the request so I would not end up here in the hands of these people. Of the people from here who knew me, you know? I was a little over a year on that front up there.

Even the leftists who were mobilized into the army suffered harassment. Although they were not persecuted by Falangist officers from their own town, the reports of the Castilleja authorities followed them. Aurelio Monge Romero described the treatment he received during training. *They sent bad reports from here about me when I was in Ronda because of the things that happened with my brothers* [Manuel, assassinated August 27, and Francisco, in prison in Seville] *and my family. That was with the war on already. But we had still not gone to the front. We were in Ronda. We were in training. And they took away my rifle and I used to follow behind the company, me and four or six others, like four or six lambs, to do the training, but without armament or anything.*

I wrote home and my mother spoke up. And they wrote good reports about me. "La Portuguesa" [María da Silva Brito], *who was the manager of the Carrascalejo estate, wrote that I had been working there and that I was . . . and another mayor* [Antoñito el de Aurora] *who used to live across from my house, in short. And then they sent a letter there and I got the letter and I gave it to the sergeant and the sergeant gave it to the lieutenant and then . . . Because they used to beat me every day too, eh?*

There in Ronda. They would start to sing the Falange hymn and all, and they would come up next to me and I would be singing like everyone else. But I was terrified and then another beating with one of those whips they had. They gave me two or three good beatings. For nothing. I was not . . . I was too young to have done anything. And then, well, when they got those letters, they gave me my rifle again.

Aurelio's sister Carmen was in Castilleja when his letter arrived. She described the confrontation between her mother, Aurelia Romero Rodríguez, and the author of the reports that were causing Aurelio so much trouble. *My brother Aurelio was serving* [in the army] *and every day the captain would beat him and he was dragging him down the street of bitterness. He was serving with Carlitos, son of Clemencia* [Carlos Rodríguez Rufino]. *And he told him he was fed up, that they would not leave him alone, and he* [Carlitos, son of Clemencia] *says, "Look, this is a very good boy, and he has a good record there, and he is a cousin of mine, and this man is very good because . . ." "The thing is he has reports from the priest that . . ."*

Well, my Aurelio wrote to my mother, "See if you cannot talk to Don Felipe because they are going to kill me here. I do not do anything and every day they give me a beating." And then my mama went to the priest's house. You will see what kind of balls my mother had. She says, "Felipe." He says, "What is the matter?" Because they were first cousins. The priest and my mother were first cousins. He says, "What is the matter?" She says, "Look, the reports you have given about my son to the army, right now . . ." He says, "Me?" She says, "You! They are dragging my son down the street of bitterness. And has my son done anything? What has my son done? He is a child. Right now you are going to write to the captain that he leave him alone because if he does not leave him alone I am coming back and I am going to kill you." My mother says, "I am going to kill you, I mean kill you." He says, "Oh hoo, Aurelia." She says, "Nothing doing. Nothing doing. Do you think it is fair what they are doing with my son, and he has not done anything, and he is a child? Are you going to do this to me now? That they kill my son on me there in the army because of your bad reports? What bad things do you have to report about my son? And now I am telling you what I am telling you, that you are going to send flying to the captain that he leave him alone, that my son has no bad reports and my son has not done anything. Because otherwise, if you do not do it, I am coming for sure and I am going to kill you." "Oh hoo," he says. "Nothing doing, nothing doing, I mean, I am going to kill you." He sent the reports there. Later my mother says, "Of course, because the poor thing had not done anything." That is what happened.

It may seem improbable that Aurelia Romero Rodríguez would threaten such a powerful figure in the town as the parish priest Don Felipe Rodríguez Sánchez, however feisty she was, and even though they were first cousins. But what this woman had suffered by that time must be taken into consideration. Her daughter Dionisia, recently married and pregnant, became a widow when Antonio Cruz Cruz was assassinated at the end of July 1936. Then, trusting the promises of the authorities, she persuaded her son Manuel to turn himself in. While Manuel was being held in the town hall, she was locked up in the school so she would not cause a commotion. When Manuel was taken to the jail in Sanlúcar la Mayor, Aurelia went to Seville with the group of parents who tried in vain to persuade the civil governor Pedro Parias to save their sons. They were thrown down the staircase by civil guards. Another son of hers, Francisco, was a prisoner in Seville. And now her son Aurelio, who was eighteen years old, was suffering beatings in the army. When she confronted Don Felipe, Aurelia Romero Rodríguez was probably ready to kill anyone or be killed herself so her children would be left in peace. I am married to one of Aurelia's great-granddaughters. My wife remembers her great-grandmother seated in the doorway that looked out on the corral behind her house. She remembers her always dressed in black and with sunken eyes. She did not have eyelashes and the family story was that she had lost them from having cried so much.

The reports from the Castilleja authorities followed local soldiers to all the frontlines of the war. Celedonio Escobar Reinoso had taken courses to become a sergeant and then asked to be transferred to the north to get as far away as possible from those in Castilleja who knew him. The influence of Castilleja's priest, Don Felipe, even reached Celedonio there, although with little effect because, apparently, the commander of Celedonio's company understood how the authorities in small towns operated. *Once I had words with another sergeant who was there in my company with me. And he said to me one day, he says, "You are a Communist." I say, "Look, I prefer being a Communist and not a friar like you." The corporal was there . . . it happened in the company office, and the corporal said to me, he says, "Do you know why that one said you were a Communist? Because when you arrived here, you had a denunciation from your town as a Communist. No, for being anti-religious."*

Because there were fiestas here they call "El Niño de las Espinas" [The Child of the Thorns]. *They celebrate them in May. And I was home on leave and instead of going to the fiestas I up and went to Seville. That is why the priest stuck me with another denunciation. He had already stuck me with two denunciations and now he stuck me with another. Then when I got back there, that was when he* [the corporal] *says to me, he says, "I asked the commander about the denunciation." The commander says to him, "There is a denunciation against Sergeant Escobar. It says he is anti-religious." He says, "See, the small towns still have not had their fill of injustice." Of course he grabbed it and tore it up. That is what the corporal told me in the office.*

Notes

1 José Manuel Martínez Bande, *La campaña de Andalucía*, 173–7.
2 Ibid., 184.

Ten

In the Town during the War

Changes in the town

It was perhaps the men serving in the war who could best perceive the changes in Castilleja del Campo. When they would return home on leave, the town of their childhood memories no longer existed. Another town, unrecognizably tragic, had taken its place. Manuel García Ramírez, a leftist serving in the rearguard, found a refuge in the army, cooking for officers who treated him well. They would allow him to go home when there were offensives because then they ate cold rations and did not need his services. He returned to Castilleja frequently and, visit after visit, he saw the same consequences of the repression. *Mourning and weeping, that is all there was.*

Miguel Rodríguez Caraballo, a right-winger serving in the Quartermaster Corps, also returned frequently to Castilleja. *Imagine the things that happened here, such a small town, where things like that should not have happened. But there is no getting around it because no one had to be killed. And they killed quite a few here and that is how it was. Sometimes because of hatreds, other times . . . almost all of them because of hatreds. That . . . and politics. Some were on one side, others on the other side, and because of that . . . but, I mean, in such a small town all of that did not have to happen. Because we are almost all family here and, in short, things happen. In other towns yes. In Manzanilla itself the others did a lot of things, no? But here they had done nothing. Here they did not burn the church or do anything. Nothing, nothing, nothing, nothing, nothing. Nor did they bother anyone.* Miguel was a peaceful man, proud of not having killed anyone in the war and horrified by the repression. *I used to come here* [on leave]. *There was a truck that used to bring them from around there to kill them. And one night there was a man who was here who has died, "El Chato"* [Severo Monge Fernández], *and he said to me, "Come on, it is about to arrive." I say, "Me? I would not watch an execution for anything in the world."*

Antonio Delgado Luque, another right-winger, did not go into the army until October 1938. Until his call-up was mobilized, he continued working in Castilleja. On one occasion a young man he was working with made a discovery that reflects the atmosphere of terror the repression had created in the town. *I remember we were working and there on the way to Carrión as you leave the town, to the right, that ridge there, it was all olive trees. And then we were tilling the soil in the olive grove. And a boy said, "Oh, oh, look what is here." The tree had a hollow in it and it was all full of newspapers like those you mentioned, "Mundo Obrero"* [Workers' World, a Communist newspaper], *and of portraits of Azaña and of . . . and of . . . yes, of Azaña and of . . . who else? Yes, others . . . Largo Caballero, Largo Caballero.*

Someone must have had them in their house and from fear, well, he grabbed them, rolled them up, and put them in the hollow of an olive tree in the countryside. That was already with the war on, you understand? We were there working, before going to the front. Of course they got rid of the pictures they had, those pictures of Alcalá-Zamora and the other one and the other and, of course, out of fear of a search, well they got rid of them. I would probably have burned them but they went and put them in the hollow of a tree.

The fear of expressing political opinions contrary to those of the new regime extended to the leftist combatants who were risking their lives fighting in Franco's forces. In a civil war in which the enemy could be the next door neighbor or a first cousin, the streets of one's home town could seem as dangerous as the trenches. Manuel Ramírez Mauricio had three leaves during the war. *The first time, I came after nine months. Later I came after sixteen months. And I came the last time when the war was already almost over. There were still forces there on the highway in case those who were in the mountains came down, the fugitives, you know? On the run. Well, they were up there so they would not be killed. And there were forces out there. When I got there where the forces were, well, I reported to the forces. And there was an uncle of mine there on guard and I was talking with them, everyone happy to see me, and me too.*

But, of course, the next morning, when I got up in the morning, it was not the same as when I had come other times, you know? I was gripped by panic. And talking with this one in the casino, talking with the other one, or the two of us together in my house, and he was saying, "Well, be careful because with this one, or with that one, do not talk too much." And we would go to the casino, and there with them drinking and all, chatting with them, you know? But without saying anything. They would ask me something, and I would answer them what I thought best, eh? For my own good.

For some on the Right, the changes in the town had their positive side. Since he was serving in Seville in the Quartermaster Corps, Leopoldo Rubio used to come back to Castilleja almost every weekend. *The town changed a lot. In politics and things. Then the people were more humble than they were before. After the Movement, then there was more restraint.*

Concern for family members at the front

The combatants' letters were censored and their families seldom knew where their loved ones were. This was especially the case for the families of the two men from Castilleja who had crossed over to the other zone, Pedro Donaire Leal and Juan Antonio Luque Romero "Antonio Canitas." Pedro's wife Rosario and his children, Matilde and Eugenio, heard nothing from him for years. The same is true for Antonio's fiancée, María Luque Reinoso, according to María's sister Marina. *And for three years my sister knew nothing, nothing, nothing about him.*

Families who had contact with the combatants had good reason to be alarmed. When Fernando Luque Reinoso came home on leave, his sisters Herminia and Marina were horrified by what he had seen. Herminia: *Each of them told what they had been through, that they used to eat right next to the dead and . . . my own brother . . . when they had no other choice and a cadaver was decomposing right there, they had to eat right next to it. The war was tremendous.* Marina recognized Castilleja's good fortune in being far from the front. *Here we did not experience the war. There near Córdoba is as close as the war came. Since they took Seville right away and all this area around here, it never came here. We did not get to experience the war except for the assassinations, except for the hatreds in the town. Nothing more than that. And it never should have happened. But other than that we did not experience the war at all.*

Anxiety for loved ones at war took a cruel turn in the case of Isidora Mistral's family. *This brother of mine went off and served as a courier, imagine. The ones who carried the dispatches from one place to another. And we were always with our heart in a fist with him out there, the poor thing. And now when the war is coming to an end, he goes and sleeps in a shanty. Water below him and water above. He took on so much dampness above and below, well, he came down with that chest thing. Tuberculosis. One of his lungs was undone. And then the other, well, it was irritated, because it was already infected below. He came back and they hospitalized him in Ronda, and he died in Ronda. And there he is, and I do not where he is buried or where he is not buried. In Ronda. My mother went there. She was by his side until he died. In every house and everywhere, it is enough to turn the world upside down like I say . . . what there is in every house is a story and a big one. And enough for a book is what there is in every family.*

Militarization of civilian life

A regime with a Fascist ideology led by generals who had come to power by declaring a state of war could not fail to influence life in the territory it controlled. Isidora Mistral described how young boys prepared, physically and psychologically, for the struggle and sacrifice that would save the fatherland. *They used to give the boys here military training. One of those instructors used to come from Carrión to train the younger boys, those "balillas"* [little bullets, a sort of Fascist scout organization]. *They were there with their uniforms on. And they had them run and jump and do those kinds of things. No weapons. But, I mean, physical training without weapons. Every Sunday after mass when they did not have school.*

Girls too could feel they were part of the war effort, although always in an auxiliary role. Isidora was a member of the Feminine Section, the Fascist women's organization. *At least twenty of us were there in that. In front of the church there is a house with a large room that has a fireplace. And we would go there to sew clothes for the "balilla" boys. And to embroider the little shields of the Falange. Some made the pants, others made the shirts, others sewed the collars, each one of us sewing something. For the boys who did not have the funds to buy the things and all. They used to bring the materials from the Falange in Seville and we would put them together.*

Collecting funds for the war became a social occasion. Herminia Luque Reinoso got to know her first boy friend, Gustavo Luque Romero, while collecting money during the "one dish day" and the "day without dessert." She explained what these were. *One day every week there was the "one dish day," when you only ate one dish at the main meal and another day was the "day without dessert." They were to save money for the war. And those days we used to go around and the people would give us money. I used to go with the other girls. Four or five of us would go out collecting that. Then there was a boy who would go with us and we became boy friend and girl friend.* The last year of the war, Gustavo went into the navy.

This social life built around the war effort seemed like a bad joke to family members of men who had been shot. They were not very enthusiastic about contributing and, since they were poor, they barely had the means. When I asked Carmen Monge Romero about the "one dish day" and "the day without dessert," she burst out laughing. *The day without dessert? For us, the day without dessert was a daily event.*

Work

When he spoke of the changes he observed in the town when on leave, Aurelio Monge Romero, like other ex-combatants, attributed those changes to the repression. But he had another explanation as well, which introduced a different topic. *The town was very sad because a lot of bad things had happened.*

And here there was nothing but four old men and the women. The young men were all gone. All of them. The women were working in the fields and the men who had not gone to war because they were men who were already forty years old. Those were the men who did the things that had to be done.

Many women worked in the fields because their husbands' pay in Franco's forces was insufficient to support their families. Carmen Muñoz Caraballo, the widow of Manuel Escobar Moreno, and others worked to support themselves and their children because their husbands had been shot. One would suppose that the demand for food to supply the army and the labor shortage caused by the massive mobilization of young men would have created a favorable labor market for the women and older men who worked the fields. But without a union or labor laws, the relationship between workers and landowners reverted to what it had been before the Republic. The landowners set the value of a day's work and dictated working conditions.

According to Carmen Monge Romero, on one occasion the working conditions of a job offered to her husband and others by the Falangist mayor José Cuevas Reinoso were dangerous in the extreme. *People in the town went during the war to ask him [Pepe Cuevas] for work because, of course, they had to eat and feed their children and here there was no work. And he told them there was a job there in Porcuna near the front. My husband went there and at least ten or twelve from here went. They had to go. And then when they had finished in the place where they were working, they said to the owner, they say, "Look . . . ," because he wanted to take them even closer to the front, because where they had been harvesting, the bullets would go . . . uuuyy . . . right over their heads and further on where they had to harvest there were even more bullets. And they told the man, "Look, we can stay here no longer because the families are earning nothing and the truth is . . ." He says, "Alright then, I am going to give you all safe-conduct passes and you can leave." In the end, he was a good man, no? Because otherwise, he would have taken them closer to the bullets and they would have killed them.*

And when they came back they barely had enough money for the trip. Because they had to feed themselves because there they did not give them anything. And they were frightened because they say, "Any night one of those attacks could come and overrun us and kill us." Because the houses were empty. Everyone in Porcuna had left. They had all fled elsewhere. And that man [José Cuevas Reinoso], well he told them . . . that man did not have children or anything . . . that man had no children . . . well he told them that is where they had to go if they wanted to work.

When Carmen Monge mentioned that José Cuevas Reinoso did not have children, it was not to explain his lack of compassion for the mothers and fathers he had sent to work near the front. She went on to relate a conversation between José Cuevas and one of his maids. Apparently, Pepe Cuevas did not have children due to health problems. As repeated by Carmen Monge, the conversation is an example of something quite common in the testimonies of leftists: the attribution of illnesses and other tribulations suffered by right-wingers to divine justice, an understandable defense mechanism for people who were never able to seek human justice. *And one day he said to a woman who was serving there, he says, "I do not know what I have done to be paying the way I am paying." La Chichinera* [María Díaz Sierra] *says, "Well you must have done something when you are paying for it." I say* [to La Chichinera], *"You tell him to tell it to Carmen, daughter of Aurelia. He will find out what he has done. Let him ask me." He was my age. That rabble.*

And I say [to La Chichinera] *that . . . "he sent my husband out so they would kill him there near the bullets. Ask the mothers and fathers he sent." That is where José María* [Tebas Escobar], *son of Elías went, "Manuel el Macando"* [Manuel Gómez Álvarez] *went, and that one, what was his name? My brother-in-law Felipe* [Muñoz Caraballo]. *A lot of people went. Lupe* [Guadalupe Monge Rodríguez] *went with Lupita* [Guadalupe Romero Monge]. *And there was no milk there . . . because she was feeding her with cow's milk and she had to come back because the poor creature was going to die there. She had to come back but Cristobalina* [Romero Monge] *stayed there and . . . who was the other woman? . . . Rosario, you know? That was how it was. They went through a lot, a lot. And that is only the good part that can be said about what the people in this town did. It is.*

There was another dangerous job for the older men who remained in the town, that of guarding the fields at night in case fugitives came down from the mountains. One of these men was Leovigildo Monge Pérez, Sr. One night he was confronted by a large band of fugitives, but was saved because one of them was a friend of his. His son Antonio described the incident because he wanted to tell me how this friend of his father had escaped being assassinated. The anecdote is not directly related to Castilleja del Campo. I include it for comic relief. *They sent my father out there at least four kilometers from here to see if any fugitives came down from the mountains. And staying one night in a house they called the plank house they came and said to him, "Hey, what are you doing here?" "Well, look, I am going to tell you. Because I am a leftist they have sent me here so I can tell them if you come here or not, but I am not going to speak of you if you leave me . . ."*

Then, one of them spoke up and it was a curious and laughable case. A man from Sanlúcar who had worked here at an estate with my father before the war and they got to know each other. Then that man said to the companions who came with him from the mountains . . . there were twenty some or thirty or forty . . . I have no idea how many there were . . . he said to them, he says, "This man I guarantee that he is on the Left because he has worked with me and we have talked and he is on the Left. Here there is no problem."

And that same man who said that, they were going to kill him in Sanlúcar la Mayor, and they took him out there to an olive grove to kill him. But they had a priest there so some of the prisoners could confess before being killed. And then the man went off a little ways in the olive trees . . . well since it was night . . . and he got down on his knees in front of the priest and he began to confess. In short, he was telling the priest all his . . . and it suddenly occurred to the man . . . he was a big strong man . . . he put his head between the priest's legs and stood up and held him hanging down his back and took off running and the priest, "For God's sake! Do not shoot! Do not shoot! For God's sake," and he up and dropped him and he kept running and he got away. Afterwards we found out it was him. Afterwards we found out that it was "El Silavario" as he was called. They told us here that it was he who had done that.

Economic repression

Leocadio Ramírez Rufino

Leocadio Ramírez Rufino's family was devastated by the repression. His brother José, the Republican mayor, his son José María Ramírez Mauricio, and his second cousin Lutgardo García Ramírez were assassinated on August 27, 1936. Another brother, Manuel, was assassinated after the taking of Aznalcóllar. And his nephew Braulio Ramírez García was under arrest and would be shot on December 28, 1936. Leocadio himself suffered a concerted campaign to break him physically and economically.

Leocadio's son Manuel Ramírez Mauricio told part of the story. *When they took over, they did whatever they felt like on the day they chose, which was to take the personnel out and kill them. From my family, between my brother, uncles, first cousins and second, eh?, there were about nine. The rest were all from outside the family. And my father, after that, they took him to the palace, the priest and the priest's brother* [Felipe and José Rodríguez Sánchez], *along with two members of the Civil Guard who were here in the garrison. And there they beat him well. It was a rare day they did not beat him. They would have him there three-quarters of an hour. And after that they would let him come back home. And the next day, or two or three days later, they would come calling on him again and they would give him another thrashing.* Surprisingly, Leocadio was later hired on a regular basis at the palace estate. *My father was dying of sorrow. He had to go there and work for the same estate where they used to beat him almost every day. And there at the end of the week he would go to collect his pay and the same one who had beaten him* [José Rodríguez Sánchez, the countess's new administrator] *was giving him his pay. And they had already killed his son and his brothers.*

What was the motive for giving him a job where they had previously beaten him? Feliciano Monge Pérez offered one explanation. *Leocadio, after they killed his son, a man who was worth a lot . . . José María was worth a lot . . . they took Leocadio and gave him a beating that almost killed him. And then the criminals, as the saying goes, to smooth the terrain a little, on the countess's estate they gave him a day's work before anyone else, so he would keep his mouth shut. He was not going to let it go by, but what could he do? A man who was ruptured, because he always had his guts hanging out, the poor thing. And there was no one who would give him a day's work and then they took him in there because of that, to shut his mouth. But man, you are going to shut my mouth having killed my son as well? Such a good boy. And my brother, and the other, and the other, I mean, really.*

Feliciano's explanation may be correct as far as it goes, but there is more to the story, as revealed in the minutes of a meeting of the administrative commission on October 24, 1936. Leocadio Ramírez Rufino had served as councilman when his brother José was mayor, from April 1931 until October 1934, and again during the Popular Front. In 1934, the town council had rescinded the "contracts for regulation of the consumption of meats and for regulation of weights and measures" and had failed to collect the "taxes on street vendors and peddlers." These were fees for the right to sell food and other items in open air markets or to peddle goods in the streets. It was an infraction, but could in no way be considered a theft that personally benefited the members of the 1934 town council. Their intention was to make it easier for those in the town and surrounding area to sell what they had grown in the parcels they had acquired through agrarian reform.

Nevertheless, a hearing was held on October 17, 1936, to investigate the matter. The Republican mayor, José Ramírez Rufino, and the councilmen Miguel Luque Romero, Miguel Monge Pérez, and Leocadio Ramírez Rufino were each fined four hundred and sixteen pesetas and ninety-four centimos for "damages caused to the Municipal Government" by their infraction from two years earlier. José Ramírez's fine was paid by his son Francisco Ramírez Rodríguez since José had already been shot. Miguel Luque Romero and Miguel Monge Pérez paid their own fines. At a time when a day's labor was worth little more than five pesetas, these fines were equivalent to more than eighty day's work. To pay them, these men probably lost most everything they had and likely went into debt to some creditor.[1]

In the case of Leocadio Ramírez, there was no way to pay the fine, no matter how many times he was beaten in the palace of the countess's estate. On October 22, he signed a letter redacted by the municipal secretary, Hilario Luque Ramírez. In it, Leocadio accepts "indirect responsibility for damages caused to this Municipal Body" and "implores the Municipal Government deign to concede him a moratorium to pay off the amount

owed" since "the exact fulfillment of this obligation is materially impossible for him due to lacking at the moment the necessary money and not
having found any person to facilitate the loan required for these ends."
Leocadio also agreed to pay half the fine on July 31, 1937, and the remainder
on December 31, 1937, with 5 percent interest.[2] For the complete texts of
the relevant items in the October 24 minutes, see Appendix G.

The administrative commission conceded the moratorium, noting that
the petitioner "lacks not only sufficient money to fulfill his obligation but
even the most indispensable to defray the sustenance of his numerous
family." Leocadio Ramírez Rufino, a day laborer who could not find work
because of his hernia, would never have been able to meet this obligation
without some kind of work. Employing him at the countess's palace was
not only *so he would keep his mouth shut*, as Feliciano Monge Pérez said, it was
also good business for the new authorities in the Castilleja del Campo
municipal government. It enabled them to collect the fine Leocadio owed.

José Pérez Rodríguez, Manuel Monge Romero, and José Ramírez Rufino

Imposing egregious fines for minor infractions was one modality of
economic persecution. Another was the confiscation of properties owned by
the adversaries of the New Order. There is evidence of such confiscations in
Castilleja del Campo. On November 19, 1938, Mayor Antonio Rodríguez
Fernández wrote a letter to Governor Pedro Gamero del Castillo. It is the
reply to a letter dated November 12. There is no copy of the governor's
letter, but Mayor Rodríguez's reply gives a good idea of its contents. The
war was drawing to a close and Spain was about to suffer severe food shortages. The governor, worried, was requesting information concerning the
harvesting of olives from confiscated properties in each of the province's
municipal districts.

Mayor Rodríguez answered that he knew of confiscation procedures
"initiated against properties belonging to the residents, José Perez
Rodriguez, Manuel Monge Romero and Jose Ramirez Rufino," but was
"unaware of the result of such procedures." Given this uncertainty, the
mayor then asked the governor to inform him how to proceed, and made it
known "that two of the aforementioned individuals do not have olive groves
and that José Ramirez, has one or two small parcels, although it is to be
supposed that their fruits be of scarce value if they exist given the scarcity
of the olive harvest in this municipal district during the present year."[3]

It is strange that, in November 1938, Mayor Rodríguez refers to olive
groves that José Ramírez Rufino "has," or that Manuel Monge Romero and

José Pérez Rodríguez "do not have," using verbs in the present tense, when these men had been assassinated more than two years before. The mayor's uncertainty regarding the outcome of the confiscation is understandable. The confiscation procedures would have been initiated when the owners were assassinated in 1936, during the term of the previous mayor, José Cuevas Reinoso. In any event, the families of the parcels' owners would have been prohibited from cultivating their land as long as the procedures were under way.[4]

The reference to the scarce value of the fruits of the confiscated parcels suggests that, during more than two years, they were neither rented out nor cultivated by the municipal government. These men's families were denied the use of their land with no benefit to anyone. According to what I have heard, a parcel where José Ramírez Rufino had planted a vineyard was eventually returned to his family. They had to pull up the dead vines and sell them for charcoal in order to pay the land taxes that had accumulated during the time they were forbidden to care for them.

Widows and orphans

The repression left twenty-six more economic victims. Twelve widows and fourteen dependent children were left to fend for themselves. For the sources of this information, and the names and ages of the widows and orphans, see Appendix H. Two men with dependents, Manuel Monge Romero and José Pérez Rodríguez, owned small rural properties. Their surviving family members, like the other widows and orphans, were left in abject poverty because their properties were confiscated. I was able to interview four of the orphans, José and Antonio León García, Otilia Escobar Muñoz, and Sara Tebas Rodríguez. I wanted to know how their mothers supported themselves and their children. Some had to move to the houses of relatives. Concepción García Baquero, the widow of the schoolteacher Joaquín León Trejo, had a brother-in-law in Seville, José. He was under arrest and would be shot on October 17, 1936. José's wife, Rosario Fernández Gordillo, and eight of their nine children continued living at the family home in the Heliópolis neighborhood, Amazonas Street, No. 13. Concepción and her children went to live with them, according to her son José. *We were staying at my uncle Don José's house in Heliópolis. They were eight, with my brother, nine, and with me, ten. That was when they killed my uncle.* Although José León Trejo's family was living through its own tragedy, they showed great generosity, according to Antonio. *Rosario, well, she called my mother and she said, she says, "Look, you come live with us. What belongs to my children, let it also belong to yours."*

Some of the widows went to work in the fields. One of these was Carmen Muñoz Caraballo, according to her daughter, Otilia Escobar Muñoz. They earned half of the five pesetas and twenty-five centimos a day that men earned. There were orphans who served in the houses of wealthy families, sometimes the same families responsible for the killings, according to Sara Tebas Rodríguez. *And my sister, the poor thing, as soon as she could, when she was a little older, went to serve in the house of . . . of one of the right-wing leaders, Pepe Cuevas* [José Cuevas Reinoso]. *That is where she went. She must have been twelve years old or thereabouts. She went to serve, earning very little, but she used to eat there and she stayed there to sleep. Because Enriqueta* [Pozo de la Cueva, sister of Eugenio Pozo de la Cueva and wife of José Cuevas Reinoso] *was a very good woman, very kind. And Pepe treated my sister very well and was very kind to her but we knew he was one of those.*

Other orphans also worked. At fourteen years of age, Antonio León García was given a very dangerous job while he was living in Seville with his Aunt Rosario. *When my father died, we had to be working. I was working making hand grenades. Imagine, making grenades to kill the Reds. That is where they put me. And we were already working at least two hours when the sun came up. Imagine. And by the time I got home, well, it would be eleven or twelve at night. You had to work on Sundays too. And if you missed work without permission the Civil Guard was there at your house. Organized like in the military, everything militarized. I left because I became afraid there, and a short while after leaving there it blew up and buried everyone who was working there. They were making bombs out of cans to use as hand grenades. They were like tomato cans. Women and old men . . . because there were no men of any other age . . . filled them with gunpowder and then the boys put in the fulminating powder and detonators and all those things.*

Antonio's mother, Concepción García Baquero, was a schoolteacher like her husband, although she had not practiced her profession while in Castilleja. After her husband was shot, she went with her five year old daughter Carmen to a village in the province of Córdoba, leaving her sons José and Antonio with her husband's sister-in-law Rosario in Seville. José León García told part of the story. *She went to work as a teacher, because she already had her degree, to a village in a township in Córdoba called La Carlota with my little sister. And from there she could hear the Córdoba front, boom, boom, boom, the artillery.*

Antonio León García and his daughter Concepción León López added more details. Antonio: *The village where they sent her was called El Arrecife and it was nothing more than four houses scattered about. There was no electricity. At night, she was alone with my little sister because we stayed with my aunt.* Concepción: *She used to tell how she had to ride a burro to get to the village and how she was very frightened there because the people did not want to rent her the house because they knew who she was, and she used to talk about that with such anguish and always crying when she remembered that with her little girl.* According to José León García, his mother could not put up with life in El Arrecife for very long. *Months. Because my cousins saw that it was little money for . . . and my aunt said, "No, come here to my house because for a plate of food you do not need to . . ."*

The orphan girls I interviewed, Otilia Escobar Muñoz and Sara Tebas Rodríguez, had been too young to remember their fathers. Besides being economic victims, their fathers' assassinations had caused them profound psychological suffering. Along with the extra cassettes and replacement batteries for the tape recorder, it was necessary to arrive at these interviews equipped with packets of Kleenex, because the interviews were punctuated by attacks of crying. The orphans who were infants during the repression were more deeply scarred than those who had been adolescents. They had not known the climate of freedom and hope during the Republic. As children they were subjected to the propaganda of a regime that justified its origins in a military uprising and civil war portrayed as necessary to save Spain by purging it of the traitorous and evil elements of the anti-Spain. How could orphans of that age defend themselves from the slander directed at fathers they had never been able to know?

They could not even talk to their mothers about the fathers they could not remember. According to Sara, *we used to ask my mother sometimes and she would not tell us anything. She was always full of fear. Terrible fear.* Otilia's mother would not talk about her husband either. *My mother never spoke about my father ever. Ever. And she had gone through so much. So much, so much, so much. But never ever. She never spoke about my father.* The anguish Otilia felt when she thought of the father she had never known led her to do something she would later regret. *When they killed my father I was only thirteen months old. The only thing I had was my father's letters and I tore them up. It must be about eight years ago. Because each time one read them, one became completely overwhelmed. I never should have done it. Letters that he wrote when he was in jail in Sanlúcar.*

At various moments during the interview, Sara felt the need to cite some positive opinion she had heard about her father so that I would know he had not been as bad as the Franco regime's propaganda had said. *In short, what can I say? Everybody told me very good things about my father. Because I do not even remember what he was like. I always say, "I feel very proud of my father." And I say that my father could not have been so bad when he had my sister, a nun, such a good woman, and my brother who was so good. And I have never been so bad either. What can I say?*

The interviews with Sara and Otilia were the most difficult of all. At one point, I asked Otilia if she wanted to stop and continue the interview another day. Then I realized that I was the one who wanted to stop. Otilia said no, that these things had to be said. Later I was collecting photographs of the men who had been shot. Someone said that Luisa Fernández Rodríguez, who was five years old when her father was assassinated, was still alive in Carrión de los Céspedes and perhaps had photographs of her father. My wife and I went to her house. When we explained who we were and what we wanted she was obviously very frightened. Fortunately, her son arrived just then and was able to calm her down. He liked the idea of his grandfather's photograph appearing in a book and I was able to make a copy of a very good photograph of José Fernández Luque. Of course it never even crossed my mind to ask Luisa for an interview.

The younger widows were also vulnerable to another type of harassment. It is such a delicate topic in a small town where everyone is family that only three of those I interviewed mentioned it, all of them men, Manuel Ramírez Mauricio, Feliciano Monge Pérez, and Narciso Luque Romero. Narciso expressed it with the most tact. *Like the criminals that they were . . . that is the word that . . . criminals, the ones from here, when they killed the poor things, a short while later they began to see if they could abuse the wives of those who had been killed.* Two of these men, Feliciano and Narciso, mentioned a specific case of a widow, not the same widow, who became pregnant after being coerced by Falangists.

Notes

1 Minutes, 24 October 1936, Item 1, Castilleja del Campo Municipal Archive.
2 Ibid, Item 5.
3 Correspondence, Castilleja del Campo Municipal Archive.
4 Francisco Espinosa Maestre, *La Guerra Civil en Huelva*, 468.

Eleven

From Civil War to Uncivil Peace

1937 and 1938

Before the battle of Madrid, Franco employed the strategy he had learned in the Moroccan War: domination of the population through superior firepower and terror. Then his high command adopted the theories of the Center for Superior Military Studies in Paris, based on the experience of the First World War: bloody frontal attacks and the stubborn defense of conquered territory. The only experiment with a motorized campaign of blitzkrieg was carried out by Italian troops in Guadalajara between March 8 and 21, 1937. It was a disaster, due to poor execution and bad weather. This new concept of mechanized warfare, which the Germans would employ during the Second World War, was forever discredited among Franco's high command. In 1937, the Nationalist generals turned to attacks on secondary fronts like Málaga, in the winter, and the northern sector, between March 31 and October 21. After taking the Basque country, Cantabria, and Asturias, Franco waged a war of attrition aimed at destroying the enemy army.

Meanwhile, in the Republican zone, the influence of Soviet military advisors increased after the battle of Madrid. They too followed the French military theories and were as conservative as Franco. By April 1937, the Republic had forces capable of offensive actions in the central sector around Madrid, and in Huesca, Aragón. The intent was to draw Franco's troops away from their offensive in the Basque country. In the summer, Republican offensives intensified in these sectors with the battles of Brunete, in July, and Belchite, from August 24 to September 6.

In 1938, the Republican strategy was marked by two great offensives: the taking of Teruel on January 7, and the crossing of the Ebro River on July 25. Franco's reaction to both offensives was to amass his best troops and crush the Republican army with frontal attacks. He retook Teruel on February 22 and continued pressuring the entire Aragon front, taking Lérida on April 3, and reaching Vinaroz on the Mediterranean on April 14. This divided the Republican zone in two. From there the Nationalists turned south toward Valencia, but met fierce resistance that halted their advance. The Republican offensive across the Ebro River on July 25 was an attempt to save Valencia and reconnect the two Republican territories. Again Franco amassed his best forces and, until November 16, the two armies engaged in bloody frontal attacks during almost four months. By the end of the battle of the Ebro, the Republican army was depleted of materiel and personnel, and the Nationalists prepared to occupy Catalonia.

1939

January and February

The Catalonian campaign began on December 23, 1938. The Republican army, outgunned and outmanned, resisted heroically, but on January 22, 1939, the Republican government was forced to flee Barcelona where it had been located since October 31, 1937. The roads toward the French border filled with refugees. Four days later, Barcelona was occupied with no resistance at all. On February 4, the Nationalists occupied Gerona and by February 10, they controlled the entire border with France. At first, the French government had refused to allow refugees to cross into France, but finally opened the border on the night of January 27. The following day fifteen thousand Spaniard crossed into France. One of these was the Castilleja native, Captain Pedro Donaire Leal. He crossed the Pyrenees on foot with other Republican officers through the Coll d'Ares at dawn on January 28.[1]

Between January 27 and February 10 almost half a million Spanish refugees crossed into France. They were interned in concentration camps, open spaces exposed to the elements, surrounded by barbed wire, and guarded by Senegalese soldiers. The refugees would suffer these conditions for a long time, but Captain Pedro Donaire Leal did not even have the option of remaining in France. A few days after his internment, a French officer arrived and announced that the French government could not harbor Spanish officers while the war was still going on. They would be returned to Spain and could choose to be repatriated to Burgos in the Nationalist zone or Valencia in the Republican zone. Captain Donaire Leal chose Burgos because it afforded a greater chance to see his parents, his wife Rosario, and his children Matilde and Eugenio.[2]

His decision was fairly realistic. To go to Valencia would have been even worse than the nightmare he went through in Catalonia. He would have been among masses of refugees with no Pyrenees to cross. Furthermore, Spanish representatives of the Franco government, accompanied by French officers, visited the camps inviting refugees to return to Spain and assuring them they would not suffer persecution. Pedro Donaire was among approximately seventy thousand men who crossed the south of France and entered Nationalist Spain through Hendaye and Irún in February and March. He and his companions were well received and treated to coffee and pastry by girls from the Falangist Feminine Section. It was a ploy to lure other refugees into the same trap. Those repatriated were given a safe conduct pass, a military passport, and even an "emergency payment" for their journey to Burgos. There they would begin an odyssey through Franco's penal system which, for many, would end in execution by firing squad. Pedro Donaire survived this ordeal. Twenty years later he would be billed for the "emergency payment."[3]

During the month of February, the military history of the civil war ended. In its place there is a sad history of vain attempts on the part of several Republicans to negotiate a peace without reprisals. On February 1, the head of the Republican government, Juan Negrín, proposed three conditions for surrender: a guarantee of the integrity of Spanish territory to avoid Italian control of the Balearic Islands or German control of Spanish mines, a guarantee that all Spaniards would choose the future form of the country's government, and a guarantee that there would be no reprisals against Republican soldiers and officers. He secretly told the French and English diplomats who were acting as intermediaries that he would only insist on the third condition.

On February 9, Franco promulgated a Law of Political Responsibilities that applied to all who were guilty of subversive activities between October 1934 and July 1936, and those who, during the war, had opposed the Nationalist Movement by force or passivity.[4] It was, in effect, a declaration that he would only accept an unconditional surrender without guarantees for anyone. Having failed to negotiate an amnesty, Negrín, backed by the Communists, chose to continue resisting in the hope that a European war would break out and save the Republic. Meanwhile, parallel negotiations were secretly going on between war-weary Republican officers, led by Colonel Segismundo Casado López, and their military counterparts in the Nationalist zone. The "Casadistas" hoped that military comradeship would allow surrender without reprisals.

March

On March 4, Republican troops whose officers supported Colonel Casado took over the naval radio station in Cartagena, on the Mediterranean coast, and called for reinforcements from the Nationalists. Franco sent three regiments by sea. Before the ships arrived, the uprising was put down by Republican troops under the command of Communist officers. The expedition was ordered back, but two ships that did not have radios did not receive the order. One of them, Castillo de Olite, was blown up as it entered the port. One thousand two hundred and twenty-three men died and about seven hundred men were captured, including the commander, Fernando López Canti, who swam to shore.[5]

The aborted uprising of "Casadistas" nearly cost the Castilleja native Conrado Rufino Romero his life. *I was in a maritime expedition that was going to Cartagena. We embarked in Málaga on merchant ships. And it was said that Cartagena had surrendered. I had the good fortune to belong to the third regiment of the 122nd Division. The first regiment went ahead of us and they sank a few ships there, because Cartagena had not surrendered. What they did in Cartagena was resist. And of course, when the other regiments realized what was happening, the second and third . . . I was in the third . . . well they turned the ships around and we disembarked in Málaga again.*

On March 5, Colonel Casado declared a military coup in Madrid against the Negrín government and formed a National Defense Council with representatives of all the components of the Popular Front except the Communists. Among the members of the council were the anarchist commander Cipriano Mera and the moderate Socialist Julián Besteiro Fernández. The next day, Negrín left Spain forever and there was a week of combat in Madrid between Communist divisions and those aligned with Casado, a civil war within the civil war with more than two hundred dead and five hundred wounded. By March 13, Communist resistance to the Casado junta was crushed.

A parody of negotiations began. The only thing the National Defense Council could offer Franco was the lives that would have been lost in a struggle to the death. Franco was not about to tie his hands with guarantees against reprisals in exchange for something that mattered little to him. In addition to holding all the cards, Franco knew that, with or without an agreement, the National Defense Council would cease to exist as soon as it surrendered. On March 14, the Nationalist government in Burgos announced the creation of Tribunals for Political Responsibilities. Their purpose would be to implement the previous month's decree that applied to those guilty of subversive activities since October 1934, a clear indication of what awaited the vanquished.

On March 19, Franco informed the National Defense Council that he was only interested in an unconditional surrender and that Casado should send one or two officers of low rank. The council sent two lieutenant colonels to Burgos on March 23. Franco's representatives promised the evacuation of all those who wanted to leave the country, but they refused to sign any document. They also demanded that all Republican aircraft be handed over on March 25. It was impossible to comply with this demand in the short time allowed, and when the representatives of both sides met again on March 25, the Nationalists broke off negotiations because the deadline had passed. That was the end of the negotiations.

On March 26, Franco's forces began to advance on several points along the front. The same day, Julián Besteiro, moderate Socialist member of Casado's National Defense Council, spoke on the radio, urging soldiers and civilians to go out to greet the Nationalists as brothers in a sign of reconciliation. Between March 28 and 31, all the fronts collapsed. On April 1, Generalissimo Francisco Franco signed his last war dispatch, which could not have been more succinct: "On today's date, with the Red army captured and disarmed, the Nationalist troops have achieved their final military objective. The war has ended."[6] Some of the ex-combatants from Castilleja related their memories of the last days of the war. Conrado Rufino Romero had gone with the maritime expedition to Cartagena in March, but had to return to Málaga. *We were there eleven days, near Málaga, and then they took us back to the Córdoba front. And we were on the Córdoba front until it collapsed. Then they took us to Granada. And the day we arrived in Granada, the bells were ringing because the war was over.*

And I have a clear recollection of what happened there. We stayed in the bullring and it rained on us all night, and the next day they took us out of Granada walking along the highway that goes straight into the Sierra Nevada, and the Republican brigades began to pass by. They came with their armament and our commander told us to leave the highway to them. We were walking along the sides as if we were guarding them. They laid down their armament. And some trucks came that they used to call recovery trucks. And they gathered up the armament and took it away. And they put them there in the bullring until they could examine the behavior of each of them and then, little by little, they would let them go.

Aurelio Monge Romero was on the Madrid front. He remembers the Republican soldiers surrendering before the Nationalists entered the capital. *We were there a year. And we were in combat too. And then the last time we were going to attack, after we had turned in all our baggage and all to attack, that same night the order came down that they were surrendering. And they surrendered. And that, well, you cannot imagine what . . . the trenches burning and throwing grenades and everybody happy. And their forces were crossing over to our side and we went out to receive them.* One of the soldiers who surrendered on the Madrid front was the Castilleja del Campo native Juan Antonio Luque Romero "Antonio Canitas," who had crossed over to the Republican zone in 1937.

Occupation of the Republican zone

Despite having ended his last dispatch with the words, "the war has ended," Franco went on the radio two days later and warned, "Spaniards, on guard! Spain continues to be at war with all its internal and external enemies."[7] This warning had multiple implications: the demobilization of Franco's army was going to be extremely slow, there was still a large area of Spain to occupy, and those who had fought for the Republic could expect harsh treatment.

Conrado Rufino Romero remembered the occupation of the Republican zone in the first weeks of the postwar, the imposition of the new political order, and indications of the food shortages that would beset the entire country after the war: *And then we kept going on, and on, and on. We got to what had still been their zone. Without resistance of any kind in those towns. And the municipal governments would be named. And the municipal courts would be established. And we would leave the next day for another town and the social aid societies would set up dining halls. Women brought food for the children and old people. I do remember that. And afterwards, from there they brought us to Seville. We were there a month or twenty days. For certain we experienced a lot of hunger there.*

If Nationalist soldiers stationed in Seville went hungry, Republican prisoners of war were even worse off. A leftist from Castilleja was a witness to their suffering. Aurelio Monge Romero had to accompany a column of prisoners from Madrid to concentration camps in Catalonia. *Later they formed a column of people who had been captured, with all the soldiers and all of those forces, and we took them under custody and we went to Catalonia to Berga and Manresa. We went the whole way walking and keeping them under guard. It took many days because we had to cook the food and we had to stop to rest at night. Rest wherever you happened to be. And sentinels on each side of those forces, because we had them under custody. And it took a while.*

And finally we arrived and, well, they went into some concentration camps they set up there. And we were the soldiers there who guarded the camps. Those prisoners suffered every necessity in the world. Because it filled one with pity to eat in front of them. You started to peel an apple or an orange and when you threw the peels in there, before they hit the ground, they would catch them and eat them up. Because they were weak from hunger and practically naked. I mean, it is best not to even think about it. What those creatures went through there.

Antonio Delgado Luque spent the first six months of the postwar in Madrid where his unit maintained order. *We camped in the University City in Madrid. And there what we did was go on patrols with the Civil Guard to maintain public order. In Madrid. And we were there some six months or thereabouts. They gave us a coverall, a blue coverall, and we served with the Civil Guard. In other words we would go out with one civil guard and two of us. And we were there until they discharged us.*

Victory celebrations

Franco's warning that Spain was still "at war with all its internal and external enemies," did not stop the victory celebrations. On April 10, a telegram arrived at the Castilleja town hall:

> Telegram 4–10-939
> From SECRETARY COLONEL GENERALISSIMO TO MAYOR.
> For CASTILLEJA DEL CAMPO from BURGOS
> H[*is*]. E[*xcellency*]. GENERALISSIMO EXPRESSING GRATITUDE KIND CONGRATULATION FOR FINAL VICTORY OF OUR ARMS OVER ENEMIES OF FATHERLAND SENDS HIS WARM GREETING TO THAT BODY AND TOWN.[8]

If a town as small as Castilleja caused an exchange of telegrams, Spain's telegraphers must have been putting in a lot of overtime in April 1939.

From mid-April to mid-May there were victory parades in all the provincial capitals of Andalusia and in Valencia. The culmination took place in Madrid on May 19. Two hundred thousand troops filed past Franco in a parade that was more than twenty-five kilometers long even as some desperate individuals still resisted. Conrado Rufino Romero took part. *In Madrid there were still gunshots from the rooftops and all. And there were four battalions from the south who marched in the parade. In Chamartín, that had not even been rebuilt yet, that is where we drilled. And four Italian battalions also marched there. Of course, the parade was enormous, no? The parade lasted . . . I do not know . . . but we, from the time we left until we got back there again, twenty-two hours. We were four hours on the Paseo de la Castellana waiting for the artillery to go by.*

Isidora Mistral showed me a photograph of herself when she was nineteen years old and the war had just ended. It was taken during an excursion to Seville with the Castilleja Feminine Section. She remembered it as an enjoyable day in spite of a mishap caused, quite possibly, by excessive celebration: *In the photo, that was the day we collected some beds and sheets and bedspreads for the field hospital in Seville. A group of us from the Feminine Section here went. And we went there to deliver everything to the field hospital. The sheets, the blankets, the crucifixes for the beds, and the beds. We collected it all in the town. And for the crucifixes we provided the money. Then we went to the provincial govern-*

ment building to greet the governor and they served us drinks and all. Everyone with their hand raised like Falangists, you know? They served us drinks.

Afterwards some Italians ran into us . . . there were still Italians . . . they ran smack into the doctor Don Juan's car. A crash. We were driving down the Paseo de las Palmeras. And the Italians' car, loaded with soldiers and things to eat and all. It comes and smacks us and pushes us up on the sidewalk. The headlights were broken and Don Juan drove up on the sidewalk in front of the Palmeras Hotel. We had been on our way to the hotel. And the Italian comes over and he says, "Damage personale? Damage personale?" And the doctor from here said, "No! No! Not personale! Automobale! Damage automobale! No damage personale at all!" He was so funny. Oy! Oy! He says to me, "Girl, this is probably the curse your mother put on us because today is Tuesday the thirteenth [equivalent to Friday the thirteenth] *and your mother did not want you to come. And this is probably your mother's curse." I say, "What are you talking about? What curse? You only want to put the blame on . . ." He was like a gypsy, very given to superstitions. So, that day we had a stupendous time but we had a scare that shook us all up. We went all dressed up like I am there in the photo, all dressed up with even my feather boa and all my accessories. Aw shit, what a time!*

Not everyone celebrated the victory. For Carmen Monge Romero, the end of the war meant the triumph of those who had assassinated her brother Manuel and her brother-in-law Antonio Cruz Cruz. Her brother Francisco was still in prison. *What happened at the end of the war? Franco became everyone's lord and master and the way things were you could not speak up anywhere because if you criticized anything, they got you. You could hardly breathe. Not like now when you can speak everywhere, eh?, about anything you want. Not then, not at all. You had to keep quiet and with your head bowed.* Sometimes celebration was obligatory, according to Manuel García Ramírez, whose brother Lutgardo was shot on August 27, 1936. *And when they played the hymn, fuck, if it caught you in the street you had to stand like this.* (He raises his pinky to illustrate the stiff posture of a soldier called to attention.) *They had us worse than slaves. Much worse. Much worse. You cannot even describe . . . the best thing is for no one to have to live through something like that.*

Demobilization

Gradually, men from Castilleja returned home. Among the first was Miguel Rodríguez Caraballo. *I was in Peñarroya when the war ended. Since I was one of the oldest, well, they discharged me among the first. Not the very first, but I was among the oldest just behind the first, from my call-up year, and they discharged me in Peñarroya.* Others were demobilized later. Antonio Delgado Luque was six months in Madrid patrolling the city with his Falangist unit. Then he returned home, although he could have joined the Civil Guard. *We were there until they discharged me as the son of a widow. And one morning a lieutenant colonel in the Civil Guard told us that whoever wanted to continue in the Civil Guard should take one step forward. It was up to us. And you were immediately enrolled in the Civil Guard. Many stayed in. Even from here. He has already died, the poor thing. That boy stayed in the Civil Guard.*

After the last offensive in the Pyrenees, Celedonio Escobar Reinoso was hospitalized. *I remember that I was in San Sebastián in the clinic with my foot frozen when the war ended. Well, I came here and they sent me back again to my battalion. It was in the province of Cuenca and from there they transferred us to Zaragoza, to a town called Caspe. In 1939, in October. I remember it was the fiesta of Pilar in Zaragoza when I was discharged. Everybody celebrating. And I remember, it turned out that I went to war in October and I came back exactly three years later. And I came back, well, to work here. That was all there was to do.*

After marching in the victory parade in Madrid, Conrado Rufino Romero returned to Seville. *When the war ended, I was at least eight months in the office there in Seville. I stayed in Seville because my Falangist unit was disbanded and incorporated into the army. I was in charge of the files. I took them to the barracks on the Plaza del Duque because I was in charge of the Falangist archive. By then all of those barracks were commanded by army officers. There was nothing left from the Falange but some signs they had there that said things to encourage the members. I remember one that said, "Life is militancy and must be lived with an unblemished spirit of service and sacrifice," for example. There were many signs like that there.*

In the summer of 1939, Franco still had an army of more than half a million soldiers and twenty-two thousand officers, approximately half of those serving in the Nationalist forces when the war ended in April. Maintaining such a large army was a severe strain on a country that needed manpower to rebuild its infrastructure and mitigate the alarming scarcity, especially of food, but for Franco it was more important to maintain a powerful repressive force.[9] The slow demobilization also reflected his imperialist ambitions. Europe was drawing closer to war. Franco had realized all his ambitions at the national level and hoped to participate beside Hitler and Mussolini in their war of conquest and share the spoils, specifically an expansion of the Spanish possessions in North Africa.[10]

The Second World War began on September 3, slowing the demobilization even further. In April 1940, a year after the civil war had ended, there were still twenty men from the town serving in the army, 25 percent of the town's ex-combatants. Others would be remobilized after that, for example Aurelio Monge Romero. *I was more than a year here working, always for the marquess* [García de Porres y Porres]. *And then I had to go back into the army. I got the news while I was out working there near the highway. The armed guard from that estate, Cecilio* [Rodríguez Rufino]*, arrived and he says, "Gentlemen, come over here, I have some bad news. They have mobilized the call-ups from 1938 to 1940." And then I had to go to Algeciras to be in the barracks there and that was that. The barracks were overcrowded. With quite a few call-ups. The 1939 call-up. And from 1940, 1941, 1942, and 1943. There were five call-ups and they did not rotate the garrison. So many soldiers! And then they discharged me and I never went back. But that was in 1943.*

The remobilization of Aurelio Monge Romero and so many others was due to the international situation. On November 8, 1942, British and American forces began Operation Torch, the amphibious invasion of North Africa. Fearing that the Anglo-American expeditionary force would enter Europe through the Iberian Peninsula, Franco issued the order for a general mobilization on November 12. Aurelio Monge and those he described as *so many soldiers* crowded into the Algeciras garrison adjacent to Gibraltar were there to be cannon fodder in the event of an invasion. They would have been hard put to defend themselves, much less repel an attack, given the state of deterioration of the arms they possessed. The civil war had left the nation defenseless.

The cost of the civil war

On the national level: death, imprisonment, exile

From the human perspective, the greatest devastation was the loss of life on both sides. Approximately a half million Spaniards lost their lives on the battlefields, during the bombardment of cities, in the repressions in both zones, or from malnutrition in the Republican zone. There were about two hundred thousand combat deaths, 10 percent of the soldiers mobilized on both sides. Two additional human tragedies must be added to the loss of life. At the end of 1939, there were almost two hundred and seventy-one thousand Spaniards, men and women, in prison.[11] Another hundred thousand were in concentration camps or forced labor battalions. Spain had been turned into a huge penal colony. The tragedy of the exiles should not be forgotten either. The country lost approximately 300,000 citizens who went into permanent exile.

The cliché of "one million dead" is an exaggeration if taken literally. If it is understood figuratively, it is fairly accurate. Adding the dead, the imprisoned, and those in exile, more than a million Spaniards had ceased to participate in the country's life. This is a startling number of individual tragedies. It was also a tragedy for Spain. The majority of these people were from the country's active population. Many of them were people of great talent. Their loss contributed to the cultural, scientific, and economic backwardness the country would experience for decades with respect to the rest of Europe.

On the local level: deaths, wounded, prisoners

No one from Castilleja died in combat. Considering that men from the town had seen action on some of the worst fronts in the war, this is truly astonishing. With a casualty rate of 10 percent on the national level, a town with eighty-one combatants would have been lucky with anything fewer than eight deaths. Castilleja had won the lottery and everyone who had been alive then knew it. For Antonio Monge Pérez, this made the repression even more tragic. [After the war] *the whole town was dressed in black. Almost everyone. In mourning for what had happened here. Not what had happened at the front. Because in truth, here, in the war, no one died at the front.*

For Marina Luque Reinoso, Castilleja had lost a historic opportunity. *They did what they did, and they did not have to have done it. Otherwise, in Castilleja nothing would have happened, because no one died in the war. But they killed the men they killed, who did not have to be killed. And it is a thing that has marked Castilleja for the rest of its life. Because if nothing had happened then, Castilleja, that had so many men in the war and in the war no one died, would have been a little town that was unique in history. If only it could have been.*

There were three deaths unrelated to combat. Isidora Mistral's brother returned from the war with tuberculosis and was one of three men who died of illness, according to Antonio Monge Pérez. *People died in the war who came home from the war sick. A first cousin of mine named Vicente* [Rodríguez Monge] *died. Another was called "Paté"* [Manuel Adorna Sánchez]. *And another they used to call* [Diego] *Mistral also came back sick from the war, tuberculosis, and in those days there was no cure, like my first cousin also, and he too died. Those three from here died. They died but it was not from wounds.*

Some of the combatants from Castilleja were wounded. Celedonio Escobar Reinoso had surgery in Zaragoza to remove a piece of shrapnel. José Escobar Moreno was maimed, according to Miguel Rodríguez Caraballo. *Some from the town did not come out of the war intact. A brother-in-law of my wife was disabled. He was shot and he had lost an arm . . . I mean, he had his arm but it was . . . the way he had it, he could not use it.* Others suffered psychologically from what they had been through in the war, according to Miguel. *And the municipal policeman who was here . . . there was nothing wrong with him but he probably had that problem from the fright.*

Two Castilleja natives, both right-wingers, were captured, one of them during a Republican attack on Cabeza del Buey. Miguel Rodríguez Caraballo was working there in a supply depot and mentioned him when he described the attack. Then, when Miguel spoke of how lucky the men from Castilleja had been in the war, he mentioned this man again as well as another who had been a prisoner: *Here we were very lucky. Very lucky. And people who were on all the fronts, no? Here there were men who were captured. José* [Luque Cuevas], *son of Lutgardo. He was one of them. That boy was a prisoner. Yes, and Juan María's son. Juan María was his father. He was a prisoner also.* Miguel Rodríguez mentioned the two prisoners as examples of Castilleja's good fortune, evidence that the town's combatants survived the war despite having been in fierce combat.

Manuel Ramírez Mauricio also mentioned the two prisoners. In his opinion, it was lucky that these two men had survived. *There were two from here they took prisoner. And they were right-wingers. Yes. Right-wingers. And nothing happened to them there. Nothing except work. Work, work, work, work, like in a concentration camp. There in a mine, and digging trenches and doing everything that had to be done. Filling sandbags with dirt to reinforce the trenches also, instead of with stones, if there were no stones, with sandbags.*

I do not know who Juan María's son was, but José, son of Lutgardo, was the brother of the Falangists Francisco Luque Cuevas "The Ill Wind," Antonio "The Chatterbox," and Manuel "The Little Ill Wind." Antonio Monge Pérez thought it lucky that a member of a family that had participated in the repression had been captured by the Republicans and survived. *Also there were some here who were taken prisoner by the Reds, as we used to call them here. But nothing happened to them. They came back here after the war. They did not kill them. In particular one I am certain of, who is still alive, whose name is José* [Luque] *Cuevas. It was precisely his brothers who had killed people here. Imagine, if they find out on that side that his brother had killed people here, and maybe even him too, we do not know. But no one said anything and he came back when the war ended and that was the end of it. He was on the Right. A Falangist. One of the main ones here. The brother of this man from here that they took prisoner, he was the principal killer.*

On all levels: silence, fear, hatred

The war had brought to power a totalitarian regime that monopolized public discourse. There was neither freedom of expression nor access to information that did not conform to official propaganda. Criticism of the regime could lead to execution, imprisonment, torture, or economic reprisals. Conrado Rufino Romero, a right-winger, lamented this lack of freedom and recognized that it lasted a long time, that not even Manuel

Fraga Iribarne's Press Law of 1966, put an end to the control of expression. *Franco. Man, there was no freedom with him. Of expression. Of expression and the press and the radio, no? Liberty was very limited. Now the one who gave freedom of the press with Franco was Fraga when he was a minister. He is the one who gave freedom of the press. What little there was came from him.* To access other points of view was a dangerous adventure, according to Manuel García Ramírez. *We used to listen in secret to Radio Pirenaica* [broadcast from the Soviet Union] *where La Pasionaria* [exiled Communist leader Dolores Ibárruri Gómez] *used to talk often or almost every day. We listened in secret. It was not even permitted to turn on your station, the American station. Not in those days.*

On the local level, censorship extended to private conversations. Manuel Ramírez Mauricio described the atmosphere in Castilleja in the immediate postwar period. *Here well, when I got home, I used to ask my father for a little bit of money, nothing, six centimos in those days. And I used to go to the casino to have a coffee or a drink with other boys who had come home from the war. We used to talk especially quietly. I mean, quietly. Three of us who were the same, you know? Leftists, eh? We used to get a table there and whisper so the others could not hear us. Then we would speak out loud, because we were talking about other things so they would not realize what we were really talking about. And that is what we had to do. They would come up next to us just to hear what we were talking about.*

Manuel García Ramírez described the same social control. The memory of those times of silence led him to express envy of those who, like his brother Lutgardo, were assassinated at the beginning of the war. *The people on the Left could not get together to talk about how things were. Oh hoo! You could not even go out to have a glass of wine, eh?, together with another. What we went through was . . . I think that the one who won the war was the one they killed on the first day. I have said it many times. I say it was better to have been killed the first day and not go through what one has gone through.*

The silence had a pernicious effect on everyone in the town. Manuel Ramírez Mauricio described a town where victors and vanquished inhabited two different worlds. *Before the war we had more freedom and we used to talk to them more, you know? We used to talk to them more when we had power, and they used to talk to us. But then, on the contrary, when all of that happened, when that revolution came here to the town and to all of Spain, well, then we had to talk to them more carefully, you know? Because we could not talk about what we had to talk about between one side and the other. There was like a secret between one side and the other then that could not be told. Them talking about whatever they wanted and us quiet, unable to speak.*

The leftist tradition in Castilleja survived in the town through clandestine meetings, described by Manuel Ramírez. *We often used to go for a walk at night. Four or five of us would go out along the highway to where there was a shack for the road workers, you know? And we used to go in there with small candles and we would put a shade around them so they would not be seen from outside and there we used to talk all we wanted. That custom lasted for a long time because we were never at ease. Because whenever we used to talk, they would gather around us because we . . . what they thought was that we were going to speak badly about Franco, you know?*

The most forbidden topic was the repression. One could not speak publicly of the victims or name those who had been responsible for the assassinations. This taboo was so deeply entrenched that it lasted even after Franco's death. The repression continues to be an uncomfortable topic today. Manuel García Ramírez could not forget the assassination of his brother Lutgardo, seek justice, or talk about it. *Since one could not breathe or speak or do anything, well we turned a blind eye to all that had happened. What could we do? What could we do? We had their foot at our throats everywhere we turned.*

With time, many right-wingers came to believe that the family members of the men who had been shot had forgotten their loss as everyone gets over the loss of a loved one. In 1990, Aniceto Luque Luque thought so. During fifty-five years, leftists had apparently never said in his presence what they said to me. *Well, of course, that fear was always there. For a while, no? The one whose parents were killed, the one whose brothers were killed, well, you can imagine. But later, well, nothing, we all got along together. Those things were gradually forgotten like everything is forgotten. Like when you have someone who dies and you have to forget it. Your wife dies on you and you have to forget it. It happens to all of us. So I see that forgetting as normal. Do you not agree?*

Marina Luque Reinoso was from a right-wing family, but she was aware that the hatred in the town would only disappear with a change of generations. *Things were not forgotten so quickly, no? Because the mothers whose sons had been killed, the sisters whose brothers had been killed, the women whose husbands and, of course, it took a while, no? There was a hatred that lasted a lifetime because the mother who held the belief that that person could have been the one who had been to blame for what happened in Castilleja, the family members would never forget, no? They have all died by now . . . those who could be held responsible are all dead. But then later, the hatred between the rest of us who were growing up and were very young back then, well all that began to be erased and then Castilleja became very peaceful and all.*

Aurelio Monge Romero was in agreement with Marina that the family members of the victims would spend their lives with hatreds that would never be forgotten. And he too believed that those memories would pass with the new generations. Far from celebrating this, he thought the repression had not only divided the town between the Right and the Left but also between generations. *In the first years things were very bad. With hatreds and many things because, of course, from the war until now, from 1936 to 1990 where we are now, there is already another generation here. But people my age cannot forget it. That is here inside us. That is here in our blood. But you go and tell it to the young people now what one has been through and what one has been seeing and has seen and the calamites one has lived through and all, and they refuse to believe it. The young people refuse to believe it.*

Notes

1 Matilde Donaire Pozo, "Largo camino hacia la paz," 22.

2 Ibid., 24.

3 Ibid., 27.

4 Francisco Moreno Gómez, "La represión en la posguerra," in Santos Juliá, *Víctimas de la Guerra Civil*, 346.

5 Josep M. Solé i Sabaté and Joan Villarroya, "Mayo de 1936–Abril de 1939," in Santos Juliá, *Víctimas de la Guerra Civil*, 266–7.

6 Manuel Tuñón de Lara, "Un ensayo de visión global, medio siglo después," in *La guerra civil española: 50 años después*, Manuel Tuñón de Lara and others, 421.

7 Francisco Franco, RNE [Radio Nacional Española], 3 April 1939, quoted in Gonzalo Acosta Bono, José Luis Gutiérrez Molina, Lola Martínez Macías, and Ángel del Río Sánchez, *El canal de los presos, 1940–1962*, 13.

8 Various documents 1920–1940, Castilleja del Campo Municipal Archive.

9 Paul Preston, *Franco: A Biography*, 329.

10 Ibid., 324–6.

11 On January 1, 1940, the Spanish prison population was 270,719. Instituto Nacional de Estadística, *Anuario Estadístico de España, 1944–1945*, 1093.

Part Four

Postwar

Twelve

Years of Hunger and Decades of Poverty

Spain in ruins

After the war, Spain's infrastructure was severely damaged, especially the transportation system and housing. Antonio Monge Pérez thought it absurd that such destruction had been self-inflicted. *We ourselves had ruined our own nation. That is like ruining our own houses because, in the end, later we all have to contribute to rebuild all that. It has to come out of us, because foreigners are not going to put it back together. If it gets put back together, it has to be by our own sweat, as is only natural.* Castilleja del Campo was fortunate. It had been at risk of material destruction on only two occasions. The first was the invasion of the miners on July 19, 1936. That day, the intervention of the Republican authorities and other leftists saved the town from damage. The second occasion was the occupation by Nationalist forces on July 24, 1936. Since there was no resistance, Castilleja was never bombed.

However, Castilleja did not escape the more than two decades of generalized poverty that afflicted the country. The worst years, 1940 to 1943, came to be called the "years of hunger." They were engraved in the memories of those I interviewed. Dulcenombre Ramírez Mauricio: *After the war, a great deal of hunger. The postwar, as people call it. Eating carob beans. And borage and thistles. Wild greens. Forage from the countryside. Because there was nothing else. No cooking oil. No bread. There was nothing. And stewed tomatoes we shared by the spoonful. Oh hoo! Such things.* Carmen Monge Romero: *We went through so much. I do not even want to remember. We ate so many carob beans. After the war it was worse because everybody was out of everything.* Marina Luque Reinoso: *My older sister [María] eventually lost thirty kilos after the war. Since she was a big eater and since she was not eating bread, she wasted away in no time and lost thirty kilos of flesh.*

The residents of agricultural communities like Castilleja were better off than the hundreds of thousands of Spaniards who spent the first years of the postwar wandering about the country in search of food. As many as 200,000 people starved to death in the immediate aftermath of the civil war.[1] Sara Tebas Rodríguez remembers the pity she felt for them. *I used to see people who were hungrier than I was. They used to come here to the Bar La Gasolinera. Those families were not from here. That poor family what they ate was bags of carob beans and the mother used to beg there and they used to give her flour so she could make a little gruel. And that is what they used to eat.*

The government confronts the crisis

Rationing

The Franco regime responded to the alarming food shortages on May 14, 1939, by imposing rationing on certain products. Theoretically, rationing serves to overcome a temporary crisis but, in the case of postwar Spain, rationing lasted more than a decade, until 1952. The regime's leaders were not economists. They were trained in military affairs and believed they could "discipline" the market, preventing high prices by mandate.[2] But fixing the price of a product without doing the same for the means of production discouraged the cultivation of rationed products.[3] In the case of wheat, for example, the requirement to turn it over to the government at a fixed price that did not cover increases in the cost of fertilizer or draft animals led many producers to reduce the amount of land dedicated to wheat in order to cultivate products that were not rationed. The result was a decrease in the production of precisely those products that were most needed.

Another strategy for producers was to consume part of their own harvest.[4] The practice was universal in Castilleja. Antonio Delgado Luque's father-in-law, Manuel Luque Delgado, was the manager of the countess's estate and had the means to hide wheat year-round, though not without risks. *Of course, here wheat was grown, as is natural, but it was rigorously controlled and you had to hand it over to the last grain. In other words, if you harvested two thousand kilos of wheat, well, you had to hide two hundred in order to eat. You had to find a place to hide it and know how to hide it so they would not find it, because the whole nation was short of bread. My father-in-law used to set some aside for himself. He had his own parcel and in his house he made . . . in the rafters there he used to put up wheat and I used to go grind it out there near Chichina. And in Escacena as well. We took it in such a way that no one could see what we were carrying. We would take it in the draft animals' gear and that is where we put the sacks of wheat, and the same with the flour. The Civil Guard had their eye out for us because all of Spain was going hungry.*

José Luque López was a medium landowner. According to his daughter Marina Luque Reinoso, he used to grind wheat in his house, enough to last a few days. *We had wheat, and they were requisitioning it then and you had to turn it over but, of course, the one who had some, well he had to hide some for his children, no? We had two stones to grind it but you had to grind it in the middle of the night when people were in bed so no one would hear you.*

Leovigildo Monge was a small landowner and a leftist. According to his son Antonio Monge Pérez, when rationing began, his father did not have the means to hide his harvest nor did he have the same impunity as right-wingers. *In my family we grew wheat but you had to hand it over because you were not allowed to keep the wheat. One had to turn it over to the government so they could distribute it. But then we were left without any. On the other hand, the rich people from here, since they were the authorities, well they kept wheat in their houses for the whole year. So that was the setup.*

Eventually, Leovigildo found an arrangement to keep a little of his harvest, but very cautiously. *Then later, although we turned it over, we had a little area there with a fence. My father bought that parcel and we had two shanties and the cows there. And we used to have a hay crib there, and we had a pair of oxen to work the fields and all, and then we hid our things there at night when we put up the hay. So as not to go hungry we would up and spread out a layer of wheat in the hay crib and then another layer of garbanzos and then later, as we went about rummaging hay for the cattle, the layers would appear, and we would set them aside, and at night we would take them home. As if we were robbing them! As if we were robbing them, imagine!*

Naturally, hiding crops for one's own use was not an option for those who did not own land, such as Carmen Monge Romero's family. *They used to hand out rations. Bread made from corn. Terrible. And rice rations, and sugar and so on. Rationed. And cooking oil. The rich people kept their crops for themselves, eh? But we poor people had nothing to keep. If they wanted to sell us a loaf of bread or a kilo of flour they charged an arm and a leg and we almost never had anything to eat.*

The black market

The amount that could be kept to feed one's family had its limits, but given the demand that existed for agricultural products, clandestine sales, known as "estraperlo," soon became a big business. Between 1939 and 1953 more wheat was sold on the black market than through official channels. On September 30, 1940, the government proclaimed a law imposing severe fines or imprisonment on those who bought or sold contraband products. During the following twelve months, fines totaling more than one hundred million pesetas were imposed and approximately five thousand people were incarcerated for trafficking on the black market. A bureaucracy known as

"Fiscalía de Tasas" [*the Tax Office*] enforced the law. Nevertheless, due to corruption in the system and the arbitrary application of punishments, the law had little effect.[5]

Isidora Mistral's family worked for José María Cuevas, the wealthiest man in the town besides the countess and the marchioness. Isidora's perspective is typical of those who could circumvent the law with little risk. *Here everyone got by very well because everyone had something and traded in wheat. They would sell it to the "estraperlistas"* [black marketeers] *and they made a lot of money.* This prosperity was not as universal as Isidora remembered. Those who benefited most from "estraperlo" were the large landowners. They had more wheat to sell and places to hide it. The Civil Guard and the bureaucrats from "Fiscalía de Tasas" turned a blind eye to their participation in the black market. Many of them made their fortunes during the years of hunger.

For small landholders, the black market was not a way to get rich. It was a question of economic survival. They had less excess to sell clandestinely after satisfying their families' needs. They were more closely watched, especially if they were leftists, and had to turn over a greater percentage of their harvest. Antonio Monge Pérez's perspective was different from that of Isidora Mistral. *Many "pelentrines"* [parvenus] *made their fortunes, you know? Because the times favored them. With the dictatorship they sold their things at whatever price they wanted and they paid the poor whatever they wanted as well.*

And it favored them because I remember that in those years of hunger wheat had to be sold through the government. They paid for it, well, some three pesetas or three and a half and, nevertheless, what you sold clandestinely they paid you up to eleven pesetas, eh? Imagine! And of course, well, it happened that there in the province of Huelva there were a lot of vineyards and they did not grow wheat, and around Pilas too, in short. And many people from the mountains came here for wheat. And in those days right there on the sidewalk, or in the countryside, they would set up scales, and they would weigh it and sell it, and they did not turn anything over to the government. They would say they had not harvested wheat, and nothing would happen. After a while that was the way it was. And a lot of people got rich. They got rich because no one bothered them.

Now, those who were poor, they could not do that because, like I told you, my father had to turn over everything. Until we set ourselves up to bury it in the hay because we could not have it in our house. We had to have it in the countryside. Everybody had to be a thief in order to . . . Yes. A thief of what was yours! Ha! Ha! Ha! A thief of what was yours! Yes! But, no. Not everybody. The rich people? They used to keep it in their houses and no one bothered them. No. Because they were in charge. They were the mayor and the councilmen and all, so everything was alright. Now, not the rest of us. The rest of us had to turn it over.

Because it had created groups with an interest in maintaining it, rationing persisted for almost a decade after the worst years of hunger, from 1940 to 1943. Landowners and traders got rich from clandestine sales. The bureaucrats in Fiscalía de Tasas, civil guards, and customs guards lined their pockets from the corruption that infested the entire system. And the wealthy classes could acquire whatever they wanted in spite of the general scarcity. Instead of achieving an equitable distribution of scarce goods, rationing became another instrument of economic repression.

Feliciano Monge Pérez spoke of this aspect of the black market. *They hit us with a denunciation in which they were going to dispossess us of what little we had in my family. They were taking our house, they were taking our little parcels, they were taking our cattle in order to leave us in a drainage ditch or under an olive tree. But my father* [Leovigildo Monge Pérez] *had a brother in Seville who was a dealer in cattle. But a dealer with important people, with people who had estates and my father went and spoke to him. His name was Miguel, the youngest of the sons. He says, "Look Miguel, what is happening to me. To me and to Basilio* [Rufino Pérez]*," who was a first cousin of his. Miguel says, "Well, look, I have a friend. I am going to talk to him and see if this cannot be worked out." The friend was in the office, Fiscalía de Tasas, and all the denunciations from small towns about things like that had to pass through there. And Miguel went and he gave him all the information about my father and his cousin. He says, "Do not worry because that has to pass through my hands and when it gets here I am going to grab it and tear it up."*

My father, the poor thing, and I were going to the Sanlúcar Fair that day, the two of us, and at a place there they call El Viso, on the old highway, we were going that way and a car was coming from Seville toward Huelva, and my uncle Miguel with the man were coming in the car. Of course, Miguel saw my father and stopped the car, and he said, "Leovigildo, come here." My father went over. He says, "I am going to give you some good news." "The fuck, what news?" He says, "Everything is all arranged." That was in the 1940s. The war was over. But they did not stop grinding you down. They did not stop grinding you down. In short. My father, the poor thing, he was crying like a baby. Because there was a lot at stake.

And my father had a friend [José "Pepe" Espejo] *in Villalba. He was one of the big rich people there. And they were good friends because he was a man who was very fond of cattle. And the cattle my father had were from the same stock as his, because he had very good cattle and he used to bring his bull to service my family's cows, in short, well, and my father told him what was happening. And he said to him, he says, "Look Leovigildo, your cows, you bring them to my place for as long as it may take. There we are not going to count one day or . . . as long as it takes and when whatever is happening is over, you come and get your cattle." And that is what he did. They were there at least five or six months. And when that affair was settled we went and got them.*

Feliciano's story illustrates how vulnerable small landholders were if they were leftists. They had to participate in illegal activities in order to feed their families. A denunciation, for political reasons, revenge, envy, or whatever, could ruin them. In this case, thanks to the intervention of his brother Miguel, of Miguel's friend in Fiscalía de Tasas, and to his friendship with a wealthy cattle owner in Villalba del Alcor, Leovigildo Monge escaped a fine that would have left his family in abject poverty.

Even more vulnerable were the foot soldiers in the army of "estraperlistas," the thousands of poor women who boarded trains every morning and headed for the cities carrying baskets of produce and returned at night with goods to sell in their communities. For these women, the black market was not a question of getting rich. It was a question of whether they and their children would eat that day. The cases I know of in Castilleja were all widows and orphans of men who had been shot. This was typical for all of Spain.[6]

Suceso Rodríguez Luque: Sara Tebas Rodríguez's testimony

Suceso Rodríguez Luque was thirty-five years old when her husband Manuel Tebas Escobar was shot on September 14, 1936. She had three children to support: Rosario, eleven years old; Elías, seven; and Sara, four. During the war she made a meager living selling lupine beans and homemade sweets for children. When postwar rationing began she could earn more trafficking on the black market. Her daughter Sara explained how it worked. *She began to go to Seville. And she would bring back half a kilo of coffee or a kilo of sugar or whatever. She would make a little paper with the price on it and we would put it out to sell to the people and they used to buy it. And she used to go to Carrión and they would give her garbanzos that people in Seville would order from her. Then they used to call them "estraperlistas." Black marketeers. It was the only way they could feed their children.*

When Sara was a teenager, she too trafficked on the black market, along with her cousin Luisa Fernández Rodríguez, whose father, José Fernández Luque, was shot on September 14, 1936. *I remember one morning here, the Civil Guard had a checkpoint. And we were on our way, my Luisa, the poor thing, and she used to go too, buying and selling things. And one morning the two of us were taking the basket and the civil guards took our garbanzos. They took us to the town hall. Oh hoo, what an embarrassment! And they had to weigh the basket and all. They kept the garbanzos. They did not give them back. And that is how we used to eat.*

Carmen Muñoz Caraballo: Otilia Escobar Muñoz's testimony

Carmen Muñoz Caraballo's husband, Manuel Escobar Moreno, was shot on August 27, 1936. According to her daughter, Carmen's first problem was to find a place to live. *When she was twenty-seven years old she was a widow and without a house and without anything. She had no place to live. Well then when my father died, she came to live in the house of her father-in-law* [José Escobar Rufino] *with my aunt whom we called "La Crespa"* [Rosario Escobar Moreno]. *And after a little while she went to live with my other grandfather* [Francisco Muñoz Casado] *who was a widower. And in that house at that time my uncle Manolo* [Muñoz Caraballo] *was living there. His wife Carmen* [Monge Romero], *Aurelia's daughter, was there. There were four or five of them, and my grandfather, and my mother, with three rooms and a little girl, and that is where she began to struggle. She went to work.*

During the war, Carmen Muñoz Caraballo worked in the fields. Afterwards, she began trafficking on the black market, which negatively affected her daughter Otilia. *I was a very bad student because, of course, my mother was never there ever. Because she used to leave on the train every morning at eight or at ten, and when she came home it was well into the evening. I had to go with her to Carrión, the two of us loaded down with cooking oil, with garbanzos, everything she took to sell. And, of course, when I got back to Castilleja it was time for school but, the way children are, half of them do not want to go to school and I was the same way. I went very seldom to school.*

The daily life of those I call the foot soldiers in the army of "estraperlistas" was full of dangers, and ploys to evade the surveillance of the civil guards and customs guards with circuitous treks in all kinds of weather, and the constant need to bribe the authorities, with the consequent loss of income for those who profited least from the contravention of the rationing laws. *When my mother used to come home at night, she came home exhausted. I had to go back then to Carrión to wait for her. We used to go by a road that goes along a ravine and takes you directly to the station. We used to take that road so we would not have to pass the Civil Guard barracks. Because the barracks are right on the highway. And sometimes we had to go along yet another road because the civil guards were there, and we had to get to the station by going through an irrigation ditch . . . sometimes it had water and other times not . . . in order to get to the train because the civil guards were there, so they would not see us.*

Every day an adventure. Every day. And not only that. When we would catch the train . . . many days I used to go with her . . . and when the train would arrive, well, we would board it. The train would pick up passengers in all the towns. In Paterna and Escacena there were many estraperlistas, as they called them then. When we would get to San Juan [del Puerto], *a woman would come around with a little bag taking up a collection for the customs guards who were waiting at the door when we would get to Huelva. To give them the little bag so they would let us pass. With the money. And at times, when we used to get to San Juan, the customs guards would board and take up their own collection, collecting our money as well. And she used to earn a pittance. Nothing. It turned out that when they caught her later on, she did not even have enough to pay the fine. Barely enough to eat, barely enough to get by, to get by until they would slap her with another fine and she would be back to nothing. That was the plan. Life has not been very good. She had a bad time of it. That kind of dog's life.*

Otilia spoke of *when they caught her later on* and her mother *did not even have enough to pay the fine.* She went on to describe the punishments her mother endured because she lacked the money to pay the fines imposed by the provincial office of Fiscalía de Tasas. *She was in jail three times. Because they caught her and the fine was a thousand pesetas. Three times. What she went through! When she was in jail I stayed with my grandfather. I stayed with my uncles. Since they did not even have enough to feed their own, well, I stayed here and there. When I was little I lived with one relative, I lived with another, and another, and another until my uncle José* [Escobar Moreno] *. . . he was living in Aznalcóllar. Because when the war started, to get rid of him they sent him into the legion. "El Regular." They sent him into the legion and he took a bullet in his arm. He could no longer use his arm.*

And he went to Aznalcóllar because he did not want to come back to Castilleja afterwards. He worked in Aznalcóllar as a mailman. Then I went to live with them there. Other times my uncle Modesto [Escobar Moreno], *who was living in León . . . all the brothers left Castilleja . . . and my uncle Modesto, well, he never came back again. He stayed in León and got married there. And when he found out, well, he would send the money for the fine and my mother would get out of jail. Struggling like that until the day she died. One time* [when my mother was in jail] *I was eight years old. Another time I was eleven. And the other time I do not remember, because that time the priest got involved. And he helped her. That time he helped her. Because then the priests had a lot of influence. They could fix things because Don Felipe was, in spite of everything, a fat cat. And he got her out.*

And the other time, when my uncle Modesto found out, well, he sent the thousand pesetas. And then it was a lot of money, a lot of money. But while the money was arriving and not arriving, she was in there a month and she came out just like an authentic fish fillet from top to bottom. She went through horrors. We went through horrors. Because she came out just like a . . . as if they had cut her with a knife under her breasts from the eczema and everything she caught there. Horrible diseases. And hunger. Hunger and then . . . (Crying.) *Do you have a Kleenex? And then we could not take anything to her at the jail because we did not have any money . . . I visited her once. I will never in my life forget it. In the jail in Seville.* (Blowing her nose.)

With bars like from here to there between us. Beyond the bars a glass window. Unforgettable. It was the worst thing I have seen in the world. I have been through it all.

Carmen Muñoz Caraballo's prison files

There are two files on Carmen Muñoz Caraballo from the Seville Provincial Prison. The first is from 1947, when Otilia was twelve years old. Carmen Muñoz was taken to the prison by the Civil Guard on May 21, "at the disposition of the Provincial Fiscalía de Tasas . . ." The fine was one thousand pesetas and she had to spend a day in jail for each ten pesetas. She was released on June 24, presumably because her brother-in-law Modesto had paid the fine.

The second file is from the following year, when Otilia was thirteen. Her mother entered the prison on April 30, 1948. The file indicates that this was her second offense and the fine imposed was one thousand five hundred pesetas, a sentence of one hundred and fifty days. She was released on May 31.[7] On both occasions, she was in jail a little over a month while her brother-in-law Modesto collected and sent the money to pay the fine. The arrest in 1948 was most likely when Otilia's mother contracted eczema. There is documentary evidence for only two arrests. The third arrest mentioned by Otilia may have been when Castilleja's priest, Felipe Rodríguez Sánchez, intervened, avoiding a trial.

Autarky

Theory, practice, and consequences of an economic system

In Castilleja del Campo, rationing and its consequences were the most visible aspect of the Franco regime's economic policies. The town was also affected by the implementation of an economic theory of Fascist inspiration, autarky, which sought economic independence for Spain.[8] Foreign investment was discouraged and imports were limited. The regime did not want to enrich investors and exporters in countries regarded as enemies, a category that, after the Second World War, included almost all nations. Autarky required bureaucratic micromanagement of the economy. The government set prices and wages in most categories of production and set an absurdly high valuation for the peseta. The aim was to stimulate industrialization to substitute imports with domestic products. The results were disastrous for the working class. From 1939 to 1950, the cost of living rose at twice the rate of wages. This is according to the regime's own official statistics, which were probably manipulated to present a rosier picture than what was actually taking place.[9]

Antonio Monge Pérez described how it affected his family. *Two or three years after the war, my eldest daughter, María, was born. We were raising her on Pelargón, a powdered milk for infants. It was the first to come here when the war was over. I believe that milk came from abroad.* [It was manufactured by the Swiss company Nestlé.] *She had an aversion to goat's milk or cow's milk and Pelargón suited her better, but we had to work . . . well, imagine, it used to cost me forty pesetas. With two day's work I did not have enough. When she was a little older a can could last her three days or four. When she was smaller it lasted her maybe four, five, six days, no? And I was here tending olive trees on the marquess's estate and I was earning eighteen pesetas. And I had to work a few days for a can of Pelargón for my daughter. And I could not protest because otherwise they stopped paying me and they did not give me work.*

Antonio Monge could not protest nor could anyone. Unions were illegal and strikes were prohibited. Workers were incorporated, together with management, into so-called "vertical syndicates" created by the "Movement," the vast Falangist bureaucracy. There were patriotic exhortations to make sacrifices in the present to create a prosperous and self-sufficient Spain in the future. It is curious how closely the regime's economic policies during its first two decades resembled the economic policies of Stalinist nations. The Franco regime blamed the country's economic difficulties on an "international siege."[10] In the 1960s, when Spain adopted more liberal economic policies, the regime claimed that autarky had been forced on Spain by external factors. The absurdity of this claim can be found in the Caudillo's own statements and actions.

The history of a corrupt system

On June 5, 1939, Franco announced that Spain's reconstruction would be carried out according to an economic policy of self-sufficiency.[11] On October 8, 1939, he signed a long document, "Fundamental principles and guidelines of a plan for the rationalization of our economy in harmony with our national reconstruction."[12] The plan would require an extensive bureaucracy to control all aspects of the economy, from the setting of prices and wages to the issuing of licenses for the importation of raw materials and machinery that could not be substituted by domestic production. On August 25, 1939, a decree had been promulgated that reserved all state employment for fervent supporters of the regime. The thousands of new administrators incorporated into the bureaucracy were selected for their pristine social and political background, not for their training or experience in economics. They were deplorably incompetent and faced insurmountable problems.

Rationing and the black market made it impossible to calculate the country's needs and resources. The regime's statistics from the 1940s are totally unreliable. In the case of wheat, they only include that part of the harvest turned over to the government, and not the part sold on the black market.[13] It was not even possible to know how many Spaniards needed to be fed. Local authorities exaggerated the number of inhabitants in their towns in order to obtain more ration cards. The 1940 census seems to have overestimated the national population by half a million.[14]

The administrators who managed the economy were as corrupt as their counterparts in Fiscalía de Tasas. Theoretically, industrialists received licenses to import only the raw materials and machinery necessary for their factories and impossible to acquire in the national market. In practice, permits were sold to the highest bidder. Much of Spain's scarce foreign currency was spent on the importation of luxury items, in great demand among the regime's new rich and the traditional wealthy classes.[15] Franco turned a blind eye to the corruption. In a conversation in April 1943, he told the poet and Falangist idealist Dionisio Ridruejo that in previous times it was customary to reward the victors with titles of nobility and estates, but since that was difficult in modern times, it was necessary for him to tolerate corruption in order to avoid discontent among his followers.[16]

Autarky, like rationing, had created powerful groups with a stake in maintaining the system, from the bureaucrats who administered it to the favored industrialists who monopolized a domestic market closed to foreign competition. Rationing was eliminated in 1952, but autarky was to last, with some modifications, until 1959. It caused Spain to suffer a longer and more severe postwar period than could be explained by the destructiveness of the civil war.[17] The victorious elite lived the good life while the standard of living of the defeated working class was deplorable. In the agricultural towns of Andalusia, like Castilleja del Campo, the effects of rationing and autarky were compounded by a return to the same working conditions the Republic had tried to rectify.

Relations between workers and employers

It is inaccurate to refer to Castilleja's workers as members of a "defeated working class." With the exception of Juan Antonio Luque Romero, who went over to the Republican side, the town's workers of military age had all served on the winning side in the civil war. Though technically victors, leftist workers like Antonio Monge Pérez were treated like losers. *For our service in the war we got nothing. After the war we had to adjust to something that . . . since the rich have always deceived us, when we were at the front the right-wingers from here were our officers. And they often said, "Well, now when we get back to the town those of us who are here at the front are the ones who are going to govern, because we will be the ones who won the war." And what happened was just the opposite. Because when we got back here, we had to go work for whatever they wanted to pay us. And absolutely nothing was resolved. It was worse than before because they gave us what they wanted to, a very low wage, and we did not even have enough to eat with and we had to accept it.*

Manuel Ramírez Mauricio described the working conditions in the postwar. *After the war, work in the fields. Tending the olive trees, harvesting garbanzos, or planting garbanzos, or sometimes harvesting barley or wheat. They used to pay twenty-one rials, you know? Five pesetas and one rial per day. Since it was not much money, you know?, well that was never enough. We used to eat, between two or three of us, a herring with half a small loaf of bread they used to give us, like a roll. That they gave us? No. We used to buy it.*

And when you were picking olives, piecework, you know? And later they would pay you. And after five days or seven, if you did not have money to buy food, you went to the estate with a little ticket they made for us and they had an account book. And there you would say, "Alright, well, give me so much money on account for what I have picked there." And that is how we got by until the olive harvest was over, and the manager would say, "Well tomorrow you come to collect what is left over here. The rest of the money that is left here." And we would go there and they paid us and with that we would get by for a little while until there was work again. And that is how we got by.

Some right-wing workers also felt marginalized. Conrado Rufino Romero did not see the national-syndicalist revolution to benefit workers that had been promoted by the Falange. Instead he saw a "Movement" rife with corruption and injustice. When the local leader of the Falange, José Cuevas Reinoso, asked him for his Falange membership dues after the war, Conrado refused to pay, arguing that his three years at the front had been sufficient dues for a lifetime. His name was removed from the list of active members. Later, in 1945 or 1946, there was a job opening on the countess's estate, because the armed guard, Francisco Luque Cuevas "The Ill Wind," had been fired for robbing the estate's beehives. Conrado applied, but was turned down because he was not a member of the Falange.

According to Conrado, some workers were able to establish themselves as permanent employees on the estates precisely because they were leftists. *There were right-wingers that what they did when the war was over was to take the most rebellious leftists under their wing in case all this changed again. So that nothing would happen to them. That happened here. Yes. Here and everywhere. Like insurance for them.* Having renounced his association with the Falange, Conrado, although a right-winger, had to resign himself to the same working conditions that leftists confronted. *Here after the war was over, work here was a disaster. There was work but you earned very little.*

If it is true, as Conrado said, that some right-wingers favored *the most rebellious leftists*, it was not a benefit extended to all leftists. Celedonio Escobar Reinoso was one of the town's most rebellious leftists because of his political and anti-religious attitudes. Far from being favored, he was marginalized economically to such an extent that life in Castilleja became impossible for him. Like Conrado, he earned very little when he worked, but he did not have the same access to work that Conrado had. *After the war, I went to work. The town was the same. The same old dog with a new collar. So they would give you a job, well, you had to be . . . for them to give me a job I had to put in twice the effort. I had to work twice as hard for them to give me a job.* Just as during the monarchy and the black biennium, the economic power of the employers gave them absolute political power. They could punish leftists by denying them work. Some workers left their hometown or even their country in search of work.

Two leftists from Castilleja who struggled to survive
Celedonio Escobar Reinoso

Celedonio Escobar was desperate for work. *I tried several times to join the Civil Guard, which was a way you could take in order to survive. According to the law they had, you know?, those who were sergeants in the army could go right into the corps without taking the exam, but it did not work for me. The Falange used to write up your background, politically, political antecedents. It did not work for me.* Then he reenlisted in the army. It must have been toward the end of 1941. The Spanish Blue Division was fighting alongside Germans on the Russian front. The division consisted exclusively of volunteers, fervent anti-Communists who wanted to avenge the Soviet intervention during the civil war. There was no risk Celedonio would be sent to the Russian front. He was not even incorporated into the army because at the time there were too many noncommissioned officers. *I remember when the war in Russia was under way, and there was no work here, well many of us enlisted then. But since I was a noncommissioned officer, well, they say, "Go home and we will call you."*

They called him in the winter of 1942/43. In the meantime, the Blue Division had suffered frightful casualties. The members of the division who returned described the fierce combat against numerically superior Soviet forces and the extreme cold. There were no longer enough volunteers to replace the many dead, wounded, sick, and captured, or those who had lost feet or hands to frostbite. The head of the Falange in Castilleja, José Cuevas Reinoso, brought Celedonio the news that the army had sent for him and urged him to volunteer for the Blue Division but Celedonio refused. *When they called me, it was at least a year later and I told him* [José Cuevas], *I say, "I am not going to Russia." That was already when the Germans' bread was beginning to turn hard on them in Russia.*

There was even one from here who went and who died there too, whose name was Antonio García, who was a sergeant like me. He was serving in Madrid and he was sent to Russia and the boy died there. And then they called for me to send me there and I said, "No, I am not going to Russia." I told him, "I will go [into the army], *but I am not going to Russia." He was the head of the Falange here. "Well, if you do not go to Russia, you are going to end badly." Because of the poverty there was here, because there was not even enough to eat, and if you were a leftist they did not give you work, so you would starve, eh? Well, he says to me, "You are going to end badly." I say, "Let it go. I am not going even if you kill me. I am not going now to Russia."*

Celedonio's refusal to volunteer for the Blue Division may have saved his life, but it cost him almost three decades of poverty. In the 1960's he tried to emigrate, but at first even that route was closed. *Then two or three times, after I was married with children, I tried to get out of Spain. That was in 1966. I was on the verge of going to the Dominican Republic with an emigration there was. And I wrote a letter to the minister. Then a lot of people from here went. They emigrated to the Dominican Republic. There was a family there that owned an estate in that Republic. I do not remember their name. And a lot of people went and they put them in the . . . the women on one side and the men on the other. And I remember when the minister answered my letter. And it turns out that the emigrants who were there . . . ". . . there has been a breach of contract and we find ourselves obligated to bring the people back here because of the bad working conditions." I remember when that minister answered my letter. What I wanted was to get out of here. I remember it well. They put a lot of obstacles in your way. You got there to the emigration office and they did not . . . they gave all the contracts to right-wingers.*

Finally, Celedonio was able to emigrate to France with others from Castilleja. He returned after six years because he did not like the cold weather or the job he had in a mine. It was not because of the way he was treated by the French, nor because he was isolated from other Spaniards. *The French had a very good opinion of Spaniards because they know the Spaniards are very hard-working people and they have always had a very good opinion of them. There were already many when we arrived. There were those from the war, political exiles. There were . . . how would I know? . . three hundred, four hundred thou-*

sand. And those people have had their children, they are married, and grandchildren. When he returned from France, Celedonio lived in Sanlúcar la Mayor where it was easier for him to find work. He was there for seven years before moving back again to his hometown after Franco's death.

Antonio García Ramírez

Like Celedonio, Antonio García was a sergeant when the war ended. He remained in the army because it afforded him the opportunity to study for a career in the postal service. He wanted to escape the poverty of being a leftist day laborer in Castilleja. His decision was logical, but it set off a series of events that would cost him his life. Celedonio Escobar mentioned him when speaking of his own refusal to join the Blue Division.

Others spoke of Antonio García to clarify their declaration that no one in Castilleja had died in combat. One was Miguel Rodríguez Caraballo. *No one died in the war. Manuel's son, but he did not die here. He died in the Blue Division in Russia. That boy disappeared and no one knows anything about him. They carried him off to Russia. They called them to formation, no?, and they counted off, "You, step forward," and the lot fell to him. A very good boy he was.* Antonio Monge Pérez's version was the same. *No one from here died at the front. The only combat death was one who died in the Blue Division. They took him off by force in the Blue Division. He did not want to go. Because they had killed his brother. That is right. And he was not a right-winger. He was a leftist. He was a Republican. And then, they selected him in Madrid, because they had them counting off one, two, three, four, five, six, seven . . . when they got to ten . . . and the poor thing, that was his fate, because they got him there, for the Blue Division. And then the poor thing died there.*

These testimonies explain how this leftist ended up in a unit that was supposed to be voluntary. Popularly called the "Blue Division," for the color of the Falangist shirt, the real name of the unit Franco sent to help Hitler was the "División Española de Voluntarios" or "DEV." Manuel García Ramírez showed me a photograph of his brother Antonio and told what he knew of his fate. *He was a sergeant by the end of the war. There he is* [in the photo] *with his stripe. And shortly after the end of the war he stayed in Madrid. He was studying for the postal service. He says, "I am not leaving the army until I finish studying for the postal service to find a job somewhere." And they took him off to Russia and that is where they left him. He used to write a lot until . . . it was during the Russian offensive when they surrounded all of that. Well, that is where he must have died. They reported him as missing.*

There was another from Castilleja also. He came back. They were about to give Antonio a leave and they did not even give him his leave. A brother of mine went to the provincial government building when the boys came back. He was asking them one by one about him. They had heard nothing there. But here [in Carrión] *there was an officer who was there in Russia, and he told me, he says, "Your brother, unfortunately, is not coming back because he was hospitalized with a leg wound and that hospital ended up in that encirclement." That was Juanito, Julio's son* [Lieutenant Colonel Juan Pérez]. *He told me. Antonio died there in the hospital. They bombarded it and it was completely destroyed. According to what that boy from here told me.* The little information Manuel García had, coincides with an incident during the battle of Krasni Bor on February 10, 1943, when a Blue Division field hospital was hit by an incendiary bomb and destroyed.[18]

During this testimony, Manuel García mentioned another Castilleja native who went to Russia in the Blue Division, but returned. In 2008, Feliciano Monge Pérez told me that this other man was Antonio Rodríguez Mantero "Antoñín," brother of "Manolín," the young Falangist who was mortally wounded during the confrontation with Communists in May 1936. Antoñín was also one of the Falangists who participated in the emasculation of the anarchist Lucrecio Paz Delgado. According to Feliciano, Antoñín had gone to Russia voluntarily to fight Communists.

Notes

1 Michael Richards, *A Time of Silence*, 92.
2 Carlos Barciela, "La España del 'estraperlo'," 109.
3 Ibid., 112.
4 Ibid., 110.
5 Ibid., 114.
6 Michael Richards, *A Time of Silence*, 139.
7 Carmen Muñoz Caraballo's file from the Seville Provincial Prison, Archive of the Second Territorial Military Tribunal.
8 Ángel Viñas, "La conexión entre autarquía y política exterior en el primer franquismo," in *Guerra, dinero, dictadura*, 205–37.
9 Paul Preston, *Franco: A Biography*, 608.
10 Ibid., 559.
11 Francisco Franco, *Palabras del Caudillo*, 157.
12 Paul Preston, *Franco: A Biography*, 344–5.
13 Carlos Barciela, "La España del 'estraperlo'," 114–15.
14 Alberto Reig Tapia, *Ideología e historia*, 73.
15 Paul Preston, *Franco: A Biography*, 559n2.
16 Michael Richards, *A Time of Silence*, 134.
17 Carlos Barciela, "La España del 'estraperlo'," 106.
18 Gerald L. Kleinfeld and Lewis A. Tambs, *Hitler's Spanish Legion*, 273.

Thirteen

Repression in the Postwar

Castilleja natives in the Franco regime's penal system

After the war, the Franco regime incarcerated hundreds of thousands of Spanish men and women in prisons, concentration camps, and labor battalions. Many were tortured. Tens of thousands were executed or died of disease or hunger. Four of these prisoners were natives of Castilleja del Campo.

Francisco Monge Romero

The only information I have about Francisco Monge is from his prison file. He was living in Espartinas, near Seville, and working as a chauffer. Arrested at the outbreak of the war, he was condemned in a court-martial on September 30, 1937, and sentenced to eight years and one day for the crime of "Incitement of Military Rebellion." It was a common justification for imprisoning those civilians who expressed opposition to the military coup against the constitutional legality of the Republic. On September 29, 1940, he was granted "conditional liberty." His sentence was expunged on September 16, 1944.[1]

Pedro Donaire Leal

The following summary of the postwar tribulations of Pedro Donaire Leal, schoolteacher and army captain, are from his prison file, the manuscript based on his memoir by his daughter, Matilde Donaire Pozo, and a conversation with Matilde and her brother, Eugenio.[2] Captain Pedro Donaire Leal had crossed the Pyrenees into France with other Republican officers on January 28, 1939. In February, the French authorities sent him back to Spain through Hendaye. From there, the Spanish authorities took him to Burgos. On March 11, he was taken by train to the Barcelona Model Prison, where he and one hundred and forty-six other men shared a room measuring 15.85 meters by 12 meters. There was one toilet, one washbasin, and a faucet. Infestations of scabies and lice were rampant. Food rations were scarce and the prisoners suffered vitamin deficiencies. On August 12, Pedro Donaire was transferred to the damp and lugubrious Montjuich Castle, where conditions were even worse. He was court-martialed on November 28, 1939, condemned for aiding and abetting rebellion, and sentenced to six years and one day of imprisonment.

At about the same time, one of his neighbors in Villanueva del Río, where Pedro had been a teacher before the war, filed a denunciation against him, motivated perhaps by Pedro's initiation as a Freemason in 1935. He belonged to the Mártires del Deber 41 lodge in Lora del Río (Seville).[3] Pedro would have to respond to the denunciation in another court-martial in Seville. His transfer began on February 13, 1940. Two civil guards took him by train to Castellón, where they were to be relieved by two other civil guards for the rest of the trip. Since the relief guards were not there, Pedro was held in the Castellón Provincial Prison for more than a week. The authorities seemed to have forgotten him. When two friends of his, who lived in Castellón, found out about his predicament, they passed the information on to the authorities and Pedro continued his journey. He entered the Seville Provincial Prison on February 22. On March 26, Pedro Donaire was granted provisional liberty because the judge in charge of his case had not ratified his detention order within the thirty days specified by the law. He reentered the prison on May 25. On June 27, he was transferred to the "Ave María" chalet, a detention center for army officers. More than a year later, on August 3, 1941, he was granted "conditional liberty."[4] His difficulties did not end there.

According to an investigation dated December 15, 1939, conducted by the National Education Ministry's Superior Ruling Commission of Investigation for Purges, Pedro Donaire Leal had been among the Republican schoolteachers deserving "definitive separation from service and dismissal from the instructional ranks, as well as disqualification from exercising any educational function." Furthermore, he found the door closed to other means of earning a living. Business owners were unwilling to employ a "red" ex-prisoner, either because of their own prejudices or from fear of reprisals. He would not find work until February 1943, when he was employed as the Seville representative of a Catalonian company that manufactured movie projectors. The work required him to travel extensively throughout Andalusia and Morocco. On these trips he experienced numerous unpleasant incidents with the police for being a person on "conditional liberty."

Although employed, Pedro Donaire, his wife, Rosario, and his two children, Matilde and Eugenio, continued living in two rooms in the house of one of his brothers-in-law. Property owners were as unwilling to rent apartments to "reds" as business owners were to employ them. Pedro confronted these prejudices many times. In an anecdote related by his son Eugenio, on one occasion a landlord began his interview with the question, "Where were you on July 18?" Pedro Donaire understood at once that he would not be able to rent the apartment and, before turning and walking out, he allowed himself the luxury of replying, "Exactly where I am right now, facing you."

Juan Antonio Luque Romero

In mid-1937, "Antonio Canitas" had crossed over to the Republican forces and was in Madrid when the war ended. On May 24, 1939, he returned to Castilleja del Campo and was arrested by two members of the Civil Guard. Turned over to the Military Tribunal number 31 in Sanlúcar la Mayor, he was interned in a concentration camp. On July 5, he was tried in Sanlúcar for military offenses in a summary proceeding. The judge was the infantry captain Enrique Bodegón de Castro. With his preventive detention ratified, Juan Antonio was transferred to the Seville Provincial Prison on July 6, 1939. He appeared before a court-martial on April 22, 1940, and was returned to the Seville Provincial Prison on July 10, 1940, sentenced to twenty years imprisonment.[5]

Oral testimonies, though somewhat vague about the chronology of Antonio's penal odyssey, provide information that is not in the documents, for example that two Castilleja residents denounced Juan Antonio and that he redeemed part of his sentence in a work battalion that constructed the canal of the lower Guadalquivir River, the so-called "Prisoners' Canal." As the only one from the town who crossed over to the other side while serving in the Nationalist army, Juan Antonio Luque Romero became an almost legendary figure in Castilleja for the stoicism with which he endured the harsh persecution he suffered in the postwar. The testimonies describe the subhuman conditions of his imprisonment, his life in the work battalion, and the true meaning of "liberty with surveillance." They also provide a portrait of this man of strong and defiant character, demonstrated especially during his court-martial, and of his honesty and charm, which earned him the confidence of people who could help him.

Marina Luque Reinoso, Juan Antonio's sister-in-law, and Narciso Luque Romero, his brother, described the various stages of his odyssey through the Franco regime's system of "justice." Marina: *My brother-in-law Antonio was in Madrid when the war ended and when they released him he came back here. Sometimes walking, other times . . . because he did not even have money for the train. Well, when he arrived in Castilleja, they hit him with a denunciation. Here in Castilleja they denounced him, saying that my brother-in-law Antonio had danced on the graves of Castilleja's right-wing dead, when here not a single one of them was killed in the war. He did not spend even one night at home. They took him to Sanlúcar. And from Sanlúcar they took him to the Seville Provincial Prison. And there, well, he was placed in a cell and every night they opened the lock as if to take him out to kill him. Or at least to scare him, no?*

Narciso: *My brother Antonio, the poor thing, never even entered the house, because the Civil Guard was there at once. They followed him here from Carrión. "But man, at least let him wash up." "No way. We have orders to take him to Sanlúcar right now." To a concentration camp they had there. They put him in a provisional concentration camp. They had . . . how should I know? . . . a thousand people at least.*

According to Narciso, the summary proceeding in Sanlúcar on July 5 for "military offenses" resulted in a death sentence. *He was several months in the concentration camp. From there they transferred him to the provincial jail in Seville. With a death sentence. He was in a cell in Seville for eight days. Whoever they put in a cell it was to kill them. What he told us later, he says, "There, every night a truck would arrive and they would park it at the door to the jail. And the commandant would start naming, for example, twenty or thirty. "Step forward, on the double." When there were twenty or thirty, "Ea, well, you can go back to bed." But not just one night. That was every night. There they killed more than half of those who were there, the poor things.*

When Juan Antonio's father, Antonio Luque Tebas, found out about the danger his son was in, he began to pull strings to save him. He went to see his son-in-law, Miguel Monge Pérez, the same cattle dealer who would later intervene to save his own brother Leovigildo and his cousin Basilio from being ruined by a fine imposed by Fiscalía de Tasas. *And then, while he was in the cell, well they informed my father because he went to see him. They say, "You cannot see him." The guard there told him. He says, "Why?" "Because your son has been placed in a cell* [where those condemned to death were separated from the general prison population housed in the courtyard]. *" He says, "And is that dangerous?" And he tells him yes. Then my father, with determination, went to see Miguel* [Monge] *Pérez, Leovigildo's brother. That man was a dealer on a large scale, a dealer in grains and animals, who knew everybody, military men as well as civilians. And he also knew the prison director. They were acquaintances.*

Then my father went to him and he says, "Look Miguel, this is what is happening to us. You see, Antonio is in jail. But the bad part is that he is in a cell and that is dangerous." He says, "Well look, tomorrow I am going to see the director. Rest easy because tomorrow I am going to see him because we have to get him out of there." Well he went . . . he behaved very well with us . . . and he talked to him. "Look, this man is a relative of mine." And he told him what he was like and what had happened to him and that they had falsely denounced him, because those denunciations were false. And, in short, he says to him there, "Alright then, nothing to it. We are going to get him out of the cell there." And so he was out of the cell but he remained in the prison until they sent him to a labor battalion.

Juan Antonio spent two years in the prison, during which time he appeared before a court-martial, on April 22, 1940. According to Narciso, the two residents of Castilleja who had denounced his brother believed their denunciation would remain anonymous, but that was not the case. *For them, he did not know. But man, that denunciation, they read it out loud to him at the tribunal, when they were going to judge him. And all the personnel that were there heard it. Because it was public. I mean, everyone who wanted to see him judged could go there. And we found out from the judge because he read it to the public. I did not go. My father went and my older brother, Miguel. The two of them went.*

Narciso repeated the dialogue between his brother and the judge, a dialogue that appears with variations in other testimonies, as evidence of Juan Antonio's bravery. *Alright, well, when the judge called his name, eh?, "Juan Antonio Luque Romero." "At your service." And he stood up, of course. "Is it true that on such and such a date, and on such and such a day, you crossed over to the reds?" He says, "Yes, sir. It is true." He says, "With your equipment and your rifle?" He says, "Yes. Whatever I had I took with me. Whatever I had." In short, the judge said, he says, "Alright Juan Antonio, well, we are going to sentence you. We are giving you forty years in prison." He says, "Very well." He says, "Well now I am going to tell you, judge, I am going to tell you that you are not as capable of giving them to me as I am of completing them . . ." The man says . . . Oh hoo. So that, ". . . because I feel young and strong . . ." Because he was young, of course. ". . . and I feel capable of completing the forty years." "Sit down man. Sit down," the judge told him. "Sit down." Later they judged him again and he got twenty years and one day.*

Juan Antonio's sister-in-law recreated the dialogue with the judge in a different way, but it is the same portrait of a man who did not mince his words. Marina Luque Reinoso believed that her brother-in-law's candor earned him the judge's sympathy. Then, according to her testimony, two right-wing residents of Castilleja wrote positive reports, refuting those who had denounced Juan Antonio. *His brother went to see it. My sister did not have the courage to go. And tied up, handcuffed to another, and there the judge told him, "Is it true that you crossed over to the red zone with your armament?" He says, "If I had an artillery piece with me, I would have taken that with me too. I would have crossed over with a cannon." The judge says, "We are going to stop right here because this man does not know what he is saying." But that is how clearly he spoke. He was saved by how clearly he spoke at the trial. And I think that is what saved him. And then he said, he says, "Do you know that you have two denunciations here?" And he told him, "From so-and-so and from so-and-so." They read the names of his denouncers saying that my brother-in-law Antonio . . . the two denouncers are dead now . . . that my brother-in-law Antonio had danced on the graves of the right-wing dead of Castilleja, when here not one was killed.*

When they asked for reports from Castilleja del Campo, then the grandfather of that girl in the bakery, Federico [Fernández Galeano], and Andrés [Luque Muñoz] from the Palace, Victoria's grandfather, went. And so, well, Victoria's grandfather and the baker lady's grandfather were the ones who sent good reports about my brother-in-law saying that . . . and they were the ones who were farthest to the Right you could find in Castilleja . . . that it was not true, that what they had said about my brother-in-law Antonio was untrue because my brother-in-law Antonio was . . . you ask anywhere in the town . . . no matter who you ask in Castilleja, you will see what he was like.

Narciso described the conditions in the Seville Provincial Prison during the years of hunger. *In that jail, they made it for two thousand men or three thousand, and they locked up five or six thousand, because they brought them in from everywhere. They brought a lot of them from the north there in order to separate them from their families. And they had them one on top of the other, those that were there, one on top of the other. And they did not give them more than water and bread because in the postwar they were short, completely lacking things to eat. Since we knew he was there, well, we used to go see him every week and we would bring him what we could, a basket of whatever, of fruit, with a blood sausage, a chorizo, because we could see that they were not giving him anything to eat. And whoever was from around here was saved because the families took it out of their own mouths to take it to them.*

But the poor things who were from the north, well, first of all their families did not know where they were because they did not tell them. They did not say, well, "Your son is in such and such a place." Or their brother or their father, no, no, no, no. And those poor things, well, what they ate was a broth with nothing in it. They were overcome with weakness and they got sick. And they would line up by threes in the evening or at midday to eat in the patio. Well my brother used to say, he says, "We were lined up there and, before you knew it, one would, poom, fall rotundly to the floor and, a second later, another in the other line, and every day a bunch of them would fall down, fainting."

Antonio's affability served him well in the prison, according to Marina. *Afterwards my brother-in-law worked as an aide to a captain. You can imagine the confidence the captain had in him, because he used to have to bring the captain his pistol, he even handed the captain his pistol inside the prison. And he used to make him coffee. The captain said to him, "Antonio, a cup of coffee, do you have one every morning?" He says, "My captain, when I make you coffee, the first cup I have already drunk myself." He was delightful.*

In the summer of 1941, Juan Antonio was transferred to a labor battalion under the jurisdiction of the Central Council for Redemption of Sentences. In the labor battalions, prisoners could work off part of their sentence, but the conditions were terrible. *Then, afterwards, they took my brother-in-law to that canal that was dug there in Alcalá. They put him there with a pick and shovel and he was working there just like a slave. And then they had some shacks and they had them sleeping there like hogs, exactly the same as hogs.*

The food in the labor battalions was almost as inadequate as in prison and the men's families had to help, according to Narciso. *My brother was there at least a year or a year and a half. And my father would take his horse, because you could not get there by car or anything, and every week he would take a basket of food. He would take the horse and he knew where he had to go and then he would stay at an inn or wherever, and in the morning he would start back here to work. Two or three days at least it took him, but he used to take him a basket every week because you cannot imagine how hard that work was and they hardly gave him anything to eat. And that probably killed him because he could not handle it. He suffered a lot. He suffered a lot.*

Eventually Juan Antonio was granted "liberty with surveillance," which meant living at the mercy of the local civil guards. Marina Luque Reinoso: *When he completed his sentence he returned to Castilleja. Antonio was a prisoner at least three or four years. Or five. Later he had to go every week to report at the barracks. He was quite a few years reporting at the Civil Guard barracks. And the civil guards . . . since the world consists entirely of good people and bad . . . because there were some civil guards who were bad and others who were better, well, then two civil guards used to come here to Castilleja and Antonio was in bed and they used to wake him up, "Antonio Luque Romero," and he would have to show himself at the window and they would aim their guns at him. Half the people do not know about that but, of course, when one has lived through it.*

Then a civil guard sergeant came here to Carrión who was very good, and then he was the one who cancelled his sentence for the rest of his life. He says, "You no longer have to come and report and now it is all over for you. Now you can go freely wherever you want." What a life he led! What a life he led! So when he was sixty-three years old he was already buried. He died in 1973.

Narciso Luque Romero's version goes into greater detail. *When he came back from the canal, he had to go to the Civil Guard barracks in Carrión de los Céspedes every week or every fifteen days. If it was pouring rain he had to go and report because otherwise he would go through what happened to his friend from Carrión. You will see. Wait until you hear. He used to show up at the door where the guard was, "Juan Antonio Luque Romero here, because I have to report." Then the guard would go in and he would go in too and they marked it down in the book.*

But by then, one year and then another, and a civil guard arrived there, a very good corporal, the only good one that has come. The rest, all terrible. But that was a good man, by the name of Bautista. I do not remember his last name, but Bautista was his first name. My brother went to report, and he says, "You, why do you have to report here every fifteen days?" He says, "Because that is the way it was ordered." He says, "Not you. They have not given you absolute liberty here?" He says, "Yes, I have finished the sentence between the prison and the canal." He says, "Then you are free, man, you are free." "The thing is I do not have anyone to pull the strings for me." He says, "You are going to do something, Antonio. If not you, look for someone who knows how, and you write a letter to the justice minister telling him all the details, all your information, and we will see what happens. Do it like that Antonio, do it like that, because this business of . . . you have already completed a good sentence."

In short, as soon as he got back, there was this Miguel Rodríguez [Caraballo], who used to work as a secretary in Carrión, at the Carrión town hall. He was a person who knew the ropes. And a very good person. He was a landowner from here. Well, he wrote the letter and Antonio gave him all the details about what had happened, that they caught him in Madrid, that he was in jail, in the labor camp, and that is how they laid it out for the justice minister in Madrid. And some days later there was a letter sent directly to my brother, eh? And, of course, it has been such a long time and . . . but, I mean, the minister wrote the letter, and it says, "You do not have to report anymore to the Carrión de los Céspedes barracks. You are totally free. You have completed the sentences they gave you and you . . . and besides, you are now like any other Spaniard."

It said a lot of things but I no longer remember. "And now I caution you Antonio about another thing. This letter, you should keep it as if it were a portrait of your mother. And when they call you for anything and you think they are going to give you a hard time, you present this letter to whomever, to the general, to the captain. 'Here, read this letter.' So never abandon this letter." And that is how it was, because he took it to Carrión and it was all over. It was all over. But, were it not for that corporal, well, he would have died reporting to Carrión because there would be no one to tell him that, like the corporal told him, "But man, I do not think it is right for you to be reporting here with your sentence completed, your whole life reporting here."

Narciso then told the story of Antonio's friend from Carrión, which illustrates how precarious life could be for those on "liberty with surveillance." *There was another who also went over to the other side, Domingo, who went over to the other side with Antonio the night they went over. That Domingo. From Carrión. Very good people. And when they caught him like they caught my brother too because they were both caught in Madrid, well, to prison too, in Seville like my brother. I do not know if he was at the canal or not . . . he probably was as well.*

Alright, well, he had to report too, like my brother. He reports one day at the barracks and the guard went and says, "Yes, yes, now you can go." But the guard was careless and did not mark him down in the book. Oh hoo! Oh hoo! But, the poor thing, he was the one who paid for it. They almost killed him. They call him, since the corporal reviewed the book and saw that he had not reported. Of course, the guard told the corporal . . . to cover up his responsibility . . . that he had not reported. He says, "No, no, no. I was on duty yesterday and he did not report."

Then they called him and they put him in a room. And they flayed him, the poor thing, with one of those horsewhips. He started in with, "Look, it is not my fault. I reported." "No, no. No, because it is not marked down in the book." What do you think of that? "But man, bring the guard who was here. See what he says." "Nothing doing. He says no." I mean, they did not kill him because, how should I know? And he reported the same as my brother the day assigned to him. But the guard forgot and did not mark it down and later the corporal reviewed the book and he says, "That Domingo is not here? He did not report yesterday?" The poor thing moved to Aznalcóllar because he was panic-stricken, and he went to live in Aznalcóllar. He rented a house there and he went there, married and all, out of fear of the guard. A very good person.

Eugenio Pozo de la Cueva

This native of Castilleja del Campo was arrested in Seville on July 27, 1936, and taken to the Falange headquarters where he was tortured to reveal the whereabouts of the Castilleja schoolteacher Joaquín León Trejo. Then he was taken to the Jáuregui Cinema, converted into a detention center, and from there to the Terceros Barracks. By November, he was imprisoned in the cellars of the Plaza de España. Later he was transferred to the Seville Provincial Prison. In January 1937, he was released, since there were no denunciations against him, nor had he been tried before any tribunal.

Eugenio was arrested again after the war, in February 1943. By then he was married and employed as a worker at the Hispano Aviación factory. He was taken to Madrid where he was incarcerated in the Porlier Provincial Prison on February 25. While he was there, his first child was born, on March 7. Eugenio Pozo was transferred from Madrid to Burgos on March 15, where he entered the Central Prison the following day. He was released on October 27 and sentenced to internal exile in Granada where, according to his niece, Matilde Donaire Pozo, ". . . he lived precariously, without work or money, sustained only by the small remittances his poor mother was able to send him."[6] Matilde did not remember the date his internal exile ended. While he was in prison, Eugenio wrote a poem to his newborn son. The dates of his imprisonment appear at the end of the manuscript. For a transcription of the poem, along with a prose translation, see Appendix I.

On April 7, 1945, Eugenio was arrested again by the secret police and incarcerated in the Seville Provincial Prison at the disposition of the Special Tribunal for the Repression of Freemasonry and Communism. On May 14, 1945, the Special Tribunal ordered his release on the condition that he "report at the greatest brevity to the Police Chief of Granada, place of his attenuated imprisonment." On May 19, Eugenio Pozo was placed at "liberty," meaning "attenuated imprisonment." [7] His exile to Granada, called in his file "attenuated imprisonment," was an especially cruel form of "liberty with surveillance." The freed person had to live 250 kilometers from his habitual residence.[8] Granada is precisely 250 kilometers from Seville, Eugenio Pozo's habitual residence. His arrest in Seville makes one suspect that he had tried to evade the surveillance of the secret police in order to see his son, who had just had his second birthday.

The reason for the eight months Eugenio spent in prison in 1943, and the internal exile he endured until at least 1945, was that he was a Freemason like his brother-in-law Pedro Donaire Leal. Eugenio had been initiated in the Isis and Osiris 6 lodge in Seville in 1935.[9] His arrest on February 25, 1943, was probably due to the discovery of his name on his lodge's membership list in the archive on Masonic activity maintained by the Special Tribunal for the Repression of Freemasonry and Communism in Salamanca.

"Liberty with surveillance for all"
The regime of investigations and reports

There was another, more generalized, form of repression in the postwar. I call it "liberty with surveillance for all." The Civil Guard, the Falange, the Special Tribunal for the Repression of Freemasonry and Communism, the Tribunals of Political Responsibilities, and many other organizations investigated and accumulated reports on the private lives of individuals.

The evidence of this surveillance is only a small part of what once existed. There was a paper shortage during the war and postwar, and municipalities often resorted to the archives, selling paper by the kilo.[10] In the case of documents referring to the Falange, there is evidence of deliberate destruction after Franco's death, especially on the eve of the first democratic municipal elections, in 1979, when the Franco regime's town councils were about to be replaced.[11] Castilleja del Campo's archive is fairly complete for the years of the Republic, but for the years of the civil war and the postwar, one sees the ravages of neglect and deliberate destruction. I have only been able to find three documents of the type that interests us here. But these give an idea of the intensity with which the private lives of the town's residents were investigated.

The first of these documents is a letter from the commandant of the Civil Guard barracks in Carrión de los Céspedes to the "Municipal Judge of the Town of Castilleja," Enrique Luque Ramírez. It is entitled "With interest in reports on a resident," and is dated November 16, 1939. The commandant had been ordered by the "Provincial Delegate of Information and Investigation" of the Falange to report "with the maximum breadth of details" on "the political-social background and moral conduct before and after the National Uprising" of the Castilleja resident Manuel Romero Rufino, an ex-combatant in Franco's forces, 1933 call-up, and a member of the Falange. Written by hand in the margin of the letter there appears "informed 11-17-939." There is no copy of the municipal judge's reply.[12]

The second document was also addressed to the "Municipal Judge of the Town of Castilleja del Campo." It too is from the commandant of the Civil Guard barracks in Carrión, Jerónimo Casas, and is entitled "With interest in reports on a resident." It is dated June 28, 1940. This time it was a military judge who requested "reports on the conduct observed for the resident of that locale, Felix García Ramírez, as well as his political social background and his present residence." Handwritten in the margin of the letter there appears "Answered June 28, 1940. Automotive Workshop Las Palmas Gran Canaria. He entered service about month Septbre 1939 in Seville Inftry n° 6." [13] Félix García Ramírez was the brother of Lutgardo García Ramírez, shot on August 27, 1936. Another brother, Antonio, was serving in the army in Madrid. He would die in Russia in the Blue Division.

The letters of this type in the Castilleja municipal archive, preserved either by chance or carelessness, must have been only the tip of the iceberg. There had probably been scores of them lost or purged. There are no copies of the reports sent by the municipal judge, but one can imagine they would be extremely subjective. The residents being investigated probably did not even know that these reports existed, much less their contents, but the treatment Manuel Romero Rufino would receive in the Falange, or Félix García Ramírez in his regiment, would depend upon the reports about their "social-political background and moral conduct" written by the municipal judge.

The third document of this type in the Castilleja archive indicates that not even the dead escaped the investigative interest of the authorities. It was sent directly to the Castilleja municipal judge from the Provincial

Court of Inquiry for Political Responsibilities in Seville, without the intervention of the Civil Guard. Dated February 27, 1941, it is a request for the "death certificate of the resident who was from that locale José Pérez Rodríguez, to whom according to reports we have received was applied the War Decree, or, if not, inform us of the municipal district in which said demise occurred." The municipal judge responded two days after the communiqué was sent, probably the same day it was received. Handwritten in the margin there appears "Answered March 1, 1941."[14]

The municipal judge did not need to make many inquiries. José Pérez Rodríguez's death was a dramatic event remembered by the whole town. He was the only victim killed in the streets of Castilleja and his death had great repercussions. Furthermore, in March 1941, the town's mayor was the same Antonio Rodríguez Fernández who had communicated with the civil governor on November 19, 1938, regarding the posthumous confiscation of a parcel belonging to José Pérez Rodríguez. Curiously, when the Castilleja municipal judge answered the communiqué from the Examining Magistrate for Political Responsibilities in Seville, no death certificate existed for José Pérez Rodríguez. His death was recorded in the civil death registry a little more than a month later, on April 10, 1941. This inscription may have been motivated by the correspondence between the Castilleja municipal judge and the Examining Magistrate for Political Responsibilities in Seville.

Besides the reports collected on individuals without their knowledge, it was sometimes the subject of investigation who had to seek out guarantees to their character in order to secure employment. This was the case for Concepción García Baquero, widow of the Castilleja schoolteacher, Joaquín León Trejo, shot on August 22, 1936. She supported herself and her daughter Carmen with a series of substitute teaching jobs in Seville until, in 1949, she found a more permanent position, according to her son Antonio. *They were giving her temporary jobs. And there was an inspector there who found her a substitute job that was going to last her a long, long time. She was at a school in Triana, San Jacinto, for fourteen or fifteen years. He found her a job substituting for a teacher who had dementia. And she was there for the fourteen years the job lasted and she used to say, "Ay, God, may the crazy woman last me a long time."* She had to seek reports from the authorities in order to teach. One of her grandsons, Diego León López, gave me photocopies of four documents his grandmother had saved.

The first document is from the mayor of Seville, who, on February 5, 1949, certified "that from the reports acquired by this City Government and documents that have been consulted, it results that Concepción García Vaquero [*sic*], resident of this city on *Feria* numb. 23, has shown and constantly shows good political and moral conduct." The second document, dated February 8, 1949, is from a corporal of the Civil Guard, Francisco Carrillo Rojas, who certified "that from the reports acquired concerning Dña Concepción García Vaquero [*sic*], . . . during her residence in this Post's district has observed good conduct and morality, lacks social-political antecedents, and is considered a fervent supporter of the Glorious National Movement."

The third document is from Eduardo López, the parish priest of San Pedro and San Juan Bautista, and is dated March 1, 1949. He certified "that according to the reports filed in this Archive in my charge Dª Concepcion Garcia Baquero, widow, Domiciled at Feria street number 23 of this parish observes very good religious and moral conduct." The last of the documents given me by Concepción's grandson is from two years later, July 4, 1951. It is from Rodolfo Valenzuela Granja, Provincial Undersecretary of the National Delegation for Information and Investigation of Falange Española. "That having consulted the existing records in the archives of the Delegation, concerning Dª Concepción García Baquero of 59 years of age, . . . by profession Elementary Teacher, and with domicile in Seville, Feria street, number 23, it results That she observes good moral and social-political conduct."

Concepción García Baquero had to turn to the Seville mayor's office and to representatives of the Civil Guard, the church, and the Falange for recommendations in order to work as a substitute elementary school teacher. Since these were the very institutions that shared responsibility for the assassination of her husband, it must have been humiliating to have to ask them to vouch for her good religious, social-political, and moral conduct. Corporal Francisco Carrillo Rojas' testimony that this widow "is considered a fervent supporter of the Glorious National Movement" that had taken her husband from her must have been especially difficult.

The entire town under surveillance: "General Cuesta's Papers," the "War Tribunal," and the "General Lawsuit"

From the earliest days of the civil war, the Nationalist authorities were eager to document the atrocities committed in each town before and during its "liberation." These activities increased in the postwar and culminated in the elaboration of the "General Lawsuit," whose purpose was to quantify the right-wing victims and catalogue the illegal and cruel acts committed during the "red domination of Spain." Castilleja del Campo did not escape this scrutiny.

A forerunner of the General Lawsuit in Andalusia was a collection of reports sent from the Civil Guard posts in response to a questionnaire prepared by the head of the General Staff of the Second Division, General José Cuesta Monereo. This documentation was later sent to the Military Historical Service where it was given the name "General Cuesta's Papers." The report on Castilleja was sent September 21, 1940, from the commandant of the Civil Guard post in Carrión, Jerónimo Casas, to the General Staff of the Second Division. His report was succinct to the point of being insulting to the town's residents, whatever their ideology:

> It was liberated on July 24, 1936, by a small column consisting of personnel from the Civil Guard, Falangists and Requetés, commanded by Don Ramón Carranza. No curious incidents worth mentioning occurred. Two of the leaders fled, but they turned themselves in a few months later [*A reference, no doubt, to Manuel Tebas Escobar and Lucrecio Paz Delgado*]. It did not suffer red or Nationalist bombardments. No outstanding or heroic act worthy of mention was performed by the residents of this locale. Nor did any resident stand out for philanthropic acts, although in general all responded willingly to the call for contributions.[15]

More interesting is the document with regard to Castilleja del Campo generated by the "War Tribunal of the Army of the South," published in 1939:

> Modest town of 800 inhabitants, 32 kilometers from the capital, it was occupied by national troops on July 24, 1936. On the 19th of the same month and year, miners from Río-Tinto, on their passage through this town, assaulted the houses of people of order, carrying off arms and munitions and employing, for that end, all types of threats and coercions.
>
> Social questions in this small locale acquired serious proportions after the disastrous elections of February 1936. Arbitrary arrests were practiced against landowners and people of the right, labor agreements were not observed, demanding day-labor at extremely elevated wages, in which the general norm was the failure to comply with the law and the persecution of any idea impregnated with a moral and religious character.[16]

The first sentence of this report confines itself to the facts, although it overestimates the town's population by a little over fifty inhabitants. The second sentence is also relatively objective, but it omits the fact that, according to the residents' testimonies, the miners from Río Tinto carried off arms belonging to leftists as well as to people on the Right. Nor does it mention that the Popular Front authorities of Castilleja restrained the miners when they passed through the town. The authors of the report were not interested in anything that could present leftists in a positive light.

It is in the last two sentences that the authors' imagination and selective memory are evident. There is no mention of the attempt on the part of Castilleja right-wingers to falsify the elections of February 1936, casting more than one ballot per voter. Then, the leftist victors in those elections are accused of practicing arbitrary arrests against landowners and people of the right. The only arrests in Castilleja del Campo during the Popular Front were those carried out by the Civil Guard against Casildo Escobar Reinoso, Manuel Luque Cuevas, and Gustavo Luque Romero, the Falangists who had accompanied Manuel Rodríguez Mantero to the highway on May 31 to confront the young Communists who were returning from a rally in Huelva.

The second example of the "serious proportions" that "social questions in this small locale acquired" during the Popular Front is full of exaggerations and omissions: "Labor agreements were not observed, demanding day-labor at extremely elevated wages, in which the general norm was the failure to comply with the law." During the Popular Front, day laborers in Castilleja earned the same wages as during the first Republican biennium, between nine and ten pesetas, in accord with the labor agreements negotiated by mixed juries. As far as the failure to comply with the law is concerned, there is no mention of the landowners' lockout during the Popular Front, a violation of the Law of Obligatory Cultivation. Nor is there any mention of the distribution of clandestine leaflets that led to a search of "La Patronal" (the landowners' center and Falange headquarters) by members of the Civil Guard on March 27.

Finally, the report mentions "the persecution of any idea impregnated with a moral and religious character" during the Popular Front. This reflects the opinion of one sector of Castilleja's residents. The parish priest Felipe Rodríguez Sánchez complained of this persecution in his letters to Cardinal Ilundáin during the first Republican biennium. But if the authors of the preliminary report on Castilleja had dealt with events after the town's occupation, they would have observed that some of the town's defenders of ideas of "a moral and religious character" were less scrupulous than their persecutors regarding the moral and religious idea expressed in the fifth commandment. Reports such as this would be important sources for the Franco regime's official histories of the Republic.

After the war, the regime's propagandists continued to look for evidence of Republican criminality in an investigation called the "Causa General" (General Lawsuit). Created by decree on April 26, 1940, this was a lawsuit filed by the Attorney General's office against the Popular Front government.[17] There is a document in the Castilleja municipal archive sent from

the "General Lawsuit of Granada, Seville, Córdoba and Huelva," Dated
October 6, 1942, it is a request for the names of all persons imprisoned
during the Popular Front, and a report on their treatment while in "red
jails," including the names of the prison directors and guards, especially
those responsible for acts of cruelty or the killing of prisoners.[18]
Handwritten in the margin of the letter are the words "Answered on Novber
6 1942 negatively."

Information in Franco's Spain

A one way street

The various repressive organizations of the Franco regime collected infor-
mation on the private lives of its citizens, but these same citizens had no
access to basic information relevant to their lives. Concepción García
Baquero's experience was typical. She had married Joaquín León Trejo in
Seville. After their sons José and Antonio were born, the family moved to
Pruna where Joaquín worked as a schoolteacher. During the first years of
the Republic, Joaquín was also the mayor of Pruna. The couple's daughter
Carmen was born there. In 1932, Joaquín accepted a teaching position in
Castilleja del Campo. He was shot on August 22, 1936.

Concepción spent the entire war without knowing where her husband
had been shot and buried. Her son José León García told how his mother
found out where her husband was. *In Seville there was a gentleman who had a
locksmith's shop. And he was a neighbor of ours, across the street, when I was born.
And he knew my grandfather and my father and all. His name was Manuel
Carrande. And this gentleman told my mother three years later, he says, "Conchita,
I know where Joaquín is." "You know where Joaquín is?" He says, "Yes." She says,
"How?" He says, "Well, by chance. But I know. And where he is buried and every-
thing."*

*This gentleman was in Castilblanco de los Arroyos with Queipo de Llano's army.
They drafted him into the army to open the treasury chests in the town halls and the
justice offices and wherever. Mobilized. Militarized. And one night he was in a
casino in Castilblanco playing cards and in come some of the men from the town at
three o'clock in the morning or thereabouts and they say, "They have just brought
three men from Seville there to kill them." They say, "One of them is Joaquín León
Trejo, the schoolteacher from Castilleja del Campo." This man said, he says, "You
mean from Pruna." They say, "No, no, from Castilleja, from Castilleja." Because
that gentleman knew we were in Pruna but he did not know that we were in
Castilleja. And they say, "Do you want to see? They are still digging the pit." And
he went there and he saw him, how they were burying him. He put him in a sack*

and helped them to bury him well. They say to him, "Do you know him?" He says, "Of course."

José León García's strange professional odyssey would lead him to work right next to the cemetery where his father was shot and the common grave where he was buried. During the war, José had learned to be a draftsman, a trade he would practice until the postwar when, after some success as an amateur actor, José decided to dedicate himself full-time to the theater. Eventually he became a famous circus clown, a profession his sons would also pursue. They would work with him as the Pepín León Trio.

I was working in a circus in Castilblanco and I have seen where they are buried. Because the circus was set up right in front of the door to the cemetery and I . . . of course, this was in the year 1963 . . . and I say, (whispering theatrically) *"Did they bring a lot of people here? Did they bring people here from Seville to shoot them? Did they bring a lot of people?" "Yes," and he says, "There where that wire fence is and those 'jaramagos'* [black mustard]*." It is all jaramagos and with a fenced enclosure like a corral. "That is where they are buried." And the cemetery wall there, the traces of where they had patched the bullet holes. Yes. I have seen it. I have been there.* In 2004, I visited the cemetery in Castilblanco de los Arroyos. It is indeed right next to a recreation area, ideal for setting up a circus. The jaramagos are still there, but not the patched bullet holes or the fenced enclosure, only rubble. I took several photographs and later showed them to José León García. He confirmed that it was, in fact, the wall against which his father had been shot.

Manufactured information: payment for lying

At some time during the postwar, papers arrived at the Castilleja del Campo town hall. The widows of the men who had been shot were asked to sign them in exchange for a small monthly pension. The widows' husbands were described as "dead in war action." It put the widows in a conflictive situation. To sign a lie of this sort would seem like a disloyalty to the memory of their husbands, but the pension, as small as it was, would help them feed their children.

According to her daughter Sara, Suceso Rodríguez Luque refused to sign it. *A paper was brought that they wanted the widows to sign. Two years or three or four must have gone by since my father's death. Which is why my mother never collected a pension because those who did not sign never received anything. All the widows from here never collected a cent because no one wanted to sign. All the widows were in agreement, since the paper did not say what it should have, because the paper did not say the truth. They discussed it among themselves and no one wanted to sign, of course, because it was a fraud what it said. Because they would sign it when it put the truth. That they had been killed. But, of course, that is not what they wanted. And we have had to be here living with them. What else could we do?*

Sara was mistaken when she said none of the widows signed the paper. Carmen Muñoz Caraballo did, according to her daughter Otilia. *There was a time when some people came here with a paper to sign saying that those men had died from being wounded in the war, and they gave a payment if the widows signed. That came . . . what year was it? . . . I do not remember. You had to deal with a lot of papers, and many widows did not want to do it. It was nonsense, because they lost everything, because it did not matter anymore. It did not matter. The papers came here to the town hall. My mother signed. But it was not true, I mean, the reality was not what they said there. It did not say, "We have killed them." Not that. Because, of course, they never concerned themselves about that.*

You got money every month. I do not know if it was twenty something or thirty something. Something like that every month. Thirty-two pesetas or something like that. A paymaster was in charge of that. We arranged the thing through a paymaster and we had to go to Seville to the paymaster's house and collect that money. I do not know if that paymaster kept some for himself. Of course, he must have kept some. Because it was not very out in the open. It was not very legal. Because otherwise it would have to come like the old age pension or like the widow's pension directly to your bank. When we used to collect it, we had to go to Seville to the paymaster's house. It was not much what you collected. But that is how we got by.

It was a form of persecution to present these widows the option of collecting a paltry sum every month in exchange for signing a lie about the circumstances of their husbands' deaths. The authorities were taking advantage of impoverished mothers who had lost their source of income when their husbands were shot. The same authorities who had caused this loss then wanted to cover up the crime with paperwork.

Notes

1 Francisco Monge Romero's file from the Seville Provincial Prison, Archive of the Second Territorial Military Tribunal.
2 Matilde Donaire Pozo, "Largo camino hacia la paz" (unpublished work, photocopy courtesy of the author).
3 Leandro Álvarez Rey, *Aproximación a un mito*, 256.
4 Pedro Donaire Leal's file from the Seville Provincial Prison, Archive of the Second Territorial Military Tribunal.
5 Juan Antonio Luque Romero's file from the Seville Provincial Prison, Archive of the Second Territorial Military Tribunal. This file does not include his sentence, which appears in a letter sent on May 11, 1940, to the Castilleja del Campo Municipal Judge. Dossier 24, Office of the Justice of the Peace, Castilleja del Campo.

6 Matilde Donaire Pozo, "Eugenio Pozo de la Cueva, mi tío."

7 Eugenio Pozo de la Cueva's file from the Seville Provincial Prison, Archive of the Second Territorial Military Tribunal.

8 Francisco Moreno Gómez, "La represión en la posguerra," in Santos Juliá, *Víctimas de la Guerra Civil*, 299.

9 Leandro Álvarez Rey, *Aproximación a un mito*, 301.

10 Francisco Espinosa Maestre, *La Guerra Civil en Huelva*, 18.

11 Ibid., 18n2; Alfonso Lazo, *Retrato de fascismo rural en Sevilla*, 14.

12 Correspondence, Castilleja del Campo Municipal Archive.

13 Ibid.

14 Ibid.

15 I am grateful to Francisco Espinosa Maestre for sending me this text together with an explanation of its historical context.

16 WAR TRIBUNAL OF THE ARMY OF THE SOUTH: SEVILLE (FEBRUARY 16 / JULY 18 / SEPTEMBER 11). 5 MONTHS OF POPULAR FRONT / 2 MONTHS OF MARXISM. Preliminary Report. Situation of the province of Seville from February 16 until its liberation. III TRIUMPHAL YEAR. I am grateful to Francisco Espinosa Maestre for sending me this text.

17 Alberto Reig Tapia, *Ideología e historia*, 22n2.

18 Correspondence, Castilleja del Campo Municipal Archive.

Fourteen

The Endless Postwar

The Franco dictatorship

The scars left by civil wars are more enduring than those left by wars between nations, because the victors and vanquished continue to live side by side. During the long Franco dictatorship, the celebrations of the July 18 coup, the April 1 "Day of Victory," and the October 1 "Day of the Caudillo," were annual reminders of the war. The streets and plazas named for the victors' heroes and martyrs were daily reminders of who had won and who had lost. Physical repression of the losers imposed silence about the past. In Castilleja del Campo, this fear did not end with Franco's death. Those in the town who are afraid to bring up "all those questions," or those who do not want others to bring them up, are still living the postwar. The winners and losers of the Spanish civil war also lived in two different economic realities.

The end of international ostracism: 1947 to 1953

The "years of hunger" were the logical result of the war, but Spain's slow recuperation was due to international events and the regime's economic policies. The Second World War and the international ostracism of the regime after the European conflict prevented Spain from receiving the foreign aid necessary for reconstruction. The regime's policy of autarky discouraged foreign investment and trade, and increased the inequality between those who could take advantage of the system's inherent corruption and everyone else.

The isolation or self-absorption of Spain had its most costly consequences in 1947. On June 5 of that year, the United States announced the Marshall Plan for the reconstruction of Western Europe, with the intention of making it a bulwark against Soviet expansion.[1] Perceived as a fascist anachronism in the new Europe, Spain was excluded.[2] It was the price all Spaniards paid for the survival of Franco's regime. Dean Acheson, secretary of state under President Truman, suggested offering Franco asylum outside Spain with the promise of economic aid after his departure.[3] It was somewhat naïve to think that the Spanish people's welfare would matter more to the Caudillo than his own personal power, and the offer was never even made.

For the time being, Franco relied on his friendship with the Argentine dictator Juan Domingo Perón. The importation on credit of foodstuffs and other Argentinean goods was a lifeline for the regime during the years 1946 to 1948. During the last of these years, Argentina provided 25 percent of the food consumed by Spaniards. In 1949, Argentinean aid diminished due to economic problems that plagued Perón's own regime. In February 1949, the Spanish economic crisis was so severe that the minister of industry and commerce, Juan Antonio Suanzes, told Franco that without aid from the United States there would be a collapse within six months.[4]

The same month, Spain negotiated a twenty-five million dollar loan from the Chase National Bank. As small as this aid was, it indicated the beginning of a change in the United States' attitude toward Spain.[5] A series of events convinced many in the United States that international Communism was a danger that justified alliances with all those who opposed its expansion. In August 1949, the Soviet Union exploded its first atomic bomb. Two months later, Mao triumphed in China. And on June 24, 1950, North Korea invaded South Korea. Some politicians in the United States were convinced that a third world war was imminent and the American military considered the Iberian Peninsula a possible bridgehead for the reconquest of a Soviet Europe.[6] The participation of Franco's Blue Division on the Russian front during the Second World War had previously been an obstacle to the regime's acceptance by the western democracies, but it came to be seen by the United States as evidence of Franco's reliability as an ally in the cold war against Communism.[7]

On November 16, 1950, President Truman authorized a loan of sixty-two and a half million dollars to Spain through the Export Import Bank and on December 27, he named Stanton Griffis ambassador to Madrid, the first American ambassador in four and a half years. Negotiations began which would culminate in the Madrid Pacts of September 26, 1953, during the Eisenhower administration. In exchange for the construction of three air bases and a naval base in Spain, the United States granted two hundred and twenty-six million dollars in technological and military aid, principally in the form of obsolete arms used in the Second World War or in Korea. The economic aid was limited to construction projects of military importance: roads, seaports, etc.

The Madrid Pacts were an executive agreement and not an official military treaty, which would have required the approval of the United States Senate, where there were still liberals who would have voted against it. Nevertheless, for internal consumption, Franco presented the accord as an authentic alliance between equals. During the celebrations of the Day of the Caudillo, October 1, 1953, Franco had himself photographed together with the American ambassador, who had to bend down to shake the diminutive dictator's hand. The photographer took the photograph from an angle that made the ambassador appear as a supplicant bowing before a sovereign.[8]

As evidence of the effectiveness of this propaganda, in 1990 a native of Castilleja, Aniceto Luque Luque, still believed it. *I remember that they came here to see Franco. As a statesman he was great and as an organizer greater still. And that man with his charisma or whatever, they came to see him here. Not there in their country. Franco never traveled out of Spain ever.* Aniceto was thinking of the visits to Spain by President Eisenhower in December 1959, by President Nixon in October 1970, and by President Ford in May 1975. But he had forgotten Franco's trips to Hendaye, France for his meeting with Hitler in October 1940, to Bordighera, Italy for a meeting with Mussolini in February 1941, and to Lisbon for a meeting with the Portuguese dictator Antonio de Oliveira Salazar in October 1949.

Apart from their propagandistic value, the Madrid Pacts meant the end of international ostracism and a considerable infusion of currency. According to official American statistics, economic aid to Spain from the United States during the next ten years would amount to one thousand six hundred and eighty-eight million dollars, as well as five hundred and twenty-one million dollars in military aid. The price for this aid was a loss of sovereignty. Franco was obliged to expose the country to the dangers of nuclear war. It was especially irresponsible to allow the construction of American bases near large population centers, for example the air base in Torrejón de Ardoz, twenty kilometers from Madrid. The pacts also included conditions that would eventually require fundamental changes in the regime's economic policies, such as setting a more realistic exchange rate for the peseta and increasing foreign trade. For a while, the regime was not prepared to abandon the autarkic system, cornerstone of Falangist ideology, and ignored these parts of the agreement.[9]

The Madrid Pacts with the United States consolidated the power of Franco's regime and gave it a certain level of international respectability, which is paradoxical in the extreme. The year before the pacts, Franco had published a book with the title *Freemasonry*, under the pseudonym Jakim Boor.[10] This diatribe appeared originally as a series of articles in the Falangist newspaper *Arriba*. Franco reiterated his belief that the United

States and England were the centers of a "Masonic International" that was conspiring with the Communist International. Nevertheless, it would be the United States that would make a pact with Franco, motivated by its confrontation with international Communism. Franco's regime was rescued by the cold war between his two bêtes noires.

The Spanish economy in neutral: 1954 to 1960

The end of international ostracism eliminated one of the factors that were putting the brakes on the Spanish economy, but the other factor, the regime's economic policies, remained. It was American aid after the Madrid Pacts that exposed the incapacity of autarky to confront the country's economic problems.[11] Between 1953 and 1956 there were constant budget deficits due to state investments in autarkic industrial monopolies. Lacking similar investments to stimulate the agricultural sector, the import of foreign foodstuffs continued to increase. Such decisions, evidence of the economic ineptitude of Franco and his ministers, produced spiraling inflation and a negative balance of payments. During 1955, for example, the cost of living index had risen by 55 percent. With wages set by the government, those who suffered most from the economic crisis were the members of the working class.[12]

Franco reacted as he always did when confronted by crises. He formed a new government, the sixth in twenty years. The cabinet he assembled on February 22, 1957, included two technocrats, members of the Catholic lay organization Opus Dei. One was the new finance minister Mariano Navarro Rubio, and the other was the new commerce minister Alberto Ullastres Calvo. Another member of Opus Dei, Laureano López Rodó, took up a new post created especially for him, director of the Office for Economic Coordination and Planning. Although it was not at the ministerial level, it would be a very influential post. During the next two years, Mariano Navarro Rubio, Alberto Ullastres Calvo, and Laureano López Rodó would advocate the administrative and economic modernization of the regime.[13] The changes they implemented would go far beyond anything Franco could have imagined when he formed the 1957 government.

In August 1957, Spain adjusted the exchange rate from five pesetas to the dollar to forty-two and Ullastres Calvo announced his intention to eliminate state control of prices.[14] External and internal developments gave the technocrats some trump cards to play. In early 1958, six European governments had ratified treaties establishing the European Economic Community, the Common Market. It was a spectacular success from the beginning, convincing many Spanish administrators that a prosperous future for the country depended on the integration of its economy into that of the rest of the western world. Throughout 1958, inflation continued to spiral out of control in Spain, resulting in a series of strikes and other indications of working-class militancy, and underscoring the need to reform the regime's economic policies.[15]

In 1959, after four years of inflation and deficits in its balance of payments, Spain was on the verge of bankruptcy and about to declare a suspension of payments. The International Monetary Fund offered to draw up a stabilization plan for the Spanish economy. Mariano Navarro Rubio and Alberto Ullastres Calvo were able to break Franco's resistance and, on March 6, the cabinet adopted the plan. There was also a new devaluation of the peseta, from forty-two pesetas to the dollar to sixty, and a reduction of public spending. According to what the head of government, Luis Carrero Blanco, told Laureano López Rodó, Franco was not happy.[16] But the Caudillo could take comfort in the fact that one of the regime's most outlandish public projects, the construction of Franco's mausoleum, the Valley of the Fallen, had been completed after nineteen years. It would be inaugurated on April 1, the Day of Victory.

The "boom": The decade of the 1960s

The stabilization plan included the elimination of state control of wages and prices, and the exposure of domestic industry to foreign competition. The immediate effect was negative, with the closure of many businesses, an immense rise in unemployment, and a small decrease in real wages.[17] The unemployment problem was solved after 1961 with the export of excess labor. The rest of Europe was experiencing unprecedented prosperity at the time and was able to absorb hundreds of thousands of Spanish workers.[18] These workers sent enough money home to provide the country an important source of foreign currency, contributing to a positive balance of payments.[19]

At the same time, other advantages of economic integration with the rest of the world became apparent. British, French, and German workers had enough disposable income to allow them to spend their vacations in Spain, which offered the attraction of its warm climate and low cost of living, with a consequent boom in tourism. With the suspension of restrictions on investment, the regime's repressive labor laws offered foreign investors the guarantee of a work force accustomed to privations and willing to work long hours for low wages. In the course of the decade, the most dramatic economic development and rise in living standard in Spain's history took place.

The boom also affected the life of agricultural workers. The exodus to foreign countries, or to Spanish cities in search of higher wages in the manufacturing or tourist industries created a labor shortage in the agricultural sector, stimulating greater mechanization and higher wages for the workers who stayed behind. Between 1962 and 1970 the number of tractors in Spain increased from one for every five hundred and sixty-three acres to one for every one hundred and twelve acres.[20] And between 1960 and 1970, the rural wage index more than tripled, from one thousand one hundred and twenty-five pesetas to three thousand seven hundred and eighty-seven.[21] It is possible that the wage increase in Castilleja was less impressive. In western Andalusia, agricultural underdevelopment persisted.[22]

The curriculum vitae of a Castilleja campesino

The stages of Spain's economic recovery in the postwar were exasperatingly slow. They are reflected in a part of Aurelio Monge Romero's testimony in which he spontaneously related his employment history. From a leftist family, his brother Manuel and his brother-in-law Antonio Cruz Cruz had both been shot. His brother Francisco was a prisoner during the war and part of the postwar. Aurelio himself suffered several beatings during his military training in Ronda because of the reports from Castilleja's parish priest. But Aurelio did not suffer economic discrimination in the postwar. He had good relations with the Marquess of Castilleja, García de Porres y Porres, heir to Elisa de Porres Osborne, and he worked as a permanent employee on the marquess's estate. Later he had two contracts to work on an estate the marquess owned in Arcos de la Frontera.

When I got married, which was in 1951, I was living in a rented house. I was earning seventeen pesetas a day, and the house cost me fifty pesetas a month. And, what did I eat? Well not very much. And that was only because my wife [Suceso Luque Luque] was serving here at the doctor's house and she used to bring home almost enough for us to eat, for the evening meal and all, and during the day I used to take a little bit of chorizo with me, a tortilla, an orange, eh? Nothing. And very inadequate clothing. But then later, in 1953, I went to Arcos de la Frontera to an estate [also the property of the marquess], and there I was earning twenty-five pesetas. Twenty-five pesetas. As a manager. I was there to be in charge of the people and tell them what they had to do.

They used to provide me bread, cooking oil, and charcoal for the fire, and there I could have a goat or two, fourteen or fifteen chickens, two or three turkeys, a pig, in short. And later on they used to give me . . . if we planted wheat, according to how much they were paying for it, they would give me a part and in the summer the same thing for cotton. And there I managed to put by a few pesetas and then I bought the house here that I bought. I was almost ten years in Arcos de la Frontera. I went there in 1953 and I finally came back in 1962. But then in the 1960s you could live better. After that I was here until these people [the marchioness's heirs] *sold out and left and then I was here for ten more years as the manager, and when I left they had to give me a million and a half pesetas and then I bought those little parcels of land that I bought and now, today, I live comfortably and well.*

Perhaps the emergence from poverty described in this testimony is not typical of Castilleja's workers, especially those who were leftists. Aurelio was helped by his good relations with the Marquess of Castilleja. But his story, with its happy ending, would not have been possible without the slow recovery of the national economy, no matter how hard he had worked and no matter how much his employer had favored him.

Political, social, and cultural consequences of the boom

When Franco changed his cabinet on February 22, 1957, it was a watershed in the regime's history, the beginning of the Caudillo's conversion from indispensable politician to figurehead. Two years later, Franco's reluctant decision to approve the Stabilization and Liberalization Plan left the daily administration of politics, as well as the economy, in the hands of experts.[23] During the 1960s, the Caudillo appeared in news photographs with greater and greater frequency as the congenial "Uncle Paco," hunting, fishing, or playing golf.

While its leader devoted himself to his pastimes, Spain was being transformed. As the most ardent defenders of autarky had suspected, economic interaction with the rest of the world was not possible without interactions of a cultural and social nature. The emigrants who returned from the rest of Europe brought more than foreign currency. They brought their experience of other lifestyles. Meanwhile, many of those who never left Spain were seduced by the hedonism of the foreign tourists who were inundating the country's beaches and streets, or by the images they saw in the cinemas and on television, or by what they heard on the radio. The new national prosperity allowed many Spaniards to aspire to these lifestyles.

The regime's monopoly of historical discourse was also threatened during the 1960s. In 1961, *Éditions Ruedo ibérico* was founded in Paris by José Martínez and other Republican exiles and, in 1962, began publishing

Spanish translations of authors like Gerald Brenan, Hugh Thomas, Herbert R. Southworth, and Stanley Payne, whose books entered Spain clandestinely. The translations of these historians and bibliographers, experts in contemporary Spanish history, were excellent. In a fruitless attempt to counteract the effect of these "subversive" authors, the Ministry of Information and Tourism, created in 1963, began to publish the *Bulletin of Bibliographic Orientation,* BOB, a series of criticisms of these books.[24] But the Pandora's Box had been opened.

The Franco regime was to last many more years and would never lose its capacity to make life miserable for the vanquished, but those who had been marginalized by the regime felt less inhibited by authorities whose legitimacy at all levels was based on a web of lies like those Otilia Escobar Muñoz encountered in Castilleja when she tried to collect a payment the church provided for the weddings of the daughters of widows. Apparently, Castilleja's priest Felipe Rodríguez Sánchez intended to avoid this expense because Otilia was the orphan of a man who had been shot. She told the story when I thought I was informing her that her father was one of the victims whose deaths had been recorded in the civil registry. Since she already knew it, I wanted to find out if it was her mother who had inscribed him.

No, my mother did not know either that he was in the registry. She did not know it until the day I went to be married. Because I had to go through a lot of red tape because I needed my father's death certificate. According to the church . . . I do not know how that came to be . . . right there in the church, for the daughters of widows, well they gave them some three thousand pesetas. In 1962, three thousand pesetas, well, they were a lot of pesetas. They told me about it and I talked to the priest and he responded with a lot of "buts." The priest handed me a lot of "buts" and he says, "Alright, well bring me your father's death certificate." That was Don Felipe.

And then he says, "Well, go to Espartinas [where her father was shot]*." And of course, I went to Espartinas and they told me, "Yes, you see, he is buried here. I do not know if it is him. There are men from Castilleja buried here in the common grave they dug, but none of their names are here." Then I went to the town hall here and I was commenting about it and then Pedro was the secretary in the municipal government and so he looked for it. He says, "Well, look child, he is the only one inscribed right now." He said to me, he says, "He is the only one there is."* The priest knew perfectly well that Otilia's father had been shot, but pretended to need proof of Otilia's father's death. The functionary Pedro Rebollo Medel also told her a little white lie for some reason. In 1962, the seven victims whose deaths were recorded had been in the registry for seventeen years. In 2000, Otilia still thought her father was the only one inscribed.

Otilia's story demonstrates what remained of the repression in Castilleja del Campo in the 1960s: lies and bureaucratic red tape. It was probably assumed that, accustomed to her marginalization as the orphan of one of the victims, she would be discouraged by the Kafkaesque formalities she had to endure in order to prove something that everyone in the town knew. On the eve of the happy occasion of her wedding, she had to relive the sad memory of never having known her father, and how his violent death had affected her childhood. But she was not intimidated by Don Felipe's many "buts," or by the evasive answers of the bureaucrats in Espartinas where her father had been shot. As far as Pedro Rebollo's little white lie is concerned, she was not even aware of it. She jumped through the hoops and received the payment she was entitled to.

In the 1960s, the parish priests in the small towns and the functionaries in the Franco bureaucracy were little more than an irritation. The Falangists were even less fearsome. During the war they could take one to a cemetery wall to be shot, and in the 1940s their denunciations could lead one to a firing squad or to prison. During the 1950s their reports could close the door to a decent job. But the abandonment of autarky had taken from the Falange its last sphere of real influence. As Spanish society changed during the boom of the 1960s, the Falange became a historical anachronism just like the Caudillo who had assured the Falange's loyalty by sharing with its members the spoils of war. As they grew old, the Falangists had to live side by side with those they had victimized. Two anecdotes related by Feliciano Monge Pérez describe confrontations with Castilleja Falangists and dramatize the contrast between their impunity during one period and their impotence during another.

The first anecdote is from shortly after the war: *One of [Francisco Luque Cuevas] "The Ill Wind's" brothers was named José. A tall man. Very tall. One morning he slapped my brother Alfonsito. It was by that well there below the highway. In those times, from abusiveness, they used to like to hit the children of poor people, of leftists. Because they knew we had to keep our mouths shut. And I arrived that morning and I found my brother crying. "What is the matter?" He says, "This one here has slapped me two or three times." I could do nothing about it. There, naturally, the wrath rose up within me and I was about to . . . but I looked up and I saw two civil guards there on the highway. I say, "Ay. As soon as I step over the line the least little bit, they will be right here." And there I had to control myself at once.*

Feliciano's second anecdote is from the 1960s. His younger brother Alfonso also plays a part, but it is another Falangist they encounter. He was the man Feliciano suspected had denounced the first victim of the repression in Castilleja, Antonio Cruz Cruz, because he wanted to possess Antonio's wife sexually. Feliciano also mentioned this Falangist as one of those who had impregnated a widow of one of the men who had been shot.

Feliciano also named him as the man responsible for the denunciation against his father Leovigildo to the office of Fiscalía de Tasas. *"Enriquillo"* [the municipal judge Enrique Luque Ramírez] *was a man who had no dignity, nor any sense of shame, nor anything at all. He did not respect human rights.*

And one day a brother of mine, Alfonsito, and I were preparing a cotton patch we had there near Castilleja. That land belonged to my family, and we had it half planted, and we were smoking a cigarette and taking a rest in the shade of a mulberry tree, because then there were mulberry trees all along the highway, and that man showed up, and I do not know why, but at that moment all the things I knew about him came to my mind. And he comes up and says, "What is it all about?" What he always used to say, "What is it all about?" I say, "Here it is not about anything. Here we are having a smoke." I say, "And you, where do you think you are going?" I said "you." [For "you," Feliciano employs the informal pronoun "tú," instead of the formal "usted." A sign of affection or equality when used with friends, "tú" is disrespectful when addressing one who is not your friend, especially if that person feels he is your superior.] *"Where are you going?" He says, "Me? No. I am just out for a stroll." I say, "Out for a stroll?" I say, "I am going to shit on your whore of a mother." Like that, right to his face. My brother sitting there and me over here. I say, "You no longer remember the bad things you have done? In my own family? And you come show up here? Get out of here. Ass-fucked rabble, evil bandit that you are." I say, "I am going to give you such a kick in the balls that you are going to land in that irrigation ditch that is over there." He says to my brother, he says, "Well, look at the way he is putting me down." I say, "The way he is putting me down? Maybe I do not have reasons for telling you this." I say, "Go on, get out of here. Go on, get out of here. Go on, get out of here, get out of here, get out of here."*

In this part of the interview, Feliciano had an impish grin as he remembered the pleasure of unleashing his pent-up anger. As he repeated the imprecations hurled at the Falangist, it was as if he were exorcising Castilleja's demons. But it would not be so easy. Confrontations of the type described by Feliciano would harden some of the town's residents in their aversion to seeing the questions of the past stirred up again, to seeing Castilleja del Campo recover its historical memory.

Notes

1 Ángel Viñas, *Guerra, dinero, dictadura*, 265.
2 Ibid., 280.
3 Paul Preston, *Franco: A Biography*, 568.
4 Ibid., 587.
5 Ángel Viñas, *Guerra, dinero, dictadura*, 287.
6 Paul Preston, *Franco: A Biography*, 598–9.

7   Xavier Moreno Juliá, *La División Azul*, 12.
8   Paul Preston, *Franco: A Biography*, 622–5.
9   Ángel Viñas, *Guerra, dinero, dictadura*, 225.
10 Jakim Boor, *Masonería*.
11 Paul Preston, *Franco: A Biography*, 635.
12 Ibid., 653.
13 Ibid., 669.
14 Ibid., 672.
15 Ibid., 675.
16 Ibid., 677–8.
17 Ibid., 678.
18 Michael Richards, *A Time of Silence*, 180.
19 Ángel Viñas, *Guerra, dinero, dictadura*, 294.
20 Stanley Payne, *The Franco Regime*, 482.
21 Ibid., 481, table 19.7.
22 Ibid., 483.
23 Paul Preston, *Franco: A Biography*, 635.
24 A   chronology   of   *Éditions   Ruedo   ibérico*   can   be   found   at
    http://www.ruedoiberico.org/ historia.

Epilogue

November 20, 1975

I asked those I interviewed about their reaction to the news, on November 20, 1975, of Franco's death. Miguel Rodríguez Caraballo, a right-winger, lamented the demise of the Caudillo, but he was not afraid. *When I heard the news it filled me with pity. But I was not afraid. Because I had not done anything to anyone and no one, I think, would do anything to me is what I thought. Here no one can say that I have harmed anyone, I mean, as far as I know. I have not harmed anyone knowingly. After Franco nothing happened here. It was a transition that was like it should be everywhere. Where no one is killed or anything.*

Having served in the Quartermaster Corps, Miguel Rodríguez Caraballo had not fired a shot during the war and, being a peaceful man, he was proud of that. His conscience was clear. He had even helped raise the "liberty with surveillance" of his neighbor Juan Antonio Luque Romero, who had deserted to the Republican zone. Then again, according to the testimony of Miguel and others, the men of the town who were shot in 1936 had not harmed anyone either. The good conscience of these men had not protected them.

Aniceto Luque Luque, another right-winger, expressed admiration for Franco, but he did not seem to give his death much importance: *That man died when his time came to him and there was a procession for him. All of Spain filed past to see his cadaver. And it took two or three days and all, there in Madrid, and nothing happened. He passed into history. Now he is a man who has passed into history and when more time goes by, it will be necessary to talk about him. Yes. He was a great servant of Spain.*

Antonio Monge Pérez, a leftist, expressed his recollection of that day with a fine irony. *My reaction? Well, yes. It was alright with me that he should die. I was not displeased. No! No!* According to Antonio, the only danger, at least in Castilleja, was that leftists would take advantage of Franco's death to seek revenge against the Right, but he was confident that they would not behave as the Right had thirty-nine years before. *No, because everything that could have been done had already been done. Because here there was nothing to stop them from doing all the strange things they wanted, like cutting the women's hair, marching them through the streets with their heads shorn, playing a drum and . . .*

what can I say? . . . and killing everyone they wanted and now, the people, what were they going to do? No one made a move. Since we knew it was a mistake to make a move, why would we? That was that. Yes.

Dulcenombre and Manuel Ramírez Mauricio spoke quite clearly. Their brother José María, as well as their uncles José and Manuel Ramírez Rufino, and their cousins Braulio Ramírez García and Lutgardo García Ramírez had been shot. Dulcenombre: *What a shame it had not happened sooner!* Manuel: *As I see it, he should have died when the war began. Yes.* Carmen Monge Romero did not mince her words either. Her brother Manuel and her brother-in-law, Antonio Cruz Cruz, had been shot. *I know that people from here went to the burial. Oh hoo! I did not even want to see it. When I found out he was dead, I was happy.* (She laughs.) *Very happy. You could not even breathe when he was alive. There were people who celebrated that he had died. Because he was very evil. He killed a lot of people.* Carmen's brother Aurelio expressed the same happiness and also expressed confidence in a better future. *I remember when they said he was dead. Since the radio was on all day, we found out and we were all happy because he had done a lot of bad things. But I was not afraid. I knew that a dictatorship like the one we had would not come again.*

Manuel García Ramírez was the most explicit of all. His brother Lutgardo had been shot and his brother Antonio had died in the Blue Division. *I received the news with great joy because if his mother had died when she was pregnant and had not sent that guy into the world here, that evil criminal . . . because he was just like Hitler and Mussolini. Exactly the same. Just as criminal. And he was lucky, that son of a bitch. He died in a chamber with the best doctors there were in Madrid. And he should have died tied to the tail of a horse and he would not have paid. And Queipo de Llano, he did not do anything in Andalusia? Here in Andalusia he is called . . . at least the leftists call him the butcher of Andalusia. Queipo de Llano, the butcher of Andalusia. He did not kill a few. And he is buried in the Basilica of the Macarena. That is where he is buried as a reward for being good.*

Manuel García was the only one who expressed fear of another military coup, but he was not referring so much to when Franco died as to the more dangerous moments of the transition to democracy. *At first I was afraid. When Suárez and later Calvo Sotelo were heads of government there were still threats from the army every day. Now since the Socialists came to power that is over. Since then you have not heard even one saber being rattled.* Manuel García was referring to the various military conspiracies to stop the process of democratization and establish a government of national salvation when Adolfo Suárez and Leopoldo Calvo Sotelo were heads of government, from the so-called "Operation Galaxy," aborted on November 17, 1978, to the coup that was planned to depose the king in October 1982.[1] The most dramatic of these anti-democratic projects was when Lieutenant Colonel Antonio Tejero Molina of the Civil Guard took over the Palace of the Cortes in the middle of a session on February 23, 1981.[2] These threats were one of the reasons for the extreme caution with which democracy was restored in Spain after Franco's death. The past was an especially delicate topic. During the entire transition, there was a tacit agreement to not use the crimes of the civil war and the dictatorship as a political weapon. The so-called "pact of silence" would leave questions that are still unresolved today.

Unresolved matters

On July 30, 1976, a Law of Amnesty was approved by the Cortes, which was not yet a democratically elected body. As stated in the law's preamble, one of its intentions was "to promote the reconciliation of all the members of the Nation." The law's preamble also recognized the need to overcome the division of the country into victors and vanquished by forgetting the injustices of the past: "As Spain heads toward full democratic normality, the moment has arrived to finalize the process of forgetting any discriminatory legacy of the past for the full fraternal coexistence of all Spaniards."[3] The Law of Amnesty was based on the erroneous assumption that memory could be legislated.

On October 15, 1977, four months after the democratic election of the Constituent Cortes, a new Law of Amnesty was passed. Its coverage was much greater than the law of 1976 and was approved by 93.3 percent of the votes, with the abstention of members of the conservative Popular Alliance. Antonio Carro Martínez, for example, was worried by the eagerness for a "clean slate." Representatives of the Left voted for the law in spite of considering it insufficient. Donato Fuejo Lago argued that "it would be necessary for the proposed law to contemplate a moral reparation . . ." Subsequently, there were several modifications to the Laws of Amnesty.[4] But they would always mandate wiping the slate clean and would never contemplate "moral reparation." The Laws of Amnesty would always be "laws of amnesia."

In a small town like Castilleja del Campo it was impossible for those who had lost family members in the repression or had suffered marginalization during the dictatorship to obey a law that demanded they forget the past. As Manuel García Ramírez said, *All that, it is better not to remember and it is impossible to forget. Whoever has been through that cannot forget it. Ever. Until one is swallowed up by the earth, one cannot forget it.* The only "moral reparation" that some in the town would receive would be the satisfaction of outliving those who had participated in the repression or had marginalized them during the dictatorship. The following testimony from Manuel Ramírez Mauricio is an example.

Many of those in the town who were bad have already died. Not many of them are left. There are still some, but very few, of those who killed people, who killed people on the Left. Now, those that remain are suffering. There are a few who remain and they are suffering. Because they are seeing what they do not have. Because they would like to have the power they had before and not what is happening here, what they do not want, this movement we have here, the power that is now in the hands of the Left here. Those who remain here, on the Right, do not want that and they are suffering. There are still a bunch of them and they are suffering.

There are a few who have not fallen yet, but they are ill, they are ill. Because one of them you can see right now who has a . . . (I look out the window.) *No, you did not see him. Well, he killed his brother, suffering, because the brother was a very good person. And because he came home every morning with his shoes and his pants covered in blood, he used to come home before going to work, and the brother used to see it, and from the impression he received, eh?, he fell ill. And they took him to a sanatorium and in the sanatorium he died. The brother. And that man is suffering. He has a bad thing there on his nose and there is no cure for it.*

And three or four others, because they used to talk so much, at least two of them got a thing there on their tongue and they died from it, you know? And now another one, he has been very ill, very very ill, and he has escaped for now but if he has the slightest relapse, he is going to fall too. Another went lame and six or eight days after they operated on him he died.

Another was the son of a highway worker and he went with his father to work on the highway. And by coincidence, on that occasion my brother went with one of those crowds where there are six or eight men, some here, some there, so they would give them work. The lineup, waiting for work. And my brother got that job, you know?, working on the highway. And after the Movement came in here . . . a neighbor heard him, because he was a neighbor of his and he heard him. He says, "Hey now, that ass-fucked son of a bitch . . ." They had already killed him, they had already killed my brother. " . . . they are not going to pick that ass-fucked son of a bitch to take away my work on the highway." A neighbor heard him and told me about it.

You know where he died? In the shade, under a poplar tree by the highway. There right outside of town. There where that billboard for Osborne Sherry is. Well, right there. He went to where there are some poplars and he was enjoying the shade and he was taking a rest from working. And there he died all of a sudden. Imagine. After gathering people, bringing people here to the highway to kill them, and now you die there by the side of the highway, the ditch where you used to bring them to kill them. That is where he died. There are so many things, so many many things one has seen, some of them one does not know about, other things, other people do not know about, and other things that still, even though there is freedom, one cannot talk about them much. Manuel Ramírez Mauricio did not enumerate the adverse fortunes of these men in a jubilant tone, nor with bitterness. He pronounced this mono-logue in a low and conspiratorial voice as if he were sharing with me the marvelous secret of divine justice.

A new town council deals with the past

A democratically elected municipal government

After the municipal elections on April 3, 1979, Castilleja del Campo had a new town council led by a mayor from the PSOE (Spanish Socialist Workers' Party), Vicente Zaragoza Alcover, and councilmen who represented several of the town's political sectors. The change is reflected in the style of the town hall minutes. During the Republic, the war, and the postwar, the minutes are opaque in the extreme. They only express the results of discussions and votes, with formulas such as " . . . the Corporation . . . after long and rea-soned discussion agreed unanimously . . . ," "The question was brought up for discussion and examined with due deliberation . . . and it was agreed unanimously to approve . . . ," " . . . after long and reasoned discussion of the particular it was agreed unanimously . . . ," etc. The reasonableness of the discussions and the unanimity of the agreements in these three exam-ples, the first from the Republic and the last two from the war, are due to the fact that these town councils were homogeneous and represented only one of the town's political factions.

After 1979, the town council was heterogeneous and its members repre-sented different points of view. The discussions were often heated and the votes divided. In the minutes, much more transparent than before, the municipal secretary named the councilmen when citing their opinions and recorded who had voted for or against what was proposed. Two especially contentious proposals dealt with the past.

The streets receive new names

On December 15, 1980, Mayor Vicente Zaragoza Alcover proposed changing the names of Castilleja del Campo's streets, avenues, and squares. It would be the first time in more than forty-four years. He wanted to elim-inate streets honoring Generals Mola, Sanjurjo, Franco, and Queipo de Llano. He also wanted to remove references to right-wing political figures: José Antonio Primo de Rivera, founder of the Falange; Pedro Parias, governor of Seville during the repression and former administrator of the

Countess of the Atalayas; and José Calvo Sotelo, the monarchist deputy assassinated on June 13, 1936. The mayor also proposed changing the street honoring the local icon of the agrarian oligarchy, the Count of the Atalayas. The new street signs would honor Juan Ramón Jiménez and Antonio Machado, poets who had opposed the Franco regime. The poet and dramatist Federico García Lorca and the proponent of Andalusian autonomy Blas Infante, both shot during the repression, would also be honored. Names that would not be changed included the Plaza de Ramón y Cajal, the Plaza de la Iglesia, Venerable Mañara Street, San Miguel Street, Cervantes Street, Captain Cortés Street, and Manuel Rodríguez Mantero Street.[5]

The mayor's proposal was rejected after several councilmen expressed their opinions. Álvaro Fernández Rodríguez, of the conservative UCD (Union of the Democratic Center), said changing the street names would cause unnecessary trouble and expense. José Luis Luque Sánchez, of the Spanish Socialist Workers' Party and also the town's mailman, said the street names did not matter to him. José María Ramírez Bravo, also of the Spanish Socialist Workers' Party, commented that the new street map still contained the "name of a person with specific political ideas."[6] He was referring to Manuel Rodríguez Mantero Street, named for the young Castilleja Falangist killed on May 31, 1936, during the confrontation with Communists from Seville.

Mayor Vicente Zaragoza probably left this street to avoid offending the young man's family members who still lived in the town, some on the same street that bore his name. Councilman Ramírez Bravo was the nephew of José María Ramírez Mauricio, the great-nephew of the Republican mayor José Ramírez Rufino and of the mayor's brother Manuel, and a cousin of Braulio Ramírez García and Lutgardo García Ramírez. All these men had been shot during the repression. It did not seem appropriate to councilman Ramírez that the Castilleja street map continue honoring a right-wing victim and ignoring his own family members.

The topic was tabled until a group of young men in the town, the nucleus of what would be the United Left party, proposed an alternative modification that was approved on July 30, 1981.[7] Like the changes proposed by the Socialist mayor, the streets, avenues, and squares honoring military men and right-wing politicians, as well as the Count of the Atalayas, were to be changed. There were plazas named for the poets Antonio Machado and Juan Ramón Jiménez, and a Constitution Street. San Miguel Street, for Castilleja's patron saint, and Ramón y Cajal Street remained. These were the similarities between the two proposals. New changes included Liberty Street and an Avenue of Andalusia, and streets for two more poets, Miguel Hernández, who died in prison during the postwar, and Vicente Aleixandre.

Dividing loyalties between religion and science, streets were named for the Virgen del Buen Suceso and for Doctor Fleming.

Two unusual changes were the renaming of Church Square as Monseñor Óscar Romero Square, and Captain Cortés Street as Martín Lutero King Street. At first glance, these changes seemed to show that this group of young leftists was not anti-religious, since Óscar Romero had been the archbishop of El Salvador and Dr. King had been a Baptist pastor. But the two men also had in common their struggles for marginalized peoples in their respective countries. In both cases, their activities led them to be shot by reactionary elements. Symbolically, they could represent the victims of the repression in Castilleja. Furthermore, their inclusion in the town's new street map gave it a decidedly international flavor. This expression of solidarity with the marginalized peoples of the world could be a manifestation of a Marxist orientation, a subtle insinuation that the struggle against oppression knows no borders.

The most contentious change was the elimination of Manuel Rodríguez Mantero Street. Unemployed men assigned to public works projects were given the task of changing the street signs and, since one of the signs for Manuel Rodríguez Mantero Street was just a few steps away from the house where the young Falangist had lived and where family members of his still lived, no one wanted the job of removing it. Finally, José Luque Monge, a man who seemed to enjoy confrontation, volunteered to do it. Indeed, family members of the young man protested while José was taking down the sign, to which he responded that he was just a worker following orders and that they should direct their protests to the town council. The Socialist mayor could say that the elimination of Manuel Rodríguez Mantero Street was not a change that he had proposed, that it was a group of young Communists who had proposed that change.

Years later, I asked one of these young men, José Antonio Borrego Suárez, if it would not have been better to leave Manuel Rodríguez Mantero Street and add a street with the name of one of the leftist victims, for example the Republican mayor José Ramírez Rufino or perhaps his nephew José María Ramírez Mauricio, who was the youngest of the men shot, of the same age as Manuel Rodríguez Mantero. He replied that in the early 1980s it would have been too confrontational to honor the victims of the repression.

The cross of the fallen

Another proposal dealing with the past was brought forth on February 8, 1985. Councilman Aniceto Luque Luque, of the conservative Union of the Democratic Center, proposed the renovation of the "cross of the fallen" that was located on the Plaza Monseñor Óscar Romero. By this time, several of the young men who had chosen the town's new street names were councilmen. They opposed spending public funds on a religious symbol and presented their objection indirectly by questioning the identity of "the fallen" who were honored by the cross. Were they all of those who had perished as a consequence of the war or only those "fallen for God and Spain," in other words, those in the Nationalist forces? Were they those who had died throughout Spain or only those from Castilleja del Campo? If it were those from Castilleja, then the only "fallen" were the seventeen leftists killed in the repression.

Assuming the latter to be the case, Antonio Gómez Luque, at the time a member of the Spanish Socialist Workers' Party but soon to lead the United Left party in Castilleja, questioned the appropriateness of honoring the town's victims with a cross, asking "if the victims' religious affiliations were known, because some of them may have been believers but not others." Aniceto Luque's proposal was rejected. Socialist councilmen Manuel Cabello Sánchez, José María Ramírez Bravo, Antonio Gómez Luque, and José Antonio Borrego Suárez voted no. Socialist mayor Vicente Zaragoza Alcover along with councilmen José Antonio Paz Rodríguez and Aniceto Luque Luque, both of the conservative Union of the Democratic Center, voted in favor.[8]

Residents of Castilleja del Campo deal with the past

When Antonio Monge Pérez chatted with me under his fig tree in August 1986, and even more so when, three and a half years later, I recorded interviews with him and others from Castilleja del Campo, their eagerness to see their recollections preserved was clear. Those on the Left wanted to pay homage to family members and friends who had been shot. Those on the Right wanted to repudiate the violent acts committed in Castilleja in the name of ideologies they had once embraced. They all wanted to leave a record of what they themselves had suffered in the war and postwar.

In winter of 1989/90, they unburdened themselves to me. Almost two decades passed before I dared publish their testimonies. The majority of those I interviewed are no longer with us and this book, which they will never see, is a tribute to their generosity and to the courage with which they circumvented the legislation of memory implicit in the Laws of Amnesty/Amnesia. If, instead of a "pact of silence," post-Franco Spain had been able to establish a commission of truth and reconciliation like the one presided by Bishop Desmond Tutu in South Africa after apartheid, and if this national commission had led to local commissions in all the towns of Spain, the people I interviewed probably would not have felt the need to talk to me and this book would not exist. Perhaps it would not have been necessary.

Notes

1 Charles T. Powell, *El piloto del cambio*, 275–312.
2 Ibid., 300–308.
3 Paloma Aguilar Fernández, *Memoria y olvido de la Guerra Civil española*, 264nn89–90.
4 Ibid., 266–71.
5 Minutes, 15 December 1980, Castilleja del Campo Municipal Archive.
6 Ibid.
7 Minutes, 30 July 1981, Castilleja del Campo Municipal Archive.
8 Minutes, 8 February 1985, Castilleja del Campo Municipal Archive.

Appendixes

Appendix A

Women of Castilleja Who Were Publicly Humiliated

I have included their nicknames, if known, and their ages in 1936:

Escobar Moreno, Rosario	La Crespa	29
Escobar Rufino, Rosario	La Picarita	64
González Garrido, Isabela	La Belenda	33
Luque Rodríguez, Francisca	La Pelusa	39
Muñoz Rufino, Elvira		33
Nieves Perea, Carmen	La Pomporita	41
Pérez Vera, Felisa		49
Rodríguez Luque, Laura	La Chica Pilar	35
Tebas Escobar, Esmoralda		36

Appendix B

Summary of the Men of Castilleja Killed in the Repression

Based on oral testimonies and documents, it is possible to draw up the following list of men, natives or residents of Castilleja del Campo, who were killed in the repression. I cannot assure that it is a complete list. Victims may be missing who were forgotten by their neighbors and whose names did not appear on any document. What I can assure is that no one appears on the list who was not a victim of the repression. The names are listed in alphabetical order according to their first surname. The data that appears in parentheses after the names of each victim indicate their age when shot, their profession, and the date and place of death:

1. Cruz Cruz, Antonio   (30/ laborer/ end of July/ unknown)
2. Escobar Moreno, Manuel   (30/ laborer/ August 27, 1936/ Espartinas)
3. Fernández Luque, José   (43/ laborer/ September 14, 1936/ Umbrete)
4. García Ramírez, Lutgardo   (29/ butcher/ August 27, 1936/ Espartinas)
5. León Trejo, Joaquín   (43/ teacher/ August 22, 1936/ Castilblanco de los Arroyos?)
6. López Moreno, José Luis   (31/ mechanic/ November 20, 1936/ Seville?)
7. Monge Escobar, Enrique   (43/ laborer/ August 27, 1936/ Espartinas)
8. Monge Romero, Manuel   (31/ laborer/ August 27, 1936/ Espartinas)
9. Nieves Perea, Cándido   (39/ laborer/ August 10, 1936/ unknown)
10. Paz Delgado, Lucrecio   (48/ laborer/ September 15, 1936/ Umbrete)
11. Pérez Rodríguez, José   (37/ laborer/ September 14, 1936/ Castilleja del Campo)

12. Ramírez García, Braulio	(25/ doctor/ December 28, 1936/ Seville?)
13. Ramírez Mauricio, José María	(21/ laborer/ August 27, 1936/ Espartinas)
14. Ramírez Rufino, José	(61/ barber /August 27, 1936/ Espartinas)
15. Ramírez Rufino, Manuel	(58/ builder/ August? 1936/ unknown)
16. Reinoso Monge, Alfredo	(26/ laborer/ August 10, 1936/ unknown)
17. Tebas Escobar, Manuel	(38/ laborer/ September 14, 1936/ Umbrete)

The average age of the men who were shot was 37. The youngest, José María Ramírez Mauricio, was 21, and his uncle, José Ramírez Rufino, was the oldest at 61. The age distribution of the victims is as follows:

20 to 29 years 4	30 to 39 years 7	40 to 49 years 4
50 to 59 years 1	Over 60 years 1	

This distribution reflects the stages of life most given to political militancy. I do not know if it is representative of the age distribution of the victims at the national level. It does coincide with the age distribution of victims that Francisco Espinosa Maestre found in the province of Huelva.[1]

The distribution of the victims by professions is more significant:

Agricultural workers	*Specialized workers*	*Professionals*
Cruz Cruz, Antonio	García Ramírez, Lutgardo	León Trejo, Joaquín
Escobar Moreno, Manuel	López Moreno, José Luis	Ramírez García, Braulio
Fernández Luque, José	Ramírez Rufino, José	
Monge Escobar, Enrique	Ramírez Rufino, Manuel	
Monge Romero, Manuel		
Nieves Perea, Cándido		
Paz Delgado, Lucrecio		
Pérez Rodríguez, José		
Ramírez Mauricio, José Mª		
Reinoso Monge, Alfredo		
Tebas Escobar, Manuel		

The repression in Castilleja del Campo reflects the class conflict underlying the ideological divisions during the Spanish civil war. Eleven of the men shot in Castilleja, almost 65 percent, were agricultural workers, the landless day laborers who eked out a living from occasional work. These were the members of the rural proletariat who filled the ranks of the anarcho-syndicalist CNT (National Confederation of Labor) and the Socialist UGT (General Workers' Union). Of the other victims, four were members of the middle class or lower middle class: a butcher, Lutgardo García Ramírez; a mechanic, José Luis López Moreno; a barber, José Ramírez Rufino; and a builder, Manuel Ramírez Rufino. This was the economic class that tended to support the various Republican parties. The remaining victims belonged to the two liberal professions that were most severely punished during the repression: education, represented by Joaquín León Trejo; and medicine, represented by Braulio Ramírez García. These professions attracted people who were progressive, anti-traditional, often anticlerical, people whose humanitarianism gave them a strong sense of solidarity with the marginalized classes.[2]

Regarding the dates of death, the end of July until December 28, 1936, all the Castilleja victims were killed during what Francisco Espinosa Maestre calls the first stage of the repression, from the military coup until January 1937.

> The first is the period of the great repression, the massive killings throughout the entire territory of the Second Division led by General Queipo de Llano. During this period the repression has a decidedly local character. Day after day hundreds of people disappear, and only a minimal percentage of them would later be inscribed in the Civil Registry. It is an organized repression in which various groupings, civilian and military, handle lists drawn up by different authorities; at the same time there is a repression that escapes all control carried out by paramilitary organizations operating on their own with the acquiescence of the New Order.[3]

After January 1937, the daily killings diminished, but a second and much longer repression began. According to Espinosa Maestre, it is the stage when ". . . the repression is partially cloaked in the appearance of legality. It is the period of the Courts-Martial."[4] Juan Ortiz Villalba describes the courts-martial as ". . . authentic parodies organized for ends that are more justificatory and propagandistic than procedural."[5] Since all the known victims of Castilleja del Campo were killed during the first stage of the repression, none passed through a courts-martial, due in part to the fact that the town's leftists never took up arms to resist the "New Order," but also because Castilleja's repression had been of such severity that many of the leftists who remained were so terrified that, by the end of 1936, they had already escaped from the town by joining or being drafted into the armed forces.

Francisco Espinosa Maestre describes the end of the first stage: "This stage ends between the months of January and February 1937 with the replacement of the most visible organizers of the repression, such as Díaz Criado in Seville, Ibáñez Gálvez in Córdoba, or Haro Lumbreras in Huelva."[6] Something similar occurred in Castilleja, but on a smaller scale. During an extraordinary session of the administrative commission on February 3, 1937, Mayor José Cuevas Reinoso was relieved of his post. The incoming mayor was Antonio Rodríguez Fernández "Antoñito, son of Aurora," the same man who had resigned on August 4, 1936, to avoid signing death warrants.[7] The physical elimination of Castilleja del Campo's leftists had ended.

The places of death of Castilleja's victims also deserve a comment. With the exception of José Pérez Rodríguez, they all perished outside the town's municipal boundaries. José Pérez was a case of obstinacy, a conscious decision to die in his hometown. The transport of prisoners outside their towns for execution was like a shell game that served to mask the dimensions of the repression, making it difficult to quantify the victims. It also protected the local authorities, mayors, Falangist leaders, priests, etc. who drew up the lists of those to be killed, allowing them to claim they were not to blame for the shooting of neighbors, that it was outside forces that were responsible. This was the deception that José Pérez Rodríguez had unmasked with his death in the streets of Castilleja.

Notes

1 Francisco Espinosa Maestre, *La guerra civil en Huelva*, 370.

2 For the repression of schoolteachers, see Julián Casanova, "Rebelión y revolución," 94; for the repression of doctors, see Juan Ortiz Villalba, *Sevilla 1936*, 267.

3 Francisco Espinosa Maestre, "Sevilla, 1936: Sublevación y represión," 238.

4 Ibid., 239.

5 Juan Ortiz Villalba, *Sevilla 1936*, 148.

6 Francisco Espinosa Maestre, "Sevilla, 1936: Sublevación y represión," 238.

7 Minutes, 3 February 1937, Castilleja del Campo Municipal Archive.

Appendix C

Sources of Information on the Victims

The Civil Death Registry

Investigations of the repression indicate that the majority of victims were never inscribed in the civil death registries.[1] Of those victims whose deaths were recorded, almost all were after the time period legally stipulated for doing so.[2] Castilleja del Campo was no exception. Of the seventeen victims from the town, only seven are inscribed, all of them past the legal deadline. The following is a list of the town's victims whose deaths were recorded, with the date of death that appears on their inscription and the date when they were inscribed. The list is in chronological order according to the date of inscription:

Name of the victim	Date of death	Date of inscription
1. Joaquín León Trejo	August 22, 1936	March 12, 1938
2. José Fernández Luque	September 14, 1936	September 4, 1939
3. José Pérez Rodríguez	September 14, 1936	April 10, 1941
4. Lucrecio Paz Delgado	September 15, 1936	July 26, 1941
5. Manuel Escobar Moreno	August 27, 1936	March 4, 1946
6. Manuel Monge Romero	August 27, 1936	March 4, 1946
7. Manuel Tebas Escobar	September 14, 1936	March 6, 1946[3]

For all but one of those inscribed, the cause of death was ". . . as a consequence of the application of the War Decree," a euphemism for executed without trial. The only variation on this formula was José Pérez Rodríguez, for whom the cause of death was ". . . as a consequence of wounds received during the application of the War Decree," reflecting the fact that he did not die from the gunshot wound to his leg, but when the Falangist Antonio Cuevas "Sangalato," from Carrión, struck him in the head with his rifle butt.

The small number of leftist victims whose deaths were inscribed in the civil death registries is evidence of the desire of the authorities at all levels to minimize the dimensions of the repression, which has hindered the work of researchers attempting to quantify the victims. My experience in Castilleja del Campo confirms the conclusion reached by Francisco Espinosa Maestre, whose investigations in the towns of the province of Huelva led him to write ". . . the important thing to point out is that the Civil Registries, which together with the *Causa General* are sufficient for the study of right-wing victims, should be considered only a starting point for the investigation of leftist victims."[4] Fortunately, the civil registries are not the only source of information on the leftist victims of the repression.

Recruitment and military service records

I knew of some of these people and what happened to them only because their names were on one or another of two documents in the town's municipal archive or, in some cases, their names appeared on both documents. About the middle of 1937, the military authorities in Seville requested a list of all the men of Castilleja del Campo from the draft call-ups encompassing the years 1919 to 1943, in other words, all those eligible to be enlisted in the armed forces during the war. A copy of the list sent in response to this request was filed in "Recruitment and Military Service Records." The list includes, call-up year by call-up year, the name and surnames, name of mother and father, date of birth and, from the 1928 call-up to the 1943 call-up, observations. Thus for the 1931 call-up there appears, for example, "1931/ Casildo Escobar Reinoso/ Manuel/ María/ August 25, 1910/ Incorp. Falange Militia Leader."[5] The purpose of these communiqués was to prevent anyone who could serve in Franco's forces from escaping their military obligation.

In 1940 the "Classificatory Tribunal For The Provinces Of Seville, Cádiz, Huelva" requested another list "of the individuals pertaining to the call-ups from 1922 to 1935, inclusive, from 1942, and from 1943." The request is also in "Recruitment and Military Service Records," in addition to a copy of this second list, which was sent to Seville on April 27, 1940. It includes, call-up by call-up, the name and surnames of all the local men of the call-ups from 1922 to 1942, with their place of birth, age, marital status, profession, address, and a comment.

When I found these lists in the municipal archive, I discovered that in the case of Castilleja del Campo, only seven of the seventeen victims were on one or another of the two lists, the same number of men who appear in the Civil Registry, but not the same men. Antonio Cruz Cruz, Joaquín León Trejo, and Cándido Nieves Perea are not on either list because they were not born in Castilleja. The names of José Fernández Luque, Enrique Monge Escobar, Lucrecio Paz Delgado, José Pérez Rodríguez, José Ramírez Rufino, Manuel Ramírez Rufino, and Manuel Tebas Escobar, all natives of Castilleja, were also missing because they were too old for military service.

The usefulness of the lists in Recruitment and Military Service Records has diminished with time. As informants who were alive at the time die off, these lists can lead researchers to include as victims people who were not shot. For example, on the list from 1940 there appears "Reinoso Monge, Juan Bautista/ Castilleja/ 39/ Single/ This town/ Atalayas St. No. 3/ Deceased."[6] The observation "Deceased," and his relationship to one of those shot (he was the brother of Alfredo Reinoso Monge), led me to suspect I had discovered another victim. Upon consulting Celedonio Escobar Reinoso, I found out that Juan Bautista was not shot. He died of tuberculosis. Celedonio also commented that Juan Bautista Reinoso Monge was indeed on the "black list" and would have been shot if he had not had a terminal illness. Rechecking the Civil Death Registry, I saw that, in fact, Juan Bautista's death had been inscribed on October 7, 1936, and the cause of his death was ". . . as a consequence of tuberculosis."[7]

In any event, these lists must be regarded as one more source but, like the Civil Registries, insufficient for an exact quantification of the victims of the repression. Combining the names of victims whose deaths were inscribed in the Civil Registry with the names on the lists in Recruitment and Military Service Records, four men would still be missing: Antonio Cruz Cruz, Cándido Nieves Perea, the Republican mayor José Ramírez Rufino, and his brother Manuel Ramírez Rufino.

Lists from the Civil Guard

I have never encountered a reference in any history of the repression to lists similar to two that are preserved in the Castilleja Office of the Justice of the Peace. The first list, which is typewritten, was sent from the Civil Guard barracks in Carrión on February 27, 1939, shortly before the end of the war. It is in response to a request the Castilleja municipal judge had sent the same day, with the motive of inscribing the names of victims in the Civil Death Registry. This motive struck me as odd because, of the thirteen men on this first list, one had already been inscribed, Joaquín León Trejo, and of the other twelve, only one would be inscribed the same year the list was received: José Fernández Luque, whose death was recorded on September 4, 1939. Six of the men on the list would never be inscribed. The text of the communiqué is:

In compliance with your respectable document dated the 27th of the present month in which you express interest in a report on the individuals to whom were applied the War Decree of the Most Excellent General in Chief of the Army of the South, for the purpose of inscription in the Civil Registry of that Locale, attached I have the pleasure of remitting on the reverse side a report on the individuals contained therein, stressing that more data cannot be provided to you since no further data exists in this Post.
May God preserve you many Years
Carrión February 27, 1939
III Triumphal Year
The Post Commandant
Alejandro Cueto Alonso (signed)
Castilleja del Campo Municipal Judge[8]

On the reverse side, also typewritten, is the title "Report of individuals from Castilleja del Campo to whom was applied the War Decree of the Most Excellent General in Chief of the Army of the South for their anarchic activities and extremist ideas." There follow two columns, one with the heading "Nanes" [*sic*], and the other with the heading "Causes the why [*sic*] the Decree was applied to him." The names in the first column appear without any apparent order, either alphabetical or by date of death.

The second list appears to be a supplement to the first list. It was sent on April 11, 1939, shortly after the war ended. It suggests that the reason for the lists was indeed related to the inscription of deaths in the Civil Registry because this second list contains more information about each victim, precisely that information required for inscriptions. Furthermore, on this second list the name of Joaquín León Trejo, already inscribed, is missing. Written by hand to leave room for more columns of information, the text begins as follows:

Alejandro Cueto Alonso, Commandant of the Civil Guard Post of this town. That in this Post under my command there exists a report on the individuals, residents of Castilleja del Campo to whom was applied the War Decree of the Most Excellent General in Chief of the Army of the South, with all their personal circumstances, which are detailed as follows.[9]

What follows consists of eight columns with the headings: "(1) No. in order," in other words, the twelve men on the list are assigned a number from one to twelve; "(2) Names and surnames"; "(3) Age Years"; "(4) Nativity," in other words, their place of birth; "(5) Status," either married, single, or widowed; "(6) Profession"; "(7) Date of the application of the Decree, Day, Month, Year"; "(8) Causes why the Decree was applied." After the list, the document concludes as follow:

> And for the record and to remit to the Municipal Judge of Castilleja del Campo I expedite this in Carrión de los Céspedes on April eleventh nineteen hundred and thirty nine. Year of Victory.
> Military Commandant
> Alejandro Cueto Alonso[10]

The names on the list appear in the chronological order of death. It begins with (1) Alfredo Reinoso Monge and (2) Cándido Nieves Perea, killed on August 10. This is the only document that states the date of death for these two men. Until I saw it, I had assumed they were shot on August 27 with the rest of the group taken away in early August. Then the names of the other six men of this group appear: (3) Enrique Monge Escobar, (4) Manuel Escobar Moreno, (5) Lutgardo García Ramírez, (6) José Ramírez Rufino, (7) José Ramírez Mauricio, and (8) Manuel Monge Romero, all shot on August 27. Finally there are the names of the four men from the second and last group: (9) Lucrecio Paz Delgado, (10) Manuel Tebas Escobar, (11) José Fernández Luque, and (12) José Pérez Rodríguez. This second list from 1939 contains only those men taken away from Castilleja in groups, one group in early August and the other on September 14. Antonio Cruz Cruz, the first to be taken away, in late July, is missing. All the victims, natives or residents of Castilleja, who were not in Castilleja del Campo when the war began, are also missing: Manuel Ramírez Rufino; Joaquín León Trejo, although included on the first list; José Luis López Moreno; and Braulio Ramírez García.

Why were only those men who were in one or another of the two groups taken from the town included on the second list? Was it because there was only information about these men in the Carrión Civil Guard Post? Then why was there information on the first list concerning the motive for applying the war decree to Joaquín León Trejo, arrested in Seville, and whose place of death was still unknown?[11] Does it mean there was a denunciation against him written by the Castilleja authorities?

Another mystery is the motive for including the reasons for applying the war decree to these men if the purpose of the lists was to provide data for inscriptions in the Civil Registry, where this information was neither required nor included. Whatever the motive for this inclusion, these "causes why the Decree was applied" give an idea of the victors' attitudes. It will be recalled that none of the Castilleja men killed in the repression were court-martialled. The causes on the two lists from the Civil Guard were based exclusively on denunciations written, no doubt, by individuals from Castilleja in the case of the twelve men on the second list, and possibly for Joaquín León Trejo, who only appeared on the first list.

What follows is a transcription of the causes. They are in the order in which the men appear on the first list in order to include Joaquín León Trejo but, except in his case, the causes are copied from the second list, not because they are different but because they contain fewer orthographic and grammatical errors:

Name and surnames	*Causes why the Decree was applied to them*
Joaquín León Trejo	Schoolteacher, dangerous extremist (D. in Seville)
Lucrecio Paz Delgado	Anarchist, collaborated with Miners from Rio Tinto
Manuel Monge Romero	Well-known dangerous extremist
Manuel Tebas Escobar	Communist, broke urn in elections and wounded . . .[12]
Enrique Monge Escobar	Communist, broke urn in elections and wounded . . .
José Ramírez Mauricio	Syndicalist, author shooting at Catequists' car
José Ramírez Rufino	Ex Mayor, President Republican Union Party
Alfredo Reinoso Monge	Instigator demonstration against dead Falangist
Lutgardo García Ramírez	Secretary revolutionary Party
Cándido Nieves Perea	Extremist, distinguishing himself death Falangist
José Fernández Luque	Dangerous extremist and propagandist
José Pérez Rodríguez	Coadjutor of the disarming of the populace by miners
Manuel Escobar Moreno	Coadjutor of the disarming of the populace by miners

The most frequent causes were ideological. Lucrecio Paz Delgado was denounced as an anarchist. Manuel Tebas Escobar and Enrique Monge Escobar were denounced as Communists. Mayor José Ramírez Rufino was denounced as "President Republican Union Party." Lutgardo García Ramírez was denounced as "Secretary revolutionary Party." Joaquín León Trejo and José Fernández Luque were denounced as "well known dangerous extremist." Candido Nieves Perea and Manuel Monge Romero, were denounced as "extremist." I do not know the political affiliations of all these men but I do know that José Ramírez Rufino and Joaquín León Trejo belonged to the Republican Union party, which was moderate, even conservative. Lutgardo García Ramírez belonged to the Republican Left party of President Manuel Azaña. Manuel Monge Romero was a Socialist.

Other denunciations were for specific incidents. José María Ramírez Mauricio was accused of being "author shooting at Catequists' car," possibly a reference to the incident mentioned by the parish priest Felipe Rodríguez Sánchez in his letter to Cardinal Ilundáin on December 23, 1932. Another specific incident that motivated a denunciation was the altercation during the elections on February 16, 1936, "broke urn in elections and wounded . . ." for Manuel Tebas Escobar and Enrique Monge Escobar. The demonstration after the shooting that mortally wounded Manuel Rodríguez Mantero also motivated denunciations: Alfredo Monge Reinoso, "instigator demonstration against dead Falangist"; and Cándido Nieves Perea, ". . . distinguishing himself death Falangist." Finally, their cooperation with the Río Tinto miners on July 19, 1936 led to denunciations of townsmen: Lucrecio Paz Delgado, ". . . collaborated with Miners from Rio Tinto"; José Pérez Rodríguez and Manuel Escobar Moreno, "coadjutor of the disarming of the populace by miners." Finally there are causes for killing residents of Castilleja for their union affiliation, political post, or profession. One of the causes for applying the war decree to José María Ramírez Mauricio was for being a "syndicalist." Causes for applying the war decree to José Ramírez Rufino and Joaquín León Trejo were for being, respectively, "Ex Mayor" and "schoolteacher."

Oral testimonies

When I began to record interviews in the winter of 1989/90, I thought I could reconstruct the town's history during the civil war on the basis of oral testimonies. I soon realized that these would be insufficient. Those I interviewed that winter were not even in agreement on the number of men assassinated. According to the testimonies, there could have been as few as fourteen or as many as twenty-two victims. When asked who the victims were, few of those I interviewed could name more than a handful with their first name and both surnames. Except when naming their own brothers, they sometimes used only the first name or perhaps the first name and first surname, but it was more frequent to use a nickname, or the relationship of the victim to another resident of the town. They would say Lucrecio or "El Cuartano" for Lucrecio Paz Delgado, and "Sangalato" or "Pérez's father" for José Pérez Rodríguez. Manuel Tebas Escobar was almost always "Sara's father" and José Fernández Luque was "Pepe, son of Simplicia" or "El Perlo." Often, when different witnesses spoke of the same man, I did not know that it was the same man because they identified him in different ways. Especially confusing was when some referred to José Pérez Rodríguez by his nickname "Sangalato" and others spoke of "Pérez's father," who was killed by "Sangalato," the Falangist Antonio Cuevas from Carrión.

Nevertheless, the oral testimonies have been indispensable. If the documents preserved in the Castilleja town hall were the only source of information for the list of victims, two would still be missing: Antonio Cruz Cruz and Manuel Ramírez Rufino. I learned of them exclusively through witnesses. They were not inscribed in the Civil Death Registry, nor were they in the Recruitment and Military Service Records, nor did they appear on the lists sent to the Castilleja municipal judge from the Carrión Civil Guard barracks. Their names would have passed into oblivion if they had not lived on in the memories of some of the town's residents. The victimization of these two men was later confirmed by a native of Castilleja who had drawn up his own list of the townsmen who were assassinated.

An extraordinary written testimony

Upon the death of her uncle, Eugenio Pozo de la Cueva, Matilde Donaire Pozo found among his papers a list of the men from Castilleja assassinated in the repression that this man, a native of the town, had typewritten. There was no indication of when Eugenio Pozo de la Cueva drew up the list, which I translate/transcribe as it appears in his typescript.

MEN OF CASTILLEJA DEL CAMPO ASSASSINATED IN AUGUST 1936, BY THE FASCISTS

1-José Ramirez Rufino	Mayor
2-Manuel Ramirez Rufino	Brother
3-Lutgardo García Ramirez	Butcher
4-Enrique Monge Escobar	Quiqui
5-Manuel Fernandez Luque	Perlo
6-Manuel Monge Romero	Aurelia
7-Manuel Escobar Moreno	Picarito
8-Manuel Teba Escobar	Picarita
9-José Pérez Rodríguez	Carpeta
10-José Mª Ramirez Mauricio	Leocadio
11-Bautista Reinoso Monge	Lole
12-Alfredo Reinoso Monge	Lole
13-Lucrecio Paz	Cuartano

14-Braulio Ramirez Garcia   Doctor
15-José Luís López (E   Orosia
16-Quiri, from Carrión, married to Dionisia Monge Romero
17-Andrés Rolo who lived in Carrión and joined an expedition from this town.
Fascists harassed, mistreated or killed by the "reds," NO ONE.

The first thing to be noted about this list is that it was written by a man who had been living away from the town for nine years when the war began and was imprisoned during the entire time that men from Castilleja del Campo were being killed. This explains the errors and omissions on the list and makes all the more extraordinary the accuracy with which he identifies so many of the victims. He includes the correct name and both surnames of ten men accurately identified as Castilleja victims of the repression. The great discovery for me was the corroboration of the assassination of Manuel Ramírez Rufino, brother of Castilleja's Republican mayor. As far as the errors and omissions are concerned, Cándido Nieves Perea and Joaquín León Trejo are missing. The latter omission is surprising since Eugenio Pozo was tortured on July 28 and 29, 1936, so he would reveal Joaquín's whereabouts. Perhaps he left him off the list along with Cándido Nieves Perea because they were not natives of Castilleja. But then why did he include Antonio Cruz Cruz and Andrés Rolo (?), who also were not natives of Castilleja?

It seems that Eugenio Pozo had information that there were seventeen men from the town who were killed and, lacking Cándido Nieves Perea and Joaquín León Trejo, he made a great effort to arrive at that number. That would explain why Eugenio included "11-Bautista Reinoso Monge," even though he was not shot like his brother Alfredo but rather died shortly after his brother, of tuberculosis. He also included "17-Andrés Rolo who lived in Carrión and joined an expedition from this town." The expedition would be the column of miners from Río Tinto who passed through Castilleja on July 19. But who was this man? And why did Eugenio Pozo include him as a victim from Castilleja? "Rolo," which Eugenio Pozo includes on his list as a surname, sounds more like a nickname to me.

There is an Andrés who appears on the list from 1940 in Military Service Records: "1925/ Sánchez Benítez, Andrés/ Aznalcóllar/ 36/ Married/ Agricultural Worker/ Carrión/ C. Llerena No. 12/ Deceased."[13] In other words, he was in the 1925 call-up, a native of Aznalcóllar, he would have been thirty-six years old in 1940, he was married, a day laborer, a resident of Carrión, and in 1940 he was dead. But if he was from Aznalcóllar and lived in Carrión de los Céspedes, why was he in the Castilleja Recruitment and Military Service Records? Perhaps he lived for some time in Castilleja del Campo. Are we in the presence of another victim from the town? The information is too tenuous to include him on the list of victims. It is not even possible to be sure that the Andrés Sánchez Benítez on the list from 1940 in Military Service Records is the same man Eugenio Pozo de la Cueva included on his list as Andrés Rolo.

It would not be surprising for Eugenio Pozo to use a nickname, Rolo, in place of surnames he had forgotten. He did the same thing with Antonio Cruz Cruz whom he called "Quiri," a nickname I had never heard. I had only heard the nickname "Adelino" for Antonio Cruz Cruz, but he is clearly identified by his marriage to Dionisia Monge Romero. Eugenio also omitted the second surnames of Lucrecio Paz Delgado and José Luis López Moreno, and he gives the first name Manuel to José Fernández Luque "El Perlo." The way Eugenio clarifies the identity of each victim is very interesting: for some he uses nicknames, Quiqui, Perlo, Cuartano; for others he uses political posts or professions, "mayor," "butcher," "doctor"; and for others he uses relationships, "brother" for Manuel Ramírez, the mayor's brother, or the name or nickname of the victim's mother or father, Aurelia, Picarito, Picarita, Lole, Orosia. I do not know what Carpeta means for José Pérez Rodríguez. There is a clear attempt here to leave as many clues as possible so the identity of these victims would not be forgotten, an indication that the desire to honor the men unjustly eliminated in the repression is nothing new in Castilleja del Campo.

Notes

1 Francisco Espinosa Maestre, *La Guerra Civil en Huelva*, 340; Santos Juliá, ed., *Víctimas de la Guerra Civil*, 409.
2 Francisco Espinosa Maestre, *La Guerra Civil en Huelva*, 337.
3 Civil Death Registry, Office of the Justice of the Peace, Castilleja del Campo.
4 Francisco Espinosa Maestre, *La Guerra Civil en Huelva*, 341.
5 Recruitment and Military Service Records, Castilleja del Campo Municipal Archive.
6 Ibid.
7 Civil Death Registry, Office of the Justice of the Peace, Castilleja del Campo.
8 Dossier 24, Office of the Justice of the Peace, Castilleja del Campo.
9 Ibid.
10 Ibid.
11 On Joaquín León Trejo's death certificate, inscribed on March 12, 1938, the space for place of death is left blank. Civil Death Registry, Office of the Justice of the Peace, Castilleja del Campo. After the cause for applying the decree to him on the first list there appears "(D. in Seville)." Dossier 24, Office of the Justice of the Peace, Castilleja del Campo. This is an error. He was probably killed in Castilblanco de los Arroyos.

12 The causes for Manuel Tebas Escobar and Enrique Monge Escobar are trun-
    cated in the document for lack of space on the paper.
13 Recruitment and Military Service Records, Castilleja del Campo Municipal
    Archive.

Appendix D

List of Ex-combatants

On April 9, 1940, one year after the war ended, the Castilleja del Campo municipal government sent two lists to the "National Service of Ex-combatants." One list bore the title "Nominal report of the individuals who have presented the declaration of Personal Affiliation form for the formation of the National Census of Ex-combatants" and the other was entitled "Nominal report on the individuals who have been listed in this Municipal Government and who based on records filed in the same or reports obtained to that effect turn out to have been combatants and have not presented the declaration of Personal Affiliation form for the formation of the census for the reasons that with respect to each one are expressed in the following."

The "declaration of Personal Affiliation form" referred to in the titles of the lists was a declaration of adherence to the new regime that the individuals had to sign in order to be included in the "National Census of Ex-combatants." The first list contains the name and surnames, and the call-up year of each individual. The second list contains name and surnames, call-up year, and "Observations," which are either "Absent from this locale" or "Serving in the Army." I have combined the two lists, which are ordered by age, from the oldest to the youngest, and not by alphabetical order. I have also added a number to make it easier to count the ex-combatants. I have included Juan Antonio Luque Romero, who was mobilized at the beginning of the war but crossed to the Republican zone in the summer of 1937, where he served in the Republican army. This disqualified him for official ex-combatant status and he was not on either of the two lists.

Name and surnames	Call-up	Observations (for those on the second list)
1 José Luque Ramírez	1915	
2 Juan A. Gómez Álvarez	1922	
3 Juan A. Tebas Rodríguez	1923	Absent from this locale
4 Joaquín Gómez Álvarez	1928	
5 Severo Luque Rodríguez	1928	

6	José Monge Rodríguez	1928	
7	Antonio Calero Cuevas	1929	
8	Juan Garrido Cruz	1929	Absent from this locale
9	Manuel Cuevas Reinoso	1930	
10	Ildefonso Herrero Venegas	1930	
11	Anastasio Rufino Romero	1931	
12	Casildo Escobar Reinoso	1931	
13	Francisco Garrido Gómez	1931	Absent from this locale
14	Manuel García Ramírez	1932	Absent from this locale
15	Juan Antonio Luque Romero	1932	*Not on either list. He deserted in 1937.*
16	Benjamín Caraballo Corchero	1932	
17	José María Fernández Rodríguez	1932	
18	Adolfo Muñoz Caraballo	1932	
19	Francisco Luque Cuevas	1932	
20	Florencio Luque Rodríguez	1933	
21	Leovigildo Monge Pérez	1933	
22	Manuel Romero Rufino	1933	
23	José Rodríguez Escobar	1933	
24	Miguel Rodríguez Caraballo	1933	
25	Vicente Rodríguez Monge	1933	
26	Severo Luque Fernández	1933	Serving in the Army
27	José Caraballo Luque	1933	Absent from this locale
28	José Luque Cuevas	1934	
29	Francisco Sánchez Blázquez	1934	
30	Arsenio Rodríguez Rufino	1934	Serving in the Army
31	Manuel Luque Romero	1935	
32	Lutgardo Moreno Rodríguez	1935	
33	Alejandro Tebas Adorna	1935	
34	Fernando Luque Reinoso	1935	
35	Enrique Delgado Romero	1935	Serving in the Army
36	Modesto Escobar Moreno	1935	Serving in the Army
37	Antonio Rodríguez Mantero	1935	Serving in the Army
38	José Luque Mauricio	1936	
39	Aniceto Luque Luque	1936	
40	Francisco Romero Rufino	1936	
41	Manuel Rodríguez Monge	1936	
42	Manuel Rodríguez Rufino	1936	
43	Marcelo Monge Luque	1936	
44	Gonzalo Calero Ramírez	1936	Serving in the Army
45	Manuel Luque Cuevas	1937	

46	Antonio Carretero Luque	1937	
47	Celedonio Escobar Reinoso	1937	
48	Braulio Luque Rufino	1937	
49	Manuel Tebas Adorna	1937	
50	Diego Madrigal Gómez	1937	
51	Rogelio Cuevas Reinoso	1937	
52	Antonio Monge Pérez	1937	
53	Manuel Luque Romero	1937	Serving in the Army
54	Angelino Luque Reinoso	1937	Serving in the Army
55	Antonio García Ramírez	1937	Serving in the Army
56	Macedonio Rodríguez Escobar	1938	
57	Manuel Moreno Muñoz	1938	
58	Victorio Luque Rodríguez	1938	
59	Baldomero Ramírez Paniagua	1938	
60	Manuel Ramírez Mauricio	1938	
61	Francisco Luque Reinoso	1938	Serving in the Army
62	Aurelio Monge Romero	1939	
63	Elio Paz Nieves	1939	
64	Manuel Romero Monge	1939	Serving in the Army
65	Eliseo García Ramírez	1939	Serving in the Army
66	Carlos Rodríguez Rufino	1939	Serving in the Army
67	José María Martín Blázquez	1939	Serving in the Army
68	Antonio Delgado Luque	1940	
69	Conrado Rufino Romero	1940	
70	Lucas Rebollo Medel	1940	
71	Juan María Sánchez Blázquez	1940	Serving in the Army
72	Manuel Adorna Sánchez	1940	Absent from this locale
73	Ramón Rufino Vázquez	1940	Serving in the Army
74	Manuel Díaz Laforet	1940	Serving in the Army
75	Antonio Luque Gómez	1941	
76	Sebastián Luque Adorna	1941	Serving in the Army
77	Félix García Ramírez	1941	Serving in the Army
78	Roberto Delgado Romero	1941	Serving in the Army
79	Gustavo Luque Romero	1942	
80	Antonio Mauricio Guerrero	1942[1]	

Note

1 Recruitment and Military Service Records, Castilleja del Campo Municipal Archive.

Appendix E

The Ex-combatants Who Were Interviewed

Of the sixteen people I interviewed in the winter of 1989/90, ten of them were men. They had all served in Franco's forces during the war. In the following list, which goes from the oldest to the youngest, I include their name, surnames, and their call-up year.[1] I have also indicated whether they had identified themselves as leftists or right-wingers and whether they had served in combat units or in the rearguard.

Manuel García Ramírez	1932	Left	Rearguard
Miguel Rodríguez Caraballo	1933	Right	Rearguard
Aniceto Luque Luque	1936	Right	Combat?
Celedonio Escobar Reinoso	1937	Left	Combat
Antonio Monge Pérez	1937	Left	Combat
Manuel Ramírez Mauricio	1938	Left	Combat
Aurelio Monge Romero	1939	Left	Combat
Antonio Delgado Luque	1940	Right	Rearguard
Conrado Rufino Romero	1940	Right	Combat
Leopoldo Rubio	xxxx	Right	Rearguard

These ten men are fairly representative of Castilleja's ex-combatants, with regard to their age distribution. At the outbreak of the war, these men ranged from seventeen years old, Antonio Delgado Luque and Conrado Rufino Romero, to twenty-five years old, Manuel García Ramírez. They all belonged to the age group that bore the heaviest burden during the war. Only six of the town's eighty ex-combatants were younger than Conrado Rufino and Antonio Delgado and only thirteen of the town's ex-combatants were older than Manuel García.

The ratio of leftists and right-wingers, 5 each, is probably not representative. I wanted as balanced a view as possible of events in the town and made a special effort to find right-wingers to interview. I suspect the majority of ex-combatants were leftists. Six of the ten ex-combatants I interviewed, just over half, said they had seen combat. The other four said they served in the rearguard. Of the five leftist ex-combatants interviewed, four had seen combat: Celedonio Escobar, Antonio Monge, Manuel Ramírez, and Aurelio Monge. They had served in Franco's forces against their will. Of the five right-wingers, one, maybe two, had seen combat. Conrado Rufino had enlisted enthusiastically in a Falangist militia. He wanted to see combat. Aniceto Luque was drafted into the army against his will. I have serious doubts about the veracity of Aniceto Luque's testimonies regarding his combat experiences. The data, limited as it is, suggests that leftists were more likely than right-wingers to be assigned to combat duty.

Note

1 The exception is Leopoldo Rubio, a right-winger who did not want his real name to appear in the book. To protect his identity, I have not indicated his call-up year. He does not appear where he should by age.

Appendix F

Castilleja Ex-combatants with a Brother Who Had Been Shot

Ex-combatant
Antonio García Ramírez
Eliseo García Ramírez
Félix García Ramírez
Manuel García Ramírez*
José Escobar Moreno
Modesto Escobar Moreno
Aurelio Monge Romero*
Manuel Ramírez Mauricio*

Brother
Lutgardo García Ramírez

Manuel Escobar Moreno

Manuel Monge Romero
José María Ramírez Mauricio

* Indicates ex-combatant who was interviewed.

Appendix G

Town Council Minutes, October 24, 1936, Items 1 and 5

1st The Corporation was informed that by each of the gentlemen Don Miguel Luque Romero, Don Miguel Monge Perez and Don Francisco Ramírez Rodríguez, the latter as responsible party for Don Jose Ramirez Rufino, there has been deposited in the Municipal Treasury the sum of four hundred and sixteen pesetas and ninety four centimos, which sum the first mentioned deposits as directly responsible and the other two as indirectly responsible for damages caused to the Municipal Government by the rescission of contracts for regulation of the consumption of meats and for regulation of weights and measures, and taxes on street vendors and peddlers during the year of nineteen thirty four in accordance with the administrative report that for said motive was opened and a hearing held on the seventeenth day of this month and whose findings are attached to the aforementioned report. There remains therefore to be deposited the sum of another four hundred and sixteen pesetas and ninety four centimos that is owed by Don Leocadio Rufino.

5th Immediately afterwards and as authorized by the Presiding Mayor an account and reading was given by me the Secretary of the following request.

"To the Municipal Government of Castilleja del Campo. Don Leocadio Ramirez Rufino, resident of this town, of legal age and an agricultural worker respectfully sets forth: 1st That according to a hearing held on the 17th day of the present month with respect to indirect responsibility for damages caused to this Municipal Body by the rescission of contracts for regulation of the consumption of meats and for regulation of weights and measures during the year 1934, responsibility that was confirmed in the administrative report which to that effect was opportunely issued, the petitioner promised to deposit with this Municipal Government in the space of five days the sum of four hundred and sixteen pesetas, ninety four

centimos. = 2nd That notwithstanding having put his greatest diligence
and good will to it, the exact fulfillment of this obligation is materially
impossible for him due to lacking at the moment the necessary money and
not having found any person to facilitate the loan required for these ends.
= In view of these reasons, = Implores the Municipal Government deign
to concede him a moratorium to pay off the amount owed in the following
installments and with the following conditions. = First installment of two
hundred and nine pesetas which he will deposit on July 31 of the following
year 1937, and final installment of two hundred and eight pesetas and
ninety four centimos, which he will deposit on December 31 of the same
year 1937. = Moreover the petitioner promises not to avail himself of the
fruits of his property of any kind until he pays off the aforementioned debt,
and deposit by way of interest for the delay five percent of the quantity
owed and to undersign the corresponding document in which the
contracted obligation is recorded. = It is a kindness that he seeks to deserve
from that dignified Body. Castilleja del Campo on October 22, 1936. =
Leocadio Ramirez. = "Signed."

Upon the conclusion of the reading of the aforementioned petition and
deeming worthy of attention the reasons alleged by the petitioner, since it
is noted by this Body that due to the deficient or almost null harvest of
cereals in the present year and which are the only means of income upon
which the petitioner depends, that the latter lacks not only sufficient money
to fulfill his obligation but even the most indispensable to defray the sustenance of his numerous family, deems therefore that it follows in all justice
to accede to his petition, the which on the other hand implies no damage
of any kind to the Municipal Government, given that the latter will perceive
the corresponding legal interest, after long and reasoned discussion of the
matter in unanimity agreed to accede to the petition of D. Leocadio Ramirez
Rufino in the request herein transcribed, conceding to him the moratorium
he seeks in the form, installments and conditions he proposes, empowering
the Mayor to formalize and undersign the corresponding payment obligation with the aforementioned debtor in the name and representation of this
Body.

Appendix H

Widows and Orphans of Castilleja del Campo's Victims

The household census of December 31, 1935, which is preserved in the Castilleja del Campo municipal archive, is a list of the town's streets in alphabetical order. For each street, the houses are arranged according to the house number. For each house the names of those who were living there are listed along with the age of each member of the household and their relationship to the family. With this census, I was able to identify the majority of widows and dependent children of the men who were assassinated in 1936. Oral testimonies allowed me to add to the list the names of the posthumous orphans Adelino Cruz Monge and Violeta Pérez Monge, who did not appear in the 1935 census. The victim Manuel Ramírez Rufino was not in the census either, because in 1935 he was living in Aznalcóllar with his wife, a native of that town. I do not know the name or age of his wife. From oral testimonies I have been able to correct a few errors in the census regarding the ages of some of the widows and orphans.

I have not included the names of adult orphans or the names of the single men who were shot: Lutgardo García Ramírez, José Luis López Moreno, Braulio Ramírez García, and José María Ramírez Mauricio; nor have I included the widower José Ramírez Rufino. The exclusion of adult orphans is not because I do not consider them victims. The children of the Republican mayor José Ramírez Rufino, Clotilde, Francisco, Irene, and Josefa Ramírez Rodríguez "Aunt Pepa," suffered the loss of a father they loved dearly. If they do not appear on the list, it is because they were already economically independent and not left to fend for themselves as children, like the orphans listed. The list includes the ages in 1936 of the men, their widows, and their orphans.

Widows and orphans of men of Castilleja del Campo assassinated during the repression

Antonio Cruz Cruz	30
Widow: Dionisia Monge Romero	24
Orphan: Adelino Cruz Monge	Posthumous
Manuel Escobar Moreno	30
Widow: Carmen Muñoz Caraballo	27
Orphan: Otilia Escobar Muñoz	1
José Fernández Luque	43
Widow: Laura Rodríguez Luque	35
Orphans: Digna Fernández Rodríguez	12
Luisa Fernández Rodríguez	5
Joaquín León Trejo 43	
Widow: Concepción García Baquero	47
Orphans: José León García	16
Antonio León García	14
Carmen León García	5
Enrique Monge Escobar	43
Maid?: Josefa Adorna Sánchez	36
Stepson: Manuel Adorna Sánchez	17
Manuel Monge Romero	31
Widow: Rosario Luque Romero	28
Orphan: Dalia Monge Luque	3
Cándido Nieves Perea	39
Widow: Manuela Sousa Bernal	23
Lucrecio Paz Delgado	48
Widow: Carmen Rufino Ruiz	47
José Pérez Rodríguez	37
Widow: Carmen Monge Pérez	26
Orphans: Juan Pérez Luque	13
Violeta Pérez Monge	Posthumous
Manuel Ramírez Rufino	58
Widow: ?	?
Alfredo Reinoso Monge	26
Widow: Dolores Carretero Luque	26
Manuel Tebas Escobar	38
Widow: Suceso Rodríguez Luque	35
Orphans: Rosario Tebas Rodríguez	11
Elías M. Tebas Rodríguez	7
Sara Tebas Rodríguez	4

Appendix I

Eugenio Pozo de la Cueva's Prison Poem to his Son

From a photocopy given me by Eugenio's niece Matilde. The dedication is "To my first son, whose birth I did not see, with all the force of my affection . . . Eugenio Pozo."

Mi bienvenida . . .
Como ilusión más grande de mi vida,
yo te esperaba lleno de impaciencia . . .
pues, siendo mi trasunto, en mi conciencia
te daba ya entrañable bienvenida.
Mas, esta ilusión mía, tan querida,
ha sido ensombrecida por mi suerte;
y así como mi padre, por su muerte,
no pudo ver mi entrada en este mundo,
por estar preso, con dolor profundo,
tampoco yo, hijo mío, pude verte.

Y cuando la amargura mi alma llena
porque el dolor se muestra tan prolijo,
viniste al mundo tú . . . ¡mi primer hijo!
llegando a mitigarme tanta pena.
¡Un hijo siempre llega en hora buena! . . .
¡Aun cuando, por desgracia, me halle preso,
me llena de contento el buen suceso! . . .
¡Mi corazón se invade de alegría!
¡¡No sabes, hijo mío, la ufanía
con que yo sabré darte el primer beso!!

My welcome . . .
As the greatest of my life's dreams, / I awaited you with impatience . . . / since you were a reflection of me, in my consciousness / I had already prepared a heartfelt welcome. / But this dream of mine, so cherished, / has

been darkened by my fate; / and just as my father, because of his death, / could not see my entry into this world, / with profound sorrow I, a prisoner, / could not see yours, my son.

And when bitterness fills my soul / because my sorrow is so great, / you came into the world . . . my first child! / managing to mitigate so much pain. / A child always comes at the right time! / Even when, by misfortune, I find myself imprisoned, / the event fills me with contentment! / Joy invades my heart! / You cannot know, my son, with what pride / I will give you the first kiss!!

Under the poem there appears "Madrid, Provincial Prison (Porlier), February 25 to March 15. Burgos, Central Prison, March 16 to October 27, 1943."

Sources and Bibliography

Sources

Archives consulted

Archiepiscopal Archive of Seville
Archive of the Second Territorial Military Tribunal
Archive of the Castilleja del Campo Office of the Justice of the Peace
Castilleja del Campo Municipal Archive
Municipal Newspaper Archive of Seville

Oral sources

Borrego Suárez, José Antonio	Conversation, spring 2000
Delgado Luque, Antonio	Interview, January 15, 1990
Donaire Pozo, Eugenio	Conversation, June 10, 2005
Donaire Pozo, Matilde	Conversation, June 10, 2005
Escobar Muñoz, Otilia	Interview, June 5, 2000
Escobar Reinoso, Celedonio	Interview, January 4, 1990
García Ramírez, Manuel	Inteviews, January 11, 1990 and spring 2000
Gómez Luque, Antonio	Conversation, summer 1996
León García, Antonio	Interview, June 20, 2000
León García, José	Interview, July 5, 2000
León López, Ana	Conversation, June 5, 2005
León López, Concepción	Interview, June 20, 2000
León López, Diego	Conversation, June 5, 2005
León López, Joaquín	Conversation, June 5, 2005
León Saenz, Alejandro	Conversations, 2001–2005
Leon, Hubert	Conversations, 2001–2005. Thanks to his webpage, I was able to locate the American descendants of Colonel Francisco León Trejo
Luque Luque, Aniceto	Interview, January 9, 1990
Luque Monge, José	Conversations, 1992–2000
Luque Reinoso, Marina	Interview, January 2, 1990
Luque Reinoso, Herminia	Interview, January 2, 1990
Luque Romero, Narciso	Interview, June 9, 2005
Mistral, Isidora[1]	Interview, January 10, 1990
Monge Pérez, Antonio	Interview, December 27, 1989

Monge Pérez, Feliciano	Interview, June 9, 2005
Monge Romero, Aurelio	Interview, January 7, 1990
Monge Romero, Carmen	Interview, January 15, 1990
Moreno Romero, Carmen	Interview, January 15, 1990
Ramírez Mauricio, Dulcenombre	Interview, January 9, 1990
Ramírez Mauricio, Manuel	Interview, December 30, 1989
Reinoso Muñoz, Guillermo	Conversations, 1992–2000
Rodríguez Caraballo, Miguel	Interview, January 16, 1990
Rodríguez Mantero, Eduardo	Conversation, June 12, 1992
Rubio, Leopoldo[2]	Interview, January 10, 1990
Rufino Romero, Conrado	Interview, January 3, 1990
Tebas Rodríguez, Sara	Interview, June 7, 2000
Vergne Graciani, María[3]	Interview, July 8, 2004

Notes to Sources

1 This is not her real name. The interview was granted on the condition of anonymity.
2 This is not his real name. The interview was granted on the condition of anonymity.
3 Interviewed by Juan Manuel Muñoz Luque.

Bibliography

Acosta Bono, Gonzalo, José Luis Gutiérrez Molina, Lola Martínez Macías, and Ángel del Río Sánchez. *El canal de los presos, 1940–1962: Trabajos forzados; De la represión política a la explotación económica*. Barcelona: Crítica, 2004.

Aguilar Fernández, Paloma. *Memoria y olvido de la Guerra Civil española*. Madrid: Alianza Editorial, 1996.

Alpert, Michael. "La historia militar." In *La guerra civil: una nueva visión del conflicto que dividió España*, edited by Stanley Payne and Javier Tusell, 123–94. Madrid: Temas de Hoy, 1996.

Álvarez Rey, Leandro. *Aproximación a un mito: masonería y política en la Sevilla del siglo XX*. Seville: Ayuntamiento, 1996.

Barciela, Carlos. "La España del 'estraperlo'." In *El primer franquismo: España durante la segunda guerra mundial*, edited by José Luis García Delgado, 106–22. Madrid: Siglo XXI, 1989.

Barragán Reina, Ramón. *Cantillana Segunda República: La esperanza rota*. Brenes, Seville: Muñoz Moya Editores Extremeños, 2006.

Blas Zabaleta, Patricio de, and Eva de Blas Martín-Merás. *Julián Besteiro: Nadar contra corriente*. Madrid: Algaba Ediciones, 2002.

Boor, Jakim. See Franco Bahamonde, Francisco.

Brenan, Gerald. *Al sur de Granada*. Barcelona: Tusquets, 2003.

——. *El laberinto español: Antecedentes sociales y políticos de la guerra civil*. Paris: Éditions Ruedo ibérico, 1962.

Cardona, Gabriel. "Las operaciones militares." In *La guerra civil española: 50 años después*, Manuel Tuñón de Lara, Julio Arióstegui, Ángel Viñas, Gabriel Cardona, and Josep M. Bricall, 199–274. Barcelona: Labor, 1985.

Casanova, Julián. *La Iglesia de Franco*. Madrid: Temas de Hoy, 2001.

———. "Rebelión y revolución." In *Víctimas de la Guerra Civil*, edited by Santos Juliá, 55–185. Madrid: Temas de Hoy, 1999.

Collier, George A. *Socialistas de la Andalucía rural: Los revolucionarios ignorados de la Segunda República*. Barcelona: Anthropos Editorial, 1997.

Donaire Pozo, Matilde I. "Eugenio Pozo de la Cueva, mi tío." Testimony, Second Sessions on Historical Memory, Castilleja del Campo, Seville, June 4, 2005.

———. "Largo camino hacia la paz" (unpublished work, photocopy courtesy of author).

Espinosa Maestre, Francisco. *Contra el olvido: Historia y memoria de la guerra civil*. Barcelona: Crítica, 2006.

———. *La columna de la muerte: El avance del ejército franquista de Sevilla a Badajoz*. Barcelona: Crítica, 2003.

———. *La guerra civil en Huelva*. Huelva: Diputación, 1996.

———. *La justicia de Queipo: Violencia selectiva y terror fascista en la II División en 1936; Sevilla, Huelva, Cádiz, Córdoba, Málaga y Badajoz*. Barcelona: Crítica, 2006.

———. *La primavera del Frente Popular: Los campesinos de Badajoz y el origen de la guerra civil, marzo-julio de 1936*. Barcelona: Crítica, 2007.

———. "Sevilla, 1936: Sublevación y represión." In *Sevilla, 36: sublevación fascista y represión*, Alfonso Braojos Garrido, Leandro Álvarez Rey, and Francisco Espinosa Maestre, 171–269. Brenes, Seville: Muñoz Moya y Montraveta, 1990.

Franco Bahamonde, Francisco [Jakim Boor, pseud.]. *Masonería*. Madrid: Gráficas Valera, 1952.

———. *Palabras del Caudillo, 1937–1943*. Madrid: Editora Nacional, 1943.

———. *Pensamiento económico*. Madrid: Organización Sindical de F.E.T. y de las J.O.N.S., 1958.

Fraser, Ronald. *Escondido*. Barcelona: Crítica, 2006.

———. *Mijas*. Barcelona: Antoni Boch, 1985.

———. *Recuérdalo tú y recuérdalo a otros: historia oral de la Guerra Civil española*. Barcelona: Crítica, 2001.

García Márquez, José María. *La UGT Sevilla: Golpe militar, resistencia y represión, 1936–1950*. Cordoba: Fundación para el Desarrollo de los Pueblos de Andalucía, 2008.

———. *La represión militar en la Puebla de Cazalla, 1936–1943*. Seville: Centro de Estudios Andaluces, 2007.

Gavira Gil, Javier. *En busca de una historia oculta: La guerra civil en Marchena, 1936–1939*. Marchena, Seville: Asociación DIME, 2007.

Gibson, Ian. *Queipo de Llano: Sevilla, verano de 1936*. Barcelona: Grijalbo, 1986.

Gutiérrez Molina, José Luis. *Casas Viejas: Del crimen a la esperanza*, 2nd ed. Cordoba: Editorial Almuzara, 2008.

———. *La tiza, la tinta y la palabra: José Sánchez Rosa, maestro y anarquista andaluz, 1864–1936*. Ubrique, Cadiz: Editorial Tréveris, 2005.

Iglesias, María Antonio. *Maestros de la República: Los otros santos, los otros mártires*. Madrid: La Esfera de los Libros, 2006.

Instituto Nacional de Estadística. *Anuario Estadístico de España, 1944–1945*. Fondo documental del Instituto Nacional de Estadística. http://www.ine.es/inebaseweb/ pdfDispatcher.do?td=162131&ext=.pdf.

Jackson, Gabriel. *The Spanish Republic and the Civil War, 1931–1939*. Princeton: Princeton University Press, 1965.

Juliá, Santos, ed. *Víctimas de la Guerra Civil*. Madrid: Temas de Hoy, 1999.

Kleinfeld, Gerald L., and Lewis A. Tambs. *Hitler's Spanish Legion: the Blue Division in Russia*. London and Amsterdam: Feffer & Simons, 1979.

Lazo, Alfonso. *Retrato de fascismo rural en Sevilla*. Seville: Universidad de Sevilla, 1998.

León Saenz, Fernando. "En Cuatro Vientos no se sublevó nadie, narrado por el coronel de Ingenieros y de Aviación D. Francisco León Trejo en 1965–67" (unpublished work, photocopy provided by Alejandro León Saenz).

———. "In Cuatro Vientos No One Rose In Rebellion, narrated by the Colonel of Engineers and Aviation D. Francisco León Trejo in 1965–67" (unpublished translation of "En Cuatro Vientos no se sublevó nadie," provided by Hubert Leon).

López Carvajal, Cristóbal. *Los días olvidados*. Jaen: Germania, 2002.

Luca de Tena, Torcuato. *Embajador en el infierno: Memorias del capitán Palacios*. Barcelona: Planeta, 1955.

Luque Varela, Juan C. *Crónica de una fiesta viva: Castilleja del Campo, tres siglos de historia*. Castilleja del Campo, Seville: Ayuntamiento, 1999.

Macarro Vera, José Manuel. *La Sevilla republicana*. Madrid: Sílex, 2003.

———. *La utopía revolucionaria: Sevilla en la Segunda República*. Seville: Monte de Piedad y Caja de Ahorros de Sevilla, 1985.

Malefakis, Edward. *Reforma agraria y revolución campesina en la España del siglo XX*. Madrid: Espasa Calpe, 2001.

Martínez Bande, José Manuel. *La campaña de Andalucía*. Madrid: San Martin, 1986.

Mintz, Jerome R. *Los anarquistas de Casas Viejas*. Granada: Diputaciones de Granada y Cádiz, 1999.

———. *The anarchists of Casas Viejas*. Bloomington: Indiana University Press, 1994.

Molina Domínguez, Guillermo A. *Víctimas y desaparecidos: La represión en Palos de la Frontera, 1936–1941*. Seville: Asociación Andaluza Memoria Histórica y Justicia, 2005.

Montero Gómez, Félix J. *Alcalá de Guadaira: 21 de julio de 1936; Historia de una venganza*. Alcalá de Guadaira, Seville: Ayuntamiento, 2007.

Moreno Gómez, Francisco. "La represión en la posguerra." In *Víctimas de la Guerra Civil*, edited by Santos Juliá, 277–405. Madrid: Temas de Hoy, 1999.

———. *La resistencia armada contra Franco*. Barcelona: Crítica, 2001.

———. *1936: El genocidio franquista en Córdoba*. Barcelona: Crítica, 2008.

Moreno Juliá, Xavier. *La División Azul: Sangre española en Rusia, 1941–1945*. Barcelona: Crítica, 2006.

Morente Valero, Francisco. *La depuración del Magisterio Nacional, 1936–1943*. Valladolid: Ámbito, 1997.

Negro Castro, Juan. *Españoles en la U.R.S.S.* Madrid: Escelicer, 1959.

Orihuela, Antonio. *Moguer, 1936*. Madrid: La Oveja Roja, 2010.

Ortiz Villalba, Juan. *Sevilla 1936: del golpe militar a la guerra civil*. Seville: Diputación, 1998.

Parejo, Nonio. *Los Presos del Canal*, DVD. Seville: Nonio Parejo y Asociados, 2003.

Payne, Stanley. *The Franco Regime, 1936–1975*. Madison: University of Wisconsin Press, 1987.

Pitt-Rivers, Julian. *Los hombres de la sierra*. Barcelona: Grijalbo, 1971.

Powell, Charles T. *El piloto del cambio: El rey, la monarquía y la transición a la democracia*. Barcelona: Planeta, 1991.

Preston, Paul. *A Concise History of the Spanish Civil War*. London: HarperCollins, 1996.

———. *Franco: A Biography*. New York: BasicBooks, 1994.

———. *Las tres Españas del 36*. Barcelona: Random House Mondadori, 1999.

Queipo de Llano y Serra, Gonzalo. "Carta a Franco . . . ," in *Estampas de la guerra*. San Sebastián, [1938?], 5:8.

Reig Tapia, Alberto. *Ideología e historia: Sobre la represión franquista y la Guerra Civil*. Madrid: Ediciones Akal, 1986.

———. *Memoria de la guerra civil: Los mitos de la tribu*. Madrid: Alianza Editorial, 1999.

Richards, Michael. *A Time of Silence: Civil War and the Culture of Repression in Franco's Spain, 1936–1945*. Cambridge: Cambridge University Press, 1998.

Rodrigo, Javier. *Hasta la raíz: Violencia durante la guerra civil y la dictadura franquista*. Madrid: Alianza Editorial, 2008.

Ros Aguado, Manuel. *La guerra secreta de Franco, 1939–1945*. Barcelona: Crítica, 2002.

Sígler Silvera, Fernando. *Su silencio es nuestra voz: De la esperanza republicana a la sublevación militar y la represión en Espera, el pueblo de la reforma agraria*. Espera, Cadiz: Ayuntamiento, 2008.

Silva, Emilio. *Las fosas de Franco: Crónica de un desagravio*. Madrid: Temas de Hoy, 2003.

Solé i Sabaté, Josep M., and Joan Villarroya. "Mayo de 1936–Abril de 1939." In *Víctimas de la Guerra Civil*, edited by Santos Juliá, 180–273. Madrid: Temas de Hoy, 1999.

Southworth, Herbert R. *Conspiracy and the Spanish Civil War: The Brainwashing of Francisco Franco*. London: Routledge, 2002.

Thomas, Hugh. *The Spanish Civil War, Revised Edition*. New York: The Modern Library, 2001.

Tuñón de Lara, Manuel. "Orígenes lejanos y próximos." In *La guerra civil española: 50 años después*, Manuel Tuñón de Lara, Julio Arióstegui, Ángel Viñas, Gabriel Cardona, and Joseph M. Bricall, 419–37. Barcelona: Labor, 1985.

Tuñón de Lara, Manuel. "Un ensayo de visión global, medio siglo después." In *La guerra civil española: 50 años después*, Manuel Tuñón de Lara, Julio Arióstegui, Ángel Viñas, Gabriel Cardona, and Joseph M. Bricall, 419–37. Barcelona: Labor, 1985.

Tusell, Javier. "La evolución política en la zona de Franco." In *La guerra civil: una nueva visión del conflicto que dividió España*, edited by Stanley Payne and Javier Tusell, 423–83. Madrid: Temas de Hoy, 1996.

Van Epp Salazar, Margaret. *Si yo te dijera . . .* Huelva: Diputación, 1998.

Varela Rendueles, José María. *Mi rebelión en Sevilla: Memorias de su gobernador rebelde*. Seville: Ayuntamiento, 1982.

Viñas, Ángel. *Guerra, dinero, dictadura: Ayuda fascista y autarquía en la España de Franco*. Barcelona: Crítica, 1984.

———. "Los condicionantes internacionales." In *La guerra civil española: 50 años después*, Manuel Tuñón de Lara, Julio Arióstegui, Ángel Viñas, Gabriel Cardona, and Joseph M. Bricall, 123–97. Barcelona: Labor, 1985.

Photographs and Documents

Photographs and documents are placed after page 81.
View of Castilleja del Campo from Montijena Hill in June 2007.

Repudio Inn, Espartinas, site of the assassinations on August 27, 1936. Seville–Huelva General Highway.

Junction to Umbrete, site of the assassinations on September 14, 1936. Seville–Huelva General Highway.

Map of the Seville–Huelva General Highway (now National Highway A-472).

Wall of the Castilblanco de los Arroyos Cemetery where Joaquín León Trejo was shot on August 22, 1936.

Antonio Cruz Cruz.
Joaquín León Trejo in the patio of his house, Castilleja del Campo, 1935.
José Fernández Luque.
Lutgardo García Ramírez.
Oil Portrait of José Pérez Rodríguez.
José Luis López Moreno.

Alfredo Reinoso Monge.
Braulio Ramírez García.
Manuel Monge Romero.
Newspaper clipping with photograph of José Ramírez Rufino.
José María Ramírez Mauricio.
Manuel Tebas Escobar.
Manuel Escobar Moreno.
Manuel Rodríguez Mantero.
Antonio García Ramírez.

Antonio García Ramírez (in the center) sent this photograph to his family from the Russian front.

Juan Antonio Luque Romero.
Pedro Donaire Leal.
Pedro Donaire Leal (a postwar picture).

José Luis López Moreno, Eugenio Pozo de la Cueva, and Manuel García Ramírez in María Luisa Park (Seville), during the Republic.
José, Carmen, and Antonio León García, one year before the assassination of their father, Joaquín León Trejo.
Concepción García Baquero.
Suceso Rodríguez Luque.
Carmen Muñoz Caraballo.

Elías, Rosario, and Sara Tebas Rodríguez, children of Manuel Tebas Escobar.
Otilia Escobar Muñoz, with black market baskets.
School photograph from the 1940s with orphans of men who were assassinated:.
Sara Tebas Rodríguez (top row, to the left),.
Dalia Monge Luque (next row).
Otilia Escobar Muñoz (next row, toward the right).

Manuel García Ramírez with photograph of his brothers Lutgardo and Antonio.
Leftists from Castilleja on the Málaga front with the Falangist militia: Standing, Celedonio Escobar Reinoso, Modesto Escobar Moreno, Antonio García Ramírez, Antonio Monge Pérez.
Evaristo García Ramírez, Antonio León García, and Narciso Luque Romero, family members of victims of the repression during the Second Sessions on Historical Memory in Castilleja del Campo, 2005.
Alejandro León Saenz, son of Colonel Francisco León Trejo, and José León García, son of the schoolteacher Joaquín León Trejo. These two cousins were reunited thanks to the author's research.

Feliciano Monge Pérez, next to the monument to the victims of the 1936 repression, erected in 2005.

Letter from José María Ramírez Mauricio to his grandmother before the 1936 elections. Translation, on pages 23–4.

Letter from Irene Ramírez Rodríguez to her father, José Ramírez Rufino, in the Sanlúcar la Mayor prison.

My dear father you do not know how sorry we were when they took all of you away but then we were glad that you were in Sanlucar papa pepa has written to me and says that you are well and at peace there papa write me four words if you want me to send money or clean clothes there and I am going to send a bundle with Manolito write regarding what I said about the clothes and money for me or curro and me to go there Regards from all and receive a hug and a kiss from your daughter Irene Ramirez.

Letter written from the Sanlúcar la Mayor prison by the Republican mayor José Ramírez Rufino.

Dear children I have received the clothes from Braulio and I know you are all well telling you that we are all displeased they are the circumstances of life. There is no reason to be concerned because soon within a few days we will all be together do not send me anything like I said in the last letter. And with nothing more for today Regards to all and kisses for the children Your Father who loves you Jose Ramirez.

Document from the Civil Guard in 1939, with the causes for the application of the war decree. Translation on page 245.

Dramatis Personae
A Biographical Index

Spaniards have two surnames, the first of which is their father's first surname and the second of which is their mother's first surname. The two surnames are sometimes joined by *y* (and). Some Spaniards, usually upper-class, use *de* (of) or a hyphen to include more than two surnames. Spanish names are alphabetized according to the first surname.